Technological Change and Economic Catch-up

To Federico

Technological Change and Economic Catch-up

The Role of Science and Multinationals

Edited by

Grazia D. Santangelo

University of Catania, Italy

Edward Elgar

Cheltenham, UK • Northampton, MA, USA

Published by
Edward Elgar Publishing Limited
Glensanda House
Montpellier Parade
Cheltenham
Glos GL50 1UA
UK

Edward Elgar Publishing, Inc.
136 West Street
Suite 202
Northampton
Massachusetts 01060
USA

A catalogue record for this book
is available from the British Library

ISBN 1 84542 482 4

Printed and bound in Great Britain by MPG Books Ltd, Bodmin, Cornwall

Contents

Contributors

Cristiano Antonelli, University of Turin, Italy

Christian Bellak, Vienna University of Economics, Austria

Mario Calderini, Polytechnic of Turin, Italy

John Cantwell, Rutgers University, USA, and University of Reading, UK

Davide Castellani, University of Urbino, Italy

Rosalia Epifanio, University of Palermo, Italy

Chiara Franzoni, CERIS – National Research Council of Italy, (CNR), Italy

Jeffrey L. Furman, Boston University and NBER, USA

Richard Hayes, Melbourne Business School, University of Melbourne, Australia

Aykut Lenger, EGE University, Turkey

Roberto Mazzoleni, Hofstra University, USA

Richard R. Nelson, Columbia University, USA

Maria da Conceição Rego, University of Évora, Portugal

Grazia D. Santangelo, University of Catania, Italy

Erol Taymaz, Middle East Technical University, Turkey

Antonello Zanfei, University of Urbino, Italy

Preface

This book is the outcome of an international workshop on 'Public Research Institutions, International Business, and Technological and Economic Catch-Up in Developing Regions' held at the Faculty of Political Science of Catania University (Italy) in March 2004.

In its spirit, the book has been faithful to the core topic of the workshop. The effort devoted to tie together the contributions to this volume was only minor, thanks to the stimulating forum of discussion the workshop provided. Far from being a round-table where just academic viewpoints were exchanged, the workshop was an occasion where academia and the business world came together to discuss themes of direct interest to both parties, such as the relationships between public research institutions and international business, and their implications for technological and economic catch-up processes. In this respect, we are in debt to Salvatore Barbagallo (Senior Manager of Technical Training and Manufacturing, External Affairs, of the Catania site of Wyeth Lederle) and Carmelo Papa (Corporate Vice-President of ST Microelectronics), who brought their experience to the discussion by participating in the business panels. Similarly, acknowledgement should be made to the colleagues who provided comments and criticism during the workshop, but who were unable to contribute to this volume. A special recognition in this regard goes to Giovanni Dosi, who lit up the forum with his sharp and exuberant participation. Needless to say, this book indirectly owes thanks to all the people at the Faculty of Political Science who made the workshop possible. Within this community, I would like just to mention the Chancellor of Catania University, Ferdinando Latteri, the Dean of the Faculty of Political Science, Giuseppe Vecchio, and Giuseppe Barone for the financial support provided to the workshop organization, as well as Valentina Barbagallo, Angelo Giangreco and Massimo Toscano for their technical assistance. A special thought goes to my child, whom I was pregnant with during the organization of the event and throughout the workshop.

Introduction

Grazia D. Santangelo

This book focuses on the role of public research institutions in helping to promote the processes of technological and economic catch-up in developing areas, and of local policy in fostering local science–technology linkages with incoming foreign-owned multinationals. The underlying idea is that public research, educational and political institutions, as well as private corporations, are key actors in technological and economic processes since they may reinforce (or reverse) local *virtuous* (*vicious*) cycles by providing capabilities in basic research, the training of highly skilled labour, and networking connections with scientific and professional communities (and therefore access to knowledge and contacts) in other parts of the world. Despite being a peculiar feature of the new innovation model of the knowledge-based economy, the close relationship between knowledge transfer, innovation and economic growth has historically been an important mechanism capable of stimulating economic take-off. Notwithstanding the difficulties of identifying the ingredients of successful recipes, a crucial conceptual cornerstone of the book is the belief that public research institutions help to create the conditions required for local knowledge development and a greater capacity for problem-solving in local enterprises through their interactions with other local actors.

This view is framed within a specific understanding of technological change against which the interplay between science and technology, and between multinationals and local actors, as well as catching-up processes, are investigated. In particular, the contributors to this volume share the belief that knowledge is largely excludable and its use partially rivals, rather than merely being a 'public good'. These characteristics can be summarized in the *tacit* nature of technological change resulting from the specificity of the learning process. Economic actors (whether firms, users, countries, regions, or public institutions – according to the level and the focus of analysis) are heterogeneous as far as their cognitive capabilities, environmental information and technological opportunities are concerned. In following an individual learning path, economic actors develop over time specific routines and rules of thumb which allow them to tackle daily uncertainty by means of innovative activity. Far from being on the shelf, these heuristics are highly tacit and embedded in the experience acquired in everyday life. That is, the transfer and adoption of new technologies implies a specific cost which may well equal the cost of first introduction (Antonelli, 1995). Accordingly, the process of heuristics development and, therefore, technological change has a strong path-dependent connotation in the sense that at any point in time the production, implementation, selection and adoption of new technologies by an economic actor greatly depends on the technology he/she has used up to then. Thus, technological change can be said to be *localized* in the sense that the exploration and development of new techniques are likely to occur in the neighbourhood of the techniques already in use.

Along these lines, new knowledge is the result of a specific and *local* learning process where it is hard to disentangle the role played by public research institutions and corporate research laboratories. In this perspective, no clear boundaries can be drawn between science and technology *ex ante*, while the two can be neatly distinguished *ex post* on the grounds of the degree of availability of the outcome of the research process. As pointed out in the pioneering work of Nelson (1959) and Arrow (1962), the 'public good' character of scientific output causes a shortage of scientific research since private actors will invest just as much as they will be able to directly exploit by economic returns. Following the argument of these two authors, no cure for this market failure can be provided by extending intellectual property rights to scientific information since this would raise the cost of other private actors interested in using it above the cost of its reproduction, the result being that too little science would be employed in the economy, with detrimental consequences for economic growth. Conversely, no such problems arise as far as technology output is concerned due to its tacit nature. However, as anticipated above, complementarities do exist between science and technology since the advances of the former may well depend on the advances of the latter. These complementarities are mirrored by the intensification of the linkages between corporate actors and public research institutions in terms of efforts of knowledge production as a result of several parallel phenomena. In the knowledge-based economy, the emergence of streams of scientific knowledge widely applicable to a broad range of production problems and the high rates of knowledge obsolescence has doubtless played a role in this story. Similarly, if the growing complex and interrelated nature of knowledge development has nowadays imposed budget constraints on corporate actors, universities are increasingly forced to look for external funding shifting towards a stronger market orientation. Firmly convinced of the complementarity of science and technology, the contributors to this volume frame their analysis of the role of public research institutions in economic growth and development within an innovation system approach. Far from being theoretically new, the concept of innovation system proposed by Freeman (1987) in the 1980s is well suited, we believe, to investigate the role of universities and public laboratories in contemporary efforts at catch-up given its emphasis on the wide range of institutions whose actions influence, focus, stimulate, or delay, innovation in an economy (at the national or regional level).

Within this systemic approach, multinational corporations (MNCs) do play a role in shaping and directing catching-up processes by interacting with local actors and, therefore, becoming part of the local system of innovation. The underlying notion of the MNC adopted throughout the book is that of an internationally dispersed network whose units source new knowledge complementary to the corporate learning path in different locations. The interplay between the multinational network and the local environment gives rise to patterns of national (regional) specialization as well as to clusters of (domestic and foreign) firms where location-specific knowledge spillovers take place. These spillover mechanisms gain great value when basic knowledge is involved due to its tacit and, then, geographically sticky nature (Cantwell and Santangelo, 1999). Despite the development of information and communication technology (ICT), empirical evidence has been provided on the significance of geographical proximity in the sourcing and transmission of context-dependent and locally embedded knowledge (Santangelo, 2002). These considerations bear great implications for the host locations (countries and regions), which, being ranked by MNCs on the grounds of their knowledge potential, compete in attracting foreign investment. Thus MNCs can play a major role in the processes of catch-up of countries (regions) behind the technological and economic frontier.

Drawing upon a specific understanding of the nature of technological change, the roles of universities and public research laboratories in catching-up processes, and the roles of international business, are developed in three parts, each of which deals with a specific aspect of the issue at hand. These three parts are preceded by the chapter by Cristiano Antonelli (Chapter 1) setting the theoretical framework underlying the whole volume as far as the nature of technological change is concerned. In particular, Antonelli's chapter proposes an analytical model of localized technological change where the dynamics of creative adoption of new technologies gives rise to an S-shaped diffusion path, and emphasizes the implications for the relations between the economics of innovation and the economics of growth. In Part I, the contribution of Richard Nelson (Chapter 2) elaborates on the roles of research in indigenous universities and public laboratories in technological and economic catch-up by drawing on some insightful commentary on historic events. Along these lines, Roberto Mazzoleni's chapter (Chapter 3) takes a close look at academic systems in Germany, France, the USA and Japan in the nineteenth century as well as the way in which they have been influenced by the emergence of national patterns and cross-border cooperation. This part closes with Mario Calderini and Chiara Franzoni's chapter (Chapter 4), which surveys recent works testing for the hypothesis of rivalry between basic and applied research, discusses their findings and limitations, and comments on the implications for the economics of science and technology, and policy intervention.

Part II focuses on the other main actor of this volume, the MNC. John Cantwell (Chapter 5) provides an overview of the relationship between MNCs and local economic systems, by discussing the origins of clusters, the principal types of spillovers and associated cluster types that have been observed, and the science–technology linkages found in clusters. Christian Bellak (Chapter 6) tests four hypotheses of firm strategies and interaction between firms on the basis of the existing (industry-comparative and firm-competitive) advantage combination on a representative sample of Austrian manufacturing firms during 1990–2000. The Turkish experience is the focus of the chapter by Aykut Lenger and Erol Taymaz (Chapter 7), who investigate the determinants of innovativeness in Turkish manufacturing industries by drawing on the system view of innovation and the micro view of dynamic capability and by paying special attention to foreign firms (i.e. MNCs), their interactions with domestic firms, and their impact on domestic capability building. Davide Castellani and Antonello Zanfei (Chapter 8) empirically investigate the significant heterogeneity in productivity and innovative behaviour of (foreign and domestic-owned) multinationals relative to domestic uninational firms in Italy and discuss the policy implications of their results.

Part III, devoted to the analysis of catch-up and innovative activity in backward locations, opens with the chapter by Furman and Hayes (Chapter 9), who investigate convergence in national innovative capacities, focusing on the country-level investments, institutional configurations and national policy decisions that shape the success of 'follower' nations in catching up to the world's leading innovator countries in terms of per capita innovative output. Rosalia Epifanio (Chapter 10) examines the role of 'context' variables for innovative activity in a lagging self-contained region such as Sicily on a sample of 72 small manufacturing firms, drawing the conclusion that such variables may constitute 'ties' or may trigger vicious mechanisms, instead of promoting dynamic positive synergies. The chapter by Maria da Conceição Rego (Chapter 11) focuses on a population of former University of Évora (Portugal) students in order to assess their connections with the city of Évora and its surrounding areas after graduation, and analyses their impact on regional economic activity and their contribution to the improvement of the regional labour force. The analysis devotes some space also to the relationships between Évora University and other regional agents, in terms of knowledge and innovation transfer.

REFERENCES

Antonelli, C. (1995), *The Economics of Localised Technological Change and Industrial Dynamics*. Dordrecht: Kluwer Academic Press.

Arrow, K. (1962), 'Economic Welfare and the Allocation of Resources for Innovation', in R. Nelson (ed.), *The Rate and Direction of Inventive Activity*. Princeton, NJ: Princeton University Press.

Cantwell, J.A. and Santangelo, G.D. (1999), 'The Frontier of International Technology Networks: Sourcing Abroad the Most Highly Tacit Capability', *Information Economics and Policy*, **11**, 101–23.

Freeman, C. (1987), 'National Systems of Innovation: the Case of Japan', in *Technology Policy and Economics Performance: Lessons from Japan*. London: Pinter Publishers.

Nelson, R.R. (1959), 'The Simple Economics of Basic Scientific Research', *Journal of Political Economy*, **67** (3), 297–306.

Santangelo, G.D. (2002), *Innovation in Multinational Corporations and the Information Age – The European Experience*. Cheltenham, UK and Northampton, MA, USA: Edward Elgar.

1. The economics of localized technological change: the role of creative adoption

Cristiano Antonelli

1. INTRODUCTION

The study of technological change has made a great deal of progress by means of artificial disjunctions between aspects that are difficult to separate.[2] The traditional divide between innovation, adoption and imitation can be reconciled in the context of the economics of localized technological change. Adoption is the result of a complex process of decision-making. Firms are induced to change their technology when product and factor market conditions do not meet their expectations and irreversible choices make adjustments expensive. Technological change consists of both the introduction of original, 'never-before-seen' technologies and the adoption of technologies that have already been put in place elsewhere. Indeed, adoption requires a number of highly specific and idiosyncratic problems of adaptation and integration to be solved. Moreover, it requires that several preliminary activities are carried out, such as search, selection, identification, adaptation and integration into the production process and the firm at large. Technological change, for each firm, is the result of both research and imitation activities. Both command resources and engender specific revenues. Localized technological change consists of creative adoption where external knowledge and embodied technologies are implemented with internal competence and idiosyncratic knowledge acquired by means of learning processes. The identification of the net profitability of adoption as defined by the gross profitability of adoption minus adoption costs constitutes the economics of creative adoption.

The rest of the chapter is structured as follows. Section 2 recalls the basic features of the economics of diffusion and adoption, and elaborates on the notions of induced adoption, adoption costs and net profitability of adoption. Section 3 presents a model of localized technological change consisting of both the induced introduction of new technologies and the induced adoption of technologies already available in the marketplace. The conclusion summarizes the results of the work.

2.   DIFFUSION, IMITATION AND ADOPTION

The distinction between innovation and imitation was first introduced by Joseph Schumpeter and eventually became a landmark in the economics of innovation and new technology. A new technology, either a new product or a new process, is first introduced by an innovator and eventually imitated by competitors. Imitators copy the innovation and in so doing enter the market and reduce the excess profits of the innovator. Imitation restores perfect competition.

The imitation process, that is the mechanism and the duration of the time span by means of which innovations are imitated, has been studied bit by bit and the notion of diffusion was eventually introduced. The economics of diffusion addresses relevant questions about the characteristics, determinants, and the effects of the diffusion process. The most controversial question is why imitation is not instantaneous and all firms adopt the innovation at the same time (Stoneman, 1976, 1983, 1987).

A long tradition of empirical and theoretical work on the economics of diffusion has made it possible to make a number of important distinctions. The first is between imitation and adoption. Adoption consists in the purchase of a new capital good, a new intermediary input or a new organizational procedure that has been supplied by upstream producers. Imitation consists of the replication of a new practice, product, process, market or organizational procedure first implemented by another firm. The adoption of a new capital good can be the result of the imitation of a process innovation. The imitation of a product innovation does not necessarily imply the adoption of new capital goods.

The second distinction concerns the mechanisms at work. Much attention has been paid to identifying the determinants of the diffusion of the demand side and the determinants of the supply side. In the first case diffusion, that is the process of delayed adoptions of a given innovation, with fixed economic characteristics, including performance and price, takes place because of dynamics on the demand side. The main engine is the well-known contagion in a population of heterogeneous agents, characterized by information asymmetries, and the eventual decay of information costs for potential adopters, driven by the dissemination of information carried out by all those who have already adopted (Griliches, 1957).

As soon as the information about the advantages provided by the innovation becomes available to the potential adopter, the adoption will take place. Diffusion, defined as a sequence of adoption lags, is fully explained by the characteristics of the spreading of the information. By the same token, technological resilience, that is non-adoption, is simply the result of lack of information (Mansfield, 1968).

Technological resilience can also be considered as the result of inappropriate levels of the profitability of adoption of a given technological innovation. The change of relevant conditions in the population of potential adopters, however, engenders an increase in the actual profitability of adoption and hence leads to the eventual diffusion. In this approach, where the dynamics takes place on the demand side, but is not reduced to the spreading of information, diffusion is regarded as the outcome of the increase in the profitability of adoption engendered by changes in the factor markets of potential adopters. The profitability of adoption of a technology is clearly affected by relative factor costs and hence by their changes, such as the increase in relative wages (Antonelli, 2003). In the same vein, the working of network externalities has a direct bearing on the profitability of adoption of a given innovation, provided that the number of its users has a direct bearing on its efficiency (Katz and Shapiro, 1986; Smith, 2004). In all these cases the drivers of the diffusion of a given technological innovation are found on the demand side.

In the supply side approach, heterogeneity of potential adopters consists in their cost conditions (David, 1969; Metcalfe, 1981). Diffusion is now defined not by the structure and the sequence of delays in the adoption of a family of closely related technologies with changing economic and technical characteristics, but rather a single and given technology with static features. Potential adopters can be ranked in terms of cost characteristics. Diffusion here is driven by the dynamics on the supply side and specifically by the introduction of an array of events including: (a) incremental changes in the prototype introduced by the innovator and/or by imitators, and (b) the decline of the market price due to (b1) the entry of new competitors and the decline of market power and hence mark-up for early innovators, or (b2) the positive effects of increasing returns either associated with sheer economies of scale and density, or with the dynamics of learning by doing. The sequence between the introduction of product innovations and the eventual introduction of process innovation to manufacture the new products, articulated by Utterback (1994), also has a direct effect on the decline of the market price for the new products and hence on the increase of their profitability of adoption. Both the decline of the market price and the introduction of incremental innovations can be seen as the effect of the entry of creative imitators in upstream markets (Stoneman, 1995, 2002).

In a complementary approach the reduction in the price of the new products and the increase in the scope of adoption is the result of the selection mechanism at work on the supply side. After the introduction of an array of competing product innovations targeting the same product market, a dominant design progressively emerges with relevant cost advantages in terms of standardization, specialization and division of labour, economies of scale, and economies of learning and density. Once again diffusion is driven by the dynamics of the supply side (Utterback, 1994).

Many efforts have been made to combine the supply and the demand side approaches into a single more comprehensive model. Much progress has been made possible by the insight of Metcalfe (1981), where the epidemic, demand-side mechanism is implemented by the shifting conditions on the supply side so as to define the traditional S-shaped process as the envelope of a double shift.

The identification of the role of adoption costs paves the way for the distinction between gross profitability of adoption and net profitability of adoption. Adoption costs are defined by the broad range of activities that are necessary to identify an innovation and adapt it to the existing production process. Adoption costs include those of search and adaptive research, the costs of scrapping the existing fixed production factors, the restructuring of the production and marketing organizations, the re-skilling of personnel, the actual purchase of the capital good and intermediary input embodying the new knowledge, the purchase of patents and licenses, and the costs of technical assistance. Net profitability of adoption is the result of the algebraic sum of the gross profitability engendered by the adoption of an innovation and the costs that it is necessary to incur in order to identify, select and finally adapt the new technology to the existing production conditions.

The imitation and the eventual adoption of a capital good or an intermediary input are not free, especially for firms. The adoption of a new technology is in fact necessarily the end result of a broader process that includes a preliminary search activity, a comparative assessment, the substitution of existing items, be they other capital goods in place, workers, suppliers, customers or other components of the current structure of the firm. Adoption can take place only when significant changes and adjustments have been made to the original setting. Such changes affect both the good incorporating the innovation and the layout of the firm as it was before the introduction of the new technology could take place. Adoption can take place only when the profitability of the new layout is confronted with that of the previous arrangement and yields a positive result. This comparative assessment includes the costs of the anticipated scrapping of the existing capital goods and the effects of all the related changes in investment behavior (Antonelli, 1993).

The adoption of a new technology is part of a broader process of technological change. Firms are reluctant to change their technology and are induced to introduce new technologies only when a clear inducement mechanism is put in place. As soon as the routines in place and hence the technology currently in use are questioned, and the inducement mechanism has been initiated by some mismatch between plans and facts, the choice between the introduction of original technologies invented here, and the adoption of not-invented-here technologies can take place.

The introduction of all kinds of technological changes by a firm is the result of a range of complementary activities that can be substituted only to a limited extent. At one extreme of the spectrum, technological change is the result almost exclusively of the generation of original knowledge and the novel introduction of a production factor never seen before. At the other extreme, there is the traditional passive and imitative adoption where the firm limits itself to purchasing a good incorporating an innovation. The wide gulf of intermediary positions deserves much closer attention. This is the region where creative adoption takes place.

The economics of localized technological change provides an appropriate analytical context for understanding the mechanisms at work in the case of creative adoption.

3.   THE ANALYSIS AND THE MODEL

3.1.   The Economics of Localized Technological Change

In the localized technological change tradition of analysis, firms can face unexpected changes in their product and factor markets, either changing their technologies or their techniques. When the actual conditions of the product and factor markets do not match expectations, firms can consider adjusting passively to the new market conditions. Alternatively, they can consider the opportunity for the introduction of new technologies (Atkinson and Stiglitz, 1969; David, 1975; Antonelli, 1995).

The changes in techniques imply that the firm is able to move on a given map of isoquants. Because of the effects of irreversibilities and limited knowledge, however, technical changes engender some switching costs and some costs in terms of missed opportunities for learning. The introduction of new technologies is a viable alternative when switching costs are high and technological opportunities are good. The introduction of new technologies, however, is not free: it requires that resources be dedicated and specific activities carried out.

A trade-off between technical change and technological change emerges: whether to change just the technique on the existing map of isoquants, or to change the technology, and hence the shape of the isoquants. The trade-off will be tilted towards the introduction of technological change when access to knowledge is easy.

Because learning is the main source of new knowledge and is mainly local, and because of the irreversibility of production factors and layout, technological change is localized: induced by changes in factor and product markets that cannot be accommodated by technical changes in a given map of isoquants, and the related price and quantity adjustments are based upon the local opportunities for learning and generating new knowledge (Antonelli, 1999, 2001).

In Figure 1.1 we see that a change in relative factor price affects the viability of previous equilibrium, E_1. The firm can either change the technique and move to E_2, or change the technology by means of the introduction of technological innovations so as to find a new equilibrium in the proximity of the isocline OE_1, in E_3 or (possibly) beyond.[3] The outcome will depend upon the levels of switching costs, that is, the amount of resources that are

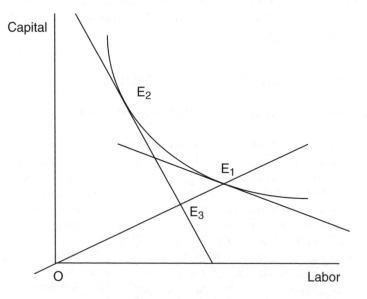

Figure 1.1   The trade-off between technical change and technological change

necessary to perform all the activities to move from E_1 to E_2, compared to the amount of resources that are necessary to innovate and move towards and beyond E_3.[4]

The resilience in the old equilibrium point E_1 is out of the question: the firm produces at costs that are well above the levels of the firms, typically new firms with lower levels of irreversible factors that are able to produce in the new equilibrium point E_2.

The firm is now exposed to a clear decline in the levels of performance and of satisfaction. A reaction is necessary: it can be a passive one and consist in the traditional technical change defined as a movement in the space of existing isoquants, or a more creative one so as to include a change in the routines and the eventual introduction of innovations. Such a change in the technology space can be the result of either the introduction of brand new technologies just invented and never seen elsewhere, or adopting technologies that have already been experienced by other competitors or supplied by vendors of capital goods and other intermediary inputs. The combination of adoption and implementation of such technologies with the knowledge and competence generated internally by means of learning processes, that is the creative adoption, is likely to be the most common strategy in these circumstances.

The difference between current profits, after the changes in the marketplace, and the profits that should have been possible without such changes indicates the amount of resource the firm is ready to commit in order to bring about the changes that are likely to restore the expected levels of profitability.

In other words, because of the mismatch between expectations and the actual conditions in the marketplace, the firm cannot stay in the position that had been planned. The introduction of technological innovations is a viable alternative to technical change. Both adjustments are possible, but are costly. Technical change, because of irreversibility of existing production factors and limited knowledge about the existing techniques, requires some switching activity. Technological change, on the other hand, by definition, is not 'on the shelf' and its introduction in turn requires some innovation activities.

Much work has been done in the localized technological change approach to inquire into the conditions, characteristics and determinants of the trade-off between technical change and technological change. The introduction of technological changes is possible only if appropriate amounts of knowledge and competence have been accumulated and are available to firms.

The conditions of the learning process and the determinants of the eventual production of knowledge, such as the characteristics of the internal organization and structure of firms, have received much attention. Also considered are the structure of the local systems of innovation, the channels of communication among firms, and between them and scientific institutions, the forms of interaction and cooperation between firms active in the same industry as well as across industries and diverse markets, and the working of labor markets as vehicles for the transmission of information and knowledge. The management and the structure of the relations among users and producers, the positive and negative effects of the spillover of proprietary knowledge among rivals and more generally the governance of the appropriability conditions and the structure of intellectual property rights all need to be taken into account. Much work has also been devoted to analysing the effects of the irreversibility and duration in historic time of capital goods and intangible assets in shaping the conduct of firms (Antonelli, 2001, 2003).

3.2. The Supply of New Technologies

Important progress can be made when localized technological change is seen as the result of a creative adoption, that is the combination of internal competence and knowledge with the external knowledge embodied in capital goods and intermediary inputs provided by upstream suppliers or available in the form of technological information, licenses and patents.

The introduction of a new technology is induced by the mismatch between expectations and actual market conditions, and the irreversibility of production choices that have been made. The firm initiates a combined process of search and research. All opportunities to change the existing map of isoquants are now considered. The introduction of a brand new technology requires research effort. The adoption of a new technology into the production process of a firm requires some effort to adapt it to the local conditions. The combination of the two activities yields the creative adoption of an existing technology to which a number of changes are made so as to make it more consistent with the specific requirements of the existing production process and hence to reduce the amount of switching costs.

The choice set is now framed. The firm faces two nested frontiers of possible changes in order to solve the mismatch between plans and real market conditions. The first frontier of possible changes is that of possible adjustments, which makes it possible to compare the results of resources invested in either technical or technological changes.

The second frontier, that of creative adoptions, compares the kinds of technological change. It defines a range of changes all stemming from creative adoptions. The range comprises the two extremes of a brand-new technology, fully original, and the 'passive' adoption of an external technology.

Both the frontiers, of possible changes and of creative adoptions, have

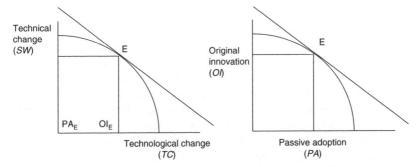

Figure 1.2   The nested frontiers of possible adjustments and creative adoptions

the usual concave shape that reflects the effects of diminishing returns in either activity. The shape is defined by the relative efficiency of the activities being considered (see Figure 1.2).

The position of the frontier of possible adjustments is defined by the amount of resources R that the firm should invest just to switch from the previous equilibrium technique to the new one. The search for the correct solution, in other words, is identified as a maximization process where the firm tries to maximize the amount of changes, including technological innovations, that can be generated with a given amount of resources set by the levels of switching costs.[5]

The firm can identify the correct solution by means of the standard maximization of the output, for two given nested frontiers, when two nested isorevenues are defined. The first isorevenue is defined by the absolute levels of the revenue generated by all adjustment activities consisting in the revenue made possible by the introduction of new techniques and the revenue made possible by the introduction of the new technologies respectively. The second isorevenue measures the bundle of revenues generated by more or less creative adoption of existing technologies, that is either the original innovation or the passive adoption.

Formally we see the following relations:

$$TC = a\,(R) \tag{1.1}$$

$$SW = b\,(R) \tag{1.2}$$

$$OI = c\,(R) \tag{1.3}$$

$$PA = d\,(R) \tag{1.4}$$

where TC measures the amount of technological innovation necessary to change the technical space that the firm can generate, taking into account the internal competence and knowledge accumulated and the external knowledge it can access; SW measures the amount of technical change necessary to move in the existing technical space and reflects the levels of irreversibility and rigidity of tangible and intangible capital; OI measures the amount of original innovation and PA measures the amount of passive adoption that can be generated with a given amount of dedicated resources (R) defined by the amount of switching activities the firm needs to complete to move from one equilibrium point to the other.

It is clear that the relationship between the four production activities is essential to define the outcome of the search process initiated by the changes in the product and factor markets. It seems clear that the larger the efficiency in the production of technological changes, the lower the efficiency of switching, and the larger the amount of innovations introduced. Correspondingly, the smaller the efficiency of internal research activities and hence the smaller the amount of original innovations, the smaller the efficiency of the adaptation activities and the smaller will be the amount of innovations each firm will generate. The firm will adjust to the new factor and product market conditions more by means of switching activities than by means of creative adoptions.

The extent to which the firm will rely on levels of creative adoption closer to passive adoption or will try to introduce original innovation, still based upon some levels of technological blending and recombination, will clearly be influenced by the relative efficiency of either activities and by the shape of the relevant isorevenue.

To make this point more compact, let us now assume that a frontier of possible adjustments can be considered, such that for a given amount of resources (R) necessary to face the mismatch, firms can generate an amount of either technological change (TC) or technical change (SW). Nested to the frontier of possible adjustments we find a frontier of creative adoptions that can be obtained with the introduction of either original innovation (OI) or passive adoption (PA). Specifically the shape and the slope of the frontier of creative adoptions reflects the effects of the technological opportunities based upon the localized competence built by means of internal learning by doing and the opportunities offered by the knowledge and the technologies generated by third parties that become available either by means of imitation or by the active push of upstream suppliers. Formally this amounts to saying that:

$$SW = e\,(TC) \qquad\qquad (1.5)$$

$$OI = f\,(PA) \qquad\qquad (1.6)$$

In order for standard optimization procedures to be operationalized, two isorevenue functions need to be set. The first, defined as the revenue of adjustments (RA), compares the revenue that adjustments by switching in the technical space (SW) yield with respect to the revenue of technological change (RTC). The second isorevenue includes the revenue generated by the introduction of original innovations (OI) and the revenues generated by the passive adoption of innovations and knowledge generated elsewhere (PA). Formally we see:

$$RA = s\ SW + t\ RTC \qquad (1.7)$$

$$RTC = r\ OI + z\ PA \qquad (1.8)$$

where s and t measure the unit revenue of switching and the unit revenue of technological change; r and z measure respectively the unit revenue of the amount of original innovations and passive adoption of external technologies and knowledge respectively, generated with the given amount of resources available to face unexpected changes in product and factor markets and the equilibrium amount of resources that can be identified to fund the introduction of technological change.

It seems clear that the slope of the isorevenue of creative adoptions exhibits the larger unit revenue stemming from the introduction of original innovations. They make it possible for the firm to command monopolistic market power and hence extra profits. By the same token, however, it should also be clear that the shape of the frontier of creative adoption should reflect the larger output – for per given levels of inputs – in terms of adoptions with respect to the output in terms of introduction of original innovations: passive adoption is easier than the introduction of original innovations.

The system of equations can be solved with the standard tangency solutions so as to define both the mixes of creative adoptions, which in each specific context firms are advised to select, and the amount of technological change with respect to switching the context suggests selecting. The system of equilibrium conditions is:

$$e'\ (TC) = t/s \qquad (1.9)$$

$$f'\ (PA) = z/r$$

subject to $TCI = OI + PA$ and $R = R_F{}^6$

The cases of either only technical change or only technological change and in turn either fully original innovations or fully passive adoptions are extreme solutions. Much of the real world can be found in between such extremes. Firms are induced to innovate by the mismatch between actual and expected conditions of their production set and their market conditions, necessarily built upon irreversible decisions taken on the basis of myopic expectations which are not met by the disequilibrium conditions in product and factor markets. The type of technological change is influenced by the relative net profitability of introduction of original innovations with respect to passive adoption of external technologies.

The slope of the innovation isorevenue reflects the relative gross profitability of introduction of invented-here technologies with respect to the gross profitability of adoption of technological innovations introduced elsewhere. According to the shape of the innovation isorevenue, both the composition of technological change, whether it consists mainly of innovations or adoptions, and the mix of possible changes, whether they consist mainly of switching activities or technological changes, are affected.

The equilibrium conditions identified in equation (1.9) capture the essence of the dynamics of localized technological changes consisting of creative adoptions engendered by the mismatch between plans and actual factor and market conditions for firms that are constrained by the irreversibility of their choices.

4. CONCLUSIONS

The economics of localized technological change provides a context in which the adoption of new technologies can be considered as the result of an active and intentional undertaking of firms. The adoption of a new technology is the result of a complex process in which an inducement mechanism has to be identified, specific activities have to be put in place, and dedicated resources have to be committed. A clear effort is needed to adapt it to the pre-existing context. There is no adoption without adaptation. In turn such an adaptation requires considerable levels of competence and creativity.

At the same the introduction of a new technology is always the result of the blending and recombination of elements of technological knowledge both as a good and embodied in capital goods and intermediary inputs, organizational procedures and routines introduced elsewhere. Each innovation builds upon previous innovations. Technological knowledge and technological change as a consequence exhibit strong elements of cumulability and both are the result of the incremental introduction of changes added on to previous advances. If there is no adoption without adaptation, it is also true that there is little innovation without some adoption.

The economics of localized technological change also provides a context in which the inducement to introduce technological changes is the result of the creative reaction of firms exposed to an increasing gap between expectations and actual conditions of profitability. When technology has to be changed, because switching costs impede standard shifts in the existing maps of isoquants and performances are falling below the expected levels, firms can rely on their competence and the knowledge acquired by means of their own internal research and development activities. However, external sources of knowledge and new technologies embodied in new capital goods and intermediary inputs do provide essential inputs to the introduction of new technologies by each firm. The introduction of technological change is the outcome of a process of creative adoption where external knowledge and new technologies made available in the markets are recombined with the knowledge generated internally by means of learning processes and research and development activities.

The traditional divide between innovation, adoption and imitation can be questioned in the context of the economics of localized technological change. Firms are induced to change their technology when product and factor market conditions do not meet their expectations and irreversible choices make adjustments expensive. Technological change is the result of the combination of research and search activities that lead to both the introduction of new technologies and to imitative adoptions. Both command resources and engender specific revenues. Localized technological change consists of creative adoption where external knowledge and embodied technologies are implemented with internal competence and idiosyncratic knowledge acquired by means of learning processes. The identification of the net profitability of adoption as defined by the gross profitability of adoption minus adoption costs constitutes the economics of technological change.

The divide between innovation and adoption is less and less realistic at a time when general-purpose technologies (Helpman, 1998), such as new information and communication technologies, characterize the rate and the direction of technological change. New information and communication technologies with high levels of fungibility characterize the present trend of innovation at the aggregate level. In this context, firms, induced to change their technology by the dynamics of localized technological change, make use of the fungibility of the new technological system and enter a process of creative adoption.

Adoption and innovation are two complementary aspects of a broader process of reaction to the mismatch between expectations and facts and eventual introduction of localized technological changes that build upon the creative adoption and recombination of internal and external technological knowledge.

NOTES

1. I acknowledge the financial support of the European Union Directorate for Research, within the context of the Key Action 'Improving the socio-economic knowledge base' to the project 'Technological Knowledge and Localised Learning: What Perspectives for a European Policy?' carried on under research contract no. HPSE-CT2001-00051 at the Fondazione Rosselli. Preliminary versions of this chapter have been presented at the international workshop on 'Public Research Institutions, International Business, and Technological and Economic Catch-Up in Developing Regions', organized by the University of Catania in March 2004 and at the tenth International J.A. Schumpeter Society meeting 'Innovation, Industrial Dynamics and Structural Transformation: Schumpeterian Legacies', Università Bocconi, Milan, June 2004. I acknowledge the funding of the Department of Economics of the University of Turin in 2002 and 2003 for the award of the research grants 'Cause ed effetti della direzione del cambiamento tecnologico' and 'Innovazione: nuove tecnologie e cambiamento strutturale'. The research work was made possible by the financial support of the Italian Ministry of Research to the national research projects 'Produzione, distribuzione della conoscenza e globalizzazione. Analisi dei processi di assimilazione, generazione e comunicazione di conoscenza tecnologica e rapporti con la dinamica industriale nei processi di crescita esterna e interna, domestica e multinazionale di imprese leader nell'industria automobilistica italiana'in 2002–3 and 'Il knowledge management come strumento di vantaggio competitivo per le imprese-rete: un confronto intersettoriale' in 2004–5. The comments and criticisms of many, including Stan Metcalfe and Grazia Santangelo, are acknowledged.
2. See Nathan Rosenberg: 'The criticisms which I have leveled thus far against the artificial segregation of invention from innovation apply equally well to the segregation of invention from diffusion. Innovation is simply the beginning of the diffusion process. However, here again we have inherited from the Schumpeterian framework a sharp disjunction which emphasizes the high levels of leadership and creativity involved in the first introduction of a new technique as compared to the mere imitative activity of subsequent adopters. Here also, as a result, the analysis of the diffusion process fails to focus upon continued technological and engineering alterations and adaptations, the cumulative effects of which decisively influence the volume and the timing of the product's sale. The diffusion process is typically dependent upon a stream of improvement in the performance characteristics of an innovation, its progressive modification and adaptation to suit the specialized requirements of various submarkets, and the availability and introduction of other complementary inputs which affect the economic usefulness of an original innovation' (Rosenberg, 1976: 75).
3. Only new solutions beyond E_3 can engender an actual increase in total factor productivity (see Antonelli, 1995 and 1999).
4. See Antonelli (1995 and 1999) for a rigorous exposition.
5. The firm can 'discover' to its surprise that the equilibrium amount of possible adjustments makes it possible to introduce a total-factor-productivity-increasing technological change which leads the firm beyond equilibrium point E_3 (see Figure 1.1). This is clearly a case for procedural rationality as opposed to substantive rationality.
6. R_F is set by the amount of resources the myopic firm, unable to anticipate the 'technological shock', should in any case invest in order to switch.

BIBLIOGRAPHY

Antonelli, C. (1990), 'Induced adoption and externalities in the regional diffusion of new information technology', *Regional Studies*, **24**, 31–40.

Antonelli, C. (1991), *The Diffusion of Advanced Telecommunications in Developing Countries*, Paris: OECD.

Antonelli, C. (1993), 'Investment and adoption in advanced telecommunications', *Journal of Economic Behavior and Organization, 20*, 227–46.

Antonelli, C. (1995), *The Economics of Localized Technological Change and Industrial Dynamics*, Boston, MA: Kluwer.

Antonelli, C. (1999), *The Microdynamics of Technological Change*, London: Routledge.

Antonelli, C. (2001), *The Microeconomics of Technological Systems*, Oxford: Oxford University Press.

Antonelli, C. (2003), *The Economics of Innovation, New Technologies and Structural Change*, London: Routledge.

Antonelli, C., Petit, P. and Tahar, G. (1992), *The Economics of Industrial Modernization*, Cambridge: Academic Press.

Arvanitis, S. and Hollenstein, H. (2001), 'The determinants of the adoption of advanced manufacturing technology', *Economics of Innovation and New Technology, 10*, 377–414.

Atkinson, A.B. and Stiglitz, J.E. (1969), 'A new view of technological change', *Economic Journal, 79*, 573–8.

Canepa, A. and Stoneman, P. (2004), 'Comparative international diffusion: patterns, determinants and policies', *Economics of Innovation and New Technology, 13*, 279–98.

David, P.A. (1969), 'A contribution to the theory of diffusion', Research Center in Economic Growth, Memorandum no. 71, Stanford University.

David, P.A. (1975), *Technical Choice, Innovation and Economic Growth*, Cambridge: Cambridge University Press.

Faria, A.P., Fenn, P. and Bruce, A. (2002), 'Determinants of the adoption of flexible production technologies: evidence from Portuguese manufacturing industry', *Economics of Innovation and New Technology, 11*, 560–80.

Griliches, Z. (1957), 'Hybrid corn: an exploration in the economics of technological change', *Econometrica, 25*, 501–22.

Helpman, E. (ed.) (1998), *General Purpose Technologies and Economic Growth*, Cambridge, MA: MIT Press.

Johnson, D.K. (2002), ' "Learning-by-licensing": R&D and technology licensing in Brazilian invention', *Economics of Innovation and New Technology, 11*, 163–77.

Katz, M.L. and Shapiro, C. (1986), 'Technology adoption in the presence of network externalities', *Journal of Political Economy, 94*, 822–41.

Mansfield, E. (1968), *Industrial Research and Technological Innovation*, New York: Norton.

Metcalfe, J.S. (1981), 'Impulse and diffusion in the study of technical change', *Futures, 13*, 347–59.

Rosenberg, N. (1976), *Perspectives on Technology*, Cambridge: Cambridge University Press.

Smith, M.Y. (2004), 'A model of linked adoption of complementary technologies', *Economics of Innovation and New Technology, 13*, 91–9.

Stoneman, P. (1976), *Technological Diffusion and the Computer Revolution*, Cambridge: Cambridge University Press.

Stoneman, P. (1983), *The Economics Analysis of Technical Change*, Oxford: Oxford University Press.

The economics of localized change

Stoneman, P. (1987), *The Economics Analysis of Technology Policy*, Oxford: Clarendon Press.

Stoneman, P. (ed.) (1995), *Handbook of the Economics of Innovation and Technological Change*, Oxford: Blackwell.

Stoneman, P. (2002), *The Economics of Technological Diffusion*, Oxford: Blackwell.

Stoneman, P. and Toivanen, O. (1997), 'The diffusion of multiple technologies: an empirical study', *Economics of Innovation and New Technology*, **5**, 1–17.

Utterback, J.M. (1994), *Mastering the Dynamics of Innovation*, Boston, MA: Harvard Business School Press.

PART I

Local Science and Technology Policy

2. The roles of research in universities and public labs in economic catch-up

Richard R. Nelson

INTRODUCTION

This chapter is concerned with the roles of research in indigenous universities and public laboratories in the processes through which countries behind the technological and economic frontier catch up. I ague that, for several reasons, the role of indigenous public research is more important today than it was in the twentieth century. I also argue that the building of an effective indigenous system of research is no easy task, while offering some guidelines that may be helpful.

However, before getting into these topics, I need to set the stage by considering the process of catch-up more generally, and in historical perspective. It is clear that the process of catch-up involves learning about and learning to master ways of doing things that are used by the leading countries of the era. However, the term catch-up seems to connote that the catching-up country simply copies, and this is misleading. While practice in advanced countries does usually serve as a model, what is achieved inevitably differs in certain ways from the template. In part this reflects that exact copying is almost impossible, and attempts to replicate at best get viably close. In part it reflects deliberate and often creative modifications aimed to tailor practice to national conditions. This is especially so regarding organizational structures and institutions.

Most of the writings on catch-up have presumed, explicitly or implicitly, that the key practices that need to be mastered are 'technologies', in a rather conventional sense of that term, with the know-how involved of the sort that is learned by engineers, and physical and biological scientists, and often embodied in physical things like machines, and specialized materials of various sorts. Certainly much of the powerful practice of advanced countries that developing ones are trying to acquire is technology of this sort: product designs, complex production processes, the seeds and pesticides and procedures used in productive agriculture, modern medical practice including the use of pharmaceuticals and sophisticated medical equipment, the technological core of modern air traffic control systems, and the like.

However, much of the relevant practice is not easily characterizable as technology in this narrow sense. Thus complex production processes generally involve large teams of workers, with a division of labor, and a management and control system to generate effective coordination. Behind the scenes is a system for hiring, rewarding, and occasionally releasing labor, and another system for assuring that the firm can finance its activities and investments. Farther back there is a system of education and training that provides, poorly or well, labor supply with the needed skills, and a system of banks and other financial institutions. As I indicated above, later in this chapter I shall focus on the set of national public institutions that do research and advanced training. All of these involve ways of doing things – practices – but technology in a narrow sense is not at their core. (For a general discussion of the relationship between technological change and institutional structures see Perez, 2002.)

Bhaven Sampat and I have proposed that it may be useful to think of the latter as being or structuring 'social' technologies, as contrasted with the 'physical' technologies that are the focus of attention in most analyses of the practices that lead to productive economic activity (Nelson and Sampat, 2001). Rather than being embodied in physical hardware and materials, social technologies are embodied in organizational forms, bodies of law, public policies, codes of good business and administrative practice, customs, expectations and norms.

The point of view that I will develop here is that, in this modern age, physical technologies may be much easier to learn and acquire than social technologies. This fact (if it is that) presents two kinds of problems for nations seeking to catch up. The first is that the effective operation of many physical technologies requires the implementation of various social technologies. Thus it may be far easier to import the machinery and acquire the engineering knowledge to produce modern automobiles or semiconductors than to set up an effective firm organization and management structure to operate the physical technology efficiently, or to set up an effective set of procedures for acquiring inputs, or for marketing.

Second, and this is where I shall focus my attention later, the broad institutional structure of a nation, and the operation of particular institutions such as its education and financial systems, and its system of public research and advanced training, strongly affects both the incentives and the ability to take on board and operate modern industrial, agricultural, or medical practice. Successful economic development generally will require the reform of traditional systems and the setting up of more modern ones, generally guided by perceptions of how those systems are structured and work in high-income countries. Some countries are able to do this effectively, taking much from abroad, and successfully tailoring the structures to work in their own cultures. But it clearly is not easy. It is far easier to advocate institutional reform, or to mount programs aimed at reform, than actually to achieve a system that successfully energizes economic catch-up. Again, effective social technologies are often very hard to copy, or to establish and maintain.

I shall elaborate these points later, and consider what I think are the reasons for them. But first, I want to lay out some features that seem clear about successful catch-up experiences in the past, and some features of the contemporary scene that are different from what they have been.

THE CATCH-UP PROCESS IN HISTORICAL PERSPECTIVE

The proposition that the economic development process of countries behind the frontier is basically that of 'catch-up' seems so compelling that one might expect that study of the processes involved would be at the center of attention of the contemporary development economics community. But this is not the case.

Understanding differences across countries in their level of economic development and the reasons for economic backwardness was of course a central concern of many of the great classical economists, particularly Adam Smith. But these questions gradually moved to the periphery of the field.

The question came back into focus after World War II. That the development problem was a catch-up problem was put forth explicitly in Alexander Gershenkron's 'Economic Backwardness in Historical Perspective' (1951), which considered the policies and new institutions of the states of continental Europe during the mid- and late nineteenth century as they strove to catch up with the UK, and reflected on the present-day relevance of this experience. However, outside of the economic historians, few development economists paid attention to the processes of catch-up *per se*, because most prevailing economic growth theory saw the principal reason for low productivity and incomes as low levels of physical and human capital, as contrasted with inadequate access to or command over technologies and other practices used in high-income countries. Relatedly, imitation of technologies, and practices more generally, in use in advanced countries generally was viewed as relatively easy, if there were no barriers like intellectual property rights, and the needed inputs, particularly physical and human capital, were available.

However, learning to do what others have already done is often not easy. Japan was successful at this at the start of the twentieth century, Korea and Taiwan later in that century, and China is proving effective at that task today. But many countries have made hardly any progress.

Moses Abramowitz's propositions about the institutional and political conditions needed for successful catch-up (1986) clearly recognized these difficulties, and generated a small research tradition specifically on the factors conducive to catch-up. However, much of the research stimulated by Abramowitz rather quickly came to concentrate on regression analysis of country-level variables. Some of this research has been quite illuminating. Thus scholars like Fagerberg and Godinho (2004), and Bernardes and Albuqurque (2003), have shown that in recent years countries that have caught up rapidly have tended to focus their higher education systems on engineering training, and have developed indigenous research efforts. However, by and large the variables in these kinds of analyses are defined at a level of aggregation too high to permit analysis of many of the relevant factors.

There are several quite detailed studies of particular countries that have been successful in catching up that do delve into the key processes and institutions involved (see, e.g., Kim, 1997, 1999). There are several fine studies that have examined how firms in developing countries have caught up in particular industries (e.g. Hobday, 1995). However, these kinds of studies have not been brought together in a systematic way.

My reading of prior relevant research leads me to propose that, in the past, all successful cases of catch-up have involved the following elements.

First, considerable cross-border flow of people, with a combination of citizens in the then backward country going to learn abroad and then returning, and people from the advanced country coming as advisers or, in some cases, to establish themselves in the developing country. Thus the core of British textile manufacturing methods was brought over to the new USA by British technicians, who stayed. Similarly, there was a significant flow of British technicians to northern Europe in the early nineteenth century, who came with the objective of setting up business on the continent. The development of Japanese industry in the late nineteenth and early twentieth centuries was helped by technical advisers from abroad, as well as by Japanese returning home after studying Western methods (Odagiri and Goto, 1996). The Korean and Taiwanese electronics industries were developed largely by men who had studied, and often worked, in the USA.

During the twentieth century companies came to play an increasing role in this cross-national learning and teaching process. The new Japanese automobile and electrical equipment companies established close interactions with companies in the USA and Europe that served as their mentors.

The development of Singapore was largely driven through the establishment branch operations by Western multinationals. Hobday (1995) has documented in detail how Korean and Taiwanese companies developed increasing competence working for American and Japanese electronics companies as original equipment manufacturers.

Over the last quarter century an important part of the transnational flow of people in the catch-up process has involved university study abroad in the relevant fields of engineering and applied science. University faculty in the successful developing countries has to a considerable degree been based on nationals who received their training abroad. I believe that this university-mediated transnational conduit of learning will be of particularly great importance during the twenty-first century for countries seeking to catch up. This certainly will be so regarding public health and medical care, as well as regarding manufacturing technology.

A second important element in countries that successfully caught up with the leaders during the nineteenth and twentieth centuries was active government support of the catch-up process, involving various forms of protection and direct and indirect subsidy. The guiding policy argument has been the need of domestic industry in the industries of the day judged critical in the development process for some protection from advanced firms in the leading nations. Alexander Hamilton's argument (1791) for infant-industry protection in the new USA was virtually identical to that put forth decades later by Friederich List (1841) regarding Germany's needs. The policies and new institutions used in continental Europe to enable catch-up with Britain are documented in Alexander Gershenkron's famous essay. The same story also fits well with the case of Japan, and of Korea and Taiwan somewhat later. In many countries these policies engendered not successful catch-up but a protected inefficient home industry. However, they also were the hallmark during the twentieth century of all the countries that have achieved their goals of catching up.

These policies obviously angered companies in the leading countries and their governments, particularly if the supported industry not only supplied its home market but began to invade the world market. While the case made after World War II for free trade was mostly concerned with eliminating protection and subsidy among the rich countries, and at that time there was sympathy for the argument that some infant-industry protection was often useful in developing countries, the international treaties that have been made have increasingly been used against import protection and subsidy in countries seeking to catch up from far behind.

My belief is that Hamilton and List were right that successful catch-up in industries where international trade is considerable requires some kind of infant-industry protection or other mode of support. The challenge is to find effective means under the new conditions.

Third, during the nineteenth and early twentieth centuries, many developing countries operated with intellectual property rights regimes which did not restrict seriously the ability of their companies to in effect copy technologies used in the advanced countries. There are many examples where licensing agreements were involved, but I believe that for the most part these were vehicles through which technology transfer was effected for a fee or other considerations, rather than instances of aggressive protection of intellectual property by the company in the advanced country.

As with infant-industry protection and subsidy, conflicts tended to emerge largely when the catching-up company began to encroach onto world markets, or even to export to the home market of the company with the patent rights. Increasing instances of this were clearly a major factor in inducing the treaty on trade-related intellectual property rights (TRIPs). But this treaty makes vulnerable to prosecution not just companies in developing countries that are exporting, but also companies that stay in their home markets.

The increased tendency of companies in high-income countries to enforce their intellectual property rights is having consequences for agricultural development, and the workings of the public health systems in developing countries, as well as for manufacturing development. Patented seed varieties are playing an increasingly important role in modern agriculture. And patented pharmaceuticals are key elements in the attack on a number of diseases that devastate poor countries. The arena of intellectual property is almost sure to become one of considerable international conflict in the immediate future. Developing countries need to learn to be able to cope with this new problem.

CHANGING CONDITIONS

As I have noted, the current and future development environment for countries trying to catch up is different from what it has been, in a number of respects. International treaties have changed the environment for catch-up in important ways. Firms in the advanced countries are likely to press hard for access to markets, and in many cases the rights to establish branches abroad. Protection and subsidy of domestic industry is likely to be met by legal and other punitive action on the part of the advanced countries, and hence will have to be more subtle, involving support of sectoral infrastructure, training and research. Firms in advanced countries also are likely to be far more aggressive and effective in protecting their intellectual property rights, and hence firms and governments in developing countries will have to develop new strategies for access on reasonable terms.

The new legal environment has come into place in a context where both business and finance are operating on a more global frame. Foreign direct investment has played a significant role in the catch-up processes of some successful countries, and is likely to play an even greater role in the future. The same applies to partnerships between firms in developing countries and companies that possess advanced know-how. At the same time, firms in developing countries can aspire realistically to sell on a world market if their wares are good enough.

Less well noticed, scientific and technical communities in different countries are now more connected than they used to be. I believe this development is very important. It is important because another major development over the past half-century has been that technologies have increasingly become associated with fields of applied science or engineering dedicated to achieving scientific understanding of the principles that are operative, to providing training for professionals who will work with the technology, and to building a scientific basis for efforts to move the technology forward. Included here are such older fields as chemical and electrical engineering, and modern fields such as computer science, biotechnology and immunology. In recent years these fields of science have become increasingly open to those who have the training and connections to get into the relevant networks.

The implications for catch-up can be profound. On the one hand, in technologies with strong scientific underpinnings, advanced training in the field has become a prerequisite for ability to understand and control; simple working experience no longer will suffice. This fact clearly challenges the capabilities for education and technical training in countries seeking to catch up. But on the other hand, I believe that a strong science base significantly reduces the importance of operating apprenticeship abroad, or tutelage by foreign industrial experts. This is not to argue that advanced formal training in a field suffices for mastery. However, in many fields it provides a substantial basis for learning by doing. Moreover, having a domestic base of good scientists provides the basis for breaking into the international networks where new technologies are being hatched.

THE INCREASED IMPORTANCE OF INDIGENOUS CAPABILITIES IN SCIENCE AND TECHNOLOGY

As a result of these changes, I propose that the development of indigenous capabilities in research and advanced training now are much more

important in enabling catch-up than used to be the case, and their importance will grow.

Christopher Freeman (1995) has proposed that Friederich List had something like a national innovation system in mind when, in the mid-nineteenth
century, he was writing about what Germany needed to do to catch up with
Great Britain. However, the modern conception of a national innovation
system was developed to be useful in thinking about the key institutions
involved in technological advance in countries at or close to the frontier (see,
e.g., Nelson, 1993). It would seem evident that, if the concept is to be useful
for orienting policy in countries significantly behind the frontier and striv-
ing to catch up, some significant reorientation is needed from the standard
format. Kim (1997, 1999), Albuquerque (2003) and Viotti (2002, 2003),
among others, have attempted to highlight some of the needed reorienta-
tions.

I propose that a suitably reoriented concept of a national innovation
system can be a useful tool for considering policies and institutions needed
for effective catch-up in the new context. In the first place, it calls attention
to the fact that the process of catch-up involves innovation in an essential
way. The innovating that drives the process of course differs from the innovating that has been the central focus of research on technological advance
in advanced economies. The new technologies, practices more generally,
that are being taken on board, while new to the country catching up, generally are well established in countries at the frontier. And much of the
innovation that is required is organizational and institutional. But what is
going on in catch-up most certainly is innovation in the sense that there is
a break from past familiar practice, considerable uncertainty about how to
make the new practice work effectively, a need for sophisticated learning
by doing and using, and a high risk of failure, as well as a major potential
payoff from success. These aspects of catch-up tend to be denied or
repressed in the standard economic development literature.

Second, the national innovation system concept focuses attention on
domestic institutions involved in science and technology. While in earlier
eras such a focus may not have been warranted, my proposition is that it is
an important one in the twenty-first century. Perez and Soete (1988) and
Bell and Pavitt (1993) argued this point some time ago. But I think it fair
to say that standard development economics still is mostly blind to this
possibility.

I believe that an important part of the national strategies needed to effect
catch-up will involve strong support of scientific and technical training. In
particular, I propose that indigenous universities and public laboratories
will play an increasingly important role as vehicles through which the technologies and organizational forms of the advanced countries come to be

mastered in the developing ones, as partially an organizing structure for and partially a substitute for international people flows. Indigenous universities will play a key role as the source of students who take advanced training abroad, and as the home of faculty who have been trained abroad. And it is clear that domestic universities must do the bulk of the training of people who will go to industry and other economic activities needing well-trained technical people.

I want to argue that the research capabilities of universities and other public institutions will play an important role in catch-up in the twenty-first century. Indeed, while often overlooked, indigenous research has long been an important element of catch-up in certain important fields. This is especially so in agriculture and medicine. An important part of the reason is that in these areas developing countries often could not simply copy technology and practice in countries at the frontier, but needed to develop technologies suited to their own conditions. Soil and climate conditions tended to be different. The prevalent diseases were different. There is every reason to believe that the importance of having the capability to do effective research and development in these fields will be even greater in the future.

In contrast, while in manufacturing the technologies used in advanced countries may not have been optimal, at least they worked in the new setting with often modest modification, and they generally were available at no great expense. The experience of countries that have successfully caught up in manufacturing over the past half-century testifies to the importance of a nation's education system in providing a supply of trained engineers and applied scientists to manufacturing firms catching up. And an important part of the catch-up process has involved firms learning to do R&D on their own. However, while there are exceptions (electronics in Taiwan seems to be one) it is not clear that research *per se* in universities and national labs has played an important role in catch-up in manufacturing, beyond its role in the training function.

But circumstances may have changed. In the new regime of stronger protection of intellectual property, it is going to be increasingly important that countries trying to catch up develop their capabilities to revise and tailor manufacturing capabilities relatively early in the game. First of all, this can help companies to develop and employ technologies that avoid direct infringement of intellectual property that is likely to be enforced aggressively. Second, over the longer run the development of an intellectual property rights portfolio by firms in a developing country can provide bargaining weight in the complex cross-licensing arrangements that mark many manufacturing industries.

More generally, achieving competence in many areas of manufacturing requires staying up with a moving target. Further, as the frontier is approached, the lines between sophisticated imitation and creative design of new products and processes becomes blurred. A strong R&D capability becomes essential. To a considerable extent the R&D needs to go on in firms. However, research in universities and public laboratories can play a strong supporting role.

I also want to note here the important roles that universities have played over the years in training private and public managers. This role is likely to become increasingly important.

It is a mistake, I believe, to view a nation's system of public research and high-level training as monolithic. The roles of public sector research and the institutional structures clearly differ between manufacturing, where engineering schools and a few departments of applied science, like computer science and metallurgy, are involved, and medicine and public health, where the key actors are medical schools and disease-related public research laboratories, and agriculture, where still a different set of institutions is involved. And by and large schools of business and of public administration have their own identity.

Thus it is a mistake to view the policy challenge here as simply to strengthen university research, without attending to the areas where the priority is high, and to the often quite specialized needed institutional structures. Indeed, it needs to be recognized that many existing university systems, or parts of university systems, operate more or less in isolation from the firms, farms, hospitals and other organizations that need to learn about and come to master superior ways of doing things if economic development is to proceed effectively. For the training and research done in universities and other public research institutions to contribute to the economic development process, there needs to be effective linkages, interaction more generally, between those institutions and the organizations and sectors involved in the production of goods and services. Existing university structures in some cases may be as much a barrier as a potential vehicle for the development of an effective system of public training and research. It is important to learn how countries that have developed public training and research systems that have been important contributors to economic catch-up have been able to do so.

THE CHALLENGE OF INSTITUTIONAL DESIGN AND DEVELOPMENT

If I am right, countries aspiring to catch up technologically and economically now are faced with the challenge of building an effective system of public research and advanced training linked to their industrial, agricultural and medical care sectors, in a way that supports the technological progress of the latter. If I am right, if this is done effectively, the problem of acquiring and mastering the needed physical technologies will be easier than has been the case in the past, because of the closer connections between physical technologies and fields of science and engineering which now are largely global rather than national. However, to operate these technologies effectively will require the development of appropriate social technologies, and as I proposed at the start of this chapter, 'It is far easier to advocate institutional reform, or to mount programs aimed at reform, than actually to achieve a system that encourages economic catch-up.'

I, and the other originators of the national innovation system concept, have argued that while national systems clearly are shaped and held in place by public policies and programs, it is a mistake to see these systems as having been 'planned' in any detail. Rather, they evolved. In that process of evolution, there almost always has been a lot of looking to, and trying to draw lessons from, the experiences of other countries judged at the time to have effective policies, programs and institutions. However, attempts at direct copying have been rare, and even when there was an effort to stick close to the template, what ended up being put in place generally had only a rough resemblance to the model.

An interesting case in point was the efforts in the early years of the twentieth century of US scientists to move American universities closer to the German university system, which at that time clearly was the world's leader in terms of both scientific research in physics and chemistry, and in advanced training of researchers. But while the German system was organized around individual professors and their labs, this structure was not imitated. Rather, most American universities adopted a departmental system, involving several professors as well as more junior departmental faculty members, which permitted much greater flexibility for students and for the research enterprise, since departments could over time change their mix of expertise without having to establish particular new designated professorships. It is not at all clear that these advantages were recognized at the time. Rather, the compelling thrust undoubtedly was that the German professorial system did not fit easily into the American university scene as it was developing at that time.

Also, as Nathan Rosenberg and I have described in some detail (Rosenberg and Nelson, 1994), the American Land Grant universities, many of which were prominent in the new move to build high-level scientific research capabilities, had a long tradition of interaction with agriculture and industry, and while some of the new science departments struggled to stay 'pure', the general university environment discouraged the establishment of a durable, isolated ivory tower. The development of strong basic science at American universities clearly pulled the more application-oriented departments to strengthen their own science base. However, the outward-looking orientation remained. And it should be noted that most of the productive contact with users of university research continues to be concentrated in the specialized research and training structures relating to engineering, medicine and agriculture.

Within this case one can see a variety of reasons why building a system of public research and high-level training that contributes to economic development is not an easy matter. It seems inevitable that countries so aspiring look to countries that seem to be doing well for guidance. But it may not be clear what are the key features of a successful system that make it work well. Almost certainly the German professors at the time would have argued that good research and research training required a hierarchical system with an individual professor at the top with unquestioned authority. But this turned out to be unnecessary, at least in the American context. And national context clearly matters. The German professorial system of management of research and training simply could not take root in American soil.

This historical episode has its echoes in the present. Today it is the American university system that is serving as the model. But there certainly is no firm agreement regarding which aspects of that system have made it such an effective contributor to economic growth. Nor is it clear what aspects are particular to the American scene, and can, perhaps must, take different forms in other national settings.

Currently there is a widespread tendency to believe that the extensive patenting and licensing activities of American universities are the key to their effectiveness in contributing to economic development, and a number of countries have acted to enact their own versions of the American Bayh–Dole Act of 1980 which strongly encouraged university patenting. However, the research that I have done with my colleagues (Mowery et al., 2004; Rosenberg and Nelson, 1994) on the long history of university involvement with innovation in agriculture, manufacturing and medicine suggests strongly that patenting is not a basic cause. American universities were important contributors to technical progress long before they started patenting extensively, and a large share of their contributions today was not particularly encouraged or facilitated by patents. Rather, the basic reason for the strong contribution to economic development of the American university system is that most universities never have been ivory towers, but have long interacted with the potential users of their research. I note that the lion's share of the research that has contributed importantly to economic development has been done in agricultural departments, engineering schools and medical schools.

But to return to an opening theme, while it is sensible to look to the American university research as an inspiration, and perhaps even as a model, each country will have to find its own way.

REFERENCES

Abramowitz, M. (1986), 'Catching Up, Forging Ahead, and Falling Behind', *Journal of Economic History*, June.

Albuquerque, E. (2003), 'Immature Systems of Innovation', paper prepared for the first conference on Globelics, Rio, November.

Bell, M. and Pavitt, K. (1993), 'Technological Accumulation and Industrial Growth', *Industrial and Corporate Change*.

Bernardes, A. and Albuquerque, E. (2003), 'Cross-over, Thresholds, and Interactions Between Science and Technology: Lessons for Less-developed Countries', *Research Policy*, May.

Fagerberg, J. and Godinho, M. (2004), 'Innovation and Catch-up', in Fagerberg, J., Mowery, D. and Nelson, R. (eds), *Handbook of Innovation*, Oxford: Oxford University Press.

Freeman, C. (1995), 'The National System of Innovation in Historical Context', *Cambridge Journal of Economics*.

Gershenkron, A. (1962), 'Economic Backwardness in Historical Perspective' (1951), reprinted in Gershenkron, A., *Economic Development in Historical Perspective*, Cambridge, MA: Harvard University Press.

Hamilton, A. (1791), 'Report on Manufactures', reprinted in *The Reports of Alexander Hamilton*, New York: Harper Torchbooks, 1965.

Hobday, M. (1995), *Innovation in East Asia: The Challenge to Japan*, Aldershot, UK and Brookfield, USA: Edward Elgar.

Kim, L. (1997), *Imitation to Innovation: The Dynamics of Korea's Technological Learning*, Boston, MA: Harvard Business School Press.

Kim, L. (1999), *Learning and Innovation in Economic Development*, Cheltenham, UK and Northampton, MA, USA: Edward Elgar.

List, F. (1841), *National Systems of Political Economy*, English edition, London: Longman 1904.

Mowery, D., Nelson, R., Sampat, B. and Ziedonis, A. (2004), *Ivory Tower and Industrial Innovation: University–Industry Technology Transfer Before and After the Bayh–Dole Act in the United States*, Stanford, CA: Stanford University Press.

Nelson, R. (ed.) (1993), *National Innovation Systems*, Oxford: Oxford University Press.

Nelson, R. and Sampat, B. (2001), 'Making Sense of Institutions as a Factor Shaping Economic Performance', *Journal of Economic Behavior and Organization*.

Odagiri, H. and Goto, A. (1996), *Technology and Industrial Development in Japan*, Oxford: Clarendon Press.

Perez, C. (2002), *Technological Revolutions and Financial Capital*, Cheltenham, UK and Northampton, MA, USA: Edward Elgar.

Perez, C. and Soete, L. (1988), 'Catching up in Technology: Entry Barriers and Windows of Opportunity', in Dosi, G., Freeman, C., Nelson, R. et al., *Technical Change and Economic Theory*, London: Pinter Publishers.

Rosenberg, N. and Nelson, R. (1994), 'American Universities and Technical Advance in Industry?' *Research Policy*.

Viotti, E. (2002), 'National Learning Systems', *Technological Forecasting and Cultural Change*, September.

Viotti, E. (2003), 'Technological Learning Systems, Competition, and Development', paper prepared for the first Globelics conference, Rio, November.

3. The development of universities and public research institutions: a historical overview of its role in technological and economic catch-up

Roberto Mazzoleni

1. INTRODUCTION

Gerschenkron (1962) popularized a characterization of the economic development of countries behind the technological frontier as a process of 'catching up' with the leading economies. According to this view, the transformation of physical and social technologies in a developing economy is facilitated by the absorption of technological, scientific and institutional knowledge originating from more advanced economies. A central focus of research on economic development should be therefore an investigation of the institutions and processes that have played a significant role in enabling the flow of knowledge from advanced to developing regions. There are strong reasons to believe that universities (or more generally, higher education institutions) and public research institutes ought to figure prominently in such investigation. Indeed, the belief – commonly held among nineteenth-century policy makers – that universities and research institutions could play an important role in promoting economic development was an important stimulus to their international diffusion during the nineteenth century.

Far from being the result of a process of mere imitation, the diffusion of these institutions was characterized by the emergence of distinctive national characteristics and a considerable amount of trial-and-error adaptation to local conditions. The resulting institutional variety likely influenced the contributions made by the emerging systems of higher education and research to the diffusion of technological knowledge (through inward transfer or otherwise), and hence to the economic catch-up of the home country. More directly, the scope and quality of these contributions reflected the changing relationship between the knowledge and skills provided to students and others through educational programs and extension services on one side, and the knowledge and skills relevant to the implementation of the technologies associated with nineteenth-century economic development on the other.

Contemporary discussions highlight the differences among technologies with respect to: (a) the importance of tacit elements of technical knowledge that make its transfer a costly and uncertain activity (Nelson, 1990); and (b) the degree to which their advance relies upon knowledge associated with fields of science and engineering (Klevorick et al., 1995; Cohen et al., 2002). Similar differences existed among nineteenth-century industrial technologies. While the production of organic chemicals, refrigeration and electrical equipment has been held to represent the earliest science-based industries, important developments in the mechanical engineering industries and the iron and steel industry occurred quite independently of advances in the relevant scientific knowledge. An implication of these empirical facts is that there were then – as there are now – significant differences among technologies in the extent to which it was possible to learn about them and their implementation in a school environment. These qualifications acquire greater significance when we observe that the nineteenth century witnessed significant changes in the nature of the school environment within which knowledge about technologies was putatively imparted.

The emerging pattern of linkages between science and technology during the nineteenth-century is an important background to the development of universities and research institutions that constitutes the primary focus of this chapter. While the two processes are related, the latter cannot be exclusively understood in light of the former. Indeed, the idea that universities ought to be concerned with the application of science to practical problems, or with the nature of technology, was a matter of debate throughout the century. Important characteristics of professional school programs at the level comparable to universities, including the balance between practical work and classroom lectures or the depth and range of the education in the sciences and humanities built into the curriculum, were debated and decided upon in different ways in different places and at different times.

How did the development of educational institutions contribute to the ability of individuals and firms in catch-up economies to learn about existing technology and to acquire the competence necessary for its implementation? In general, recent historical research has been rather bearish on the role played by university science in the industrialization of continental Europe (Wengenroth, 2000). However, an adequate answer to the question should reflect the heterogeneous characteristics of different industrial technologies and of the forms of knowledge imparted in different institutions. Higher education systems of different countries differed in terms of the extent to which they contributed to the diffusion of forms of knowledge other than purely scientific, and the extent to which they communicated practical technical knowledge to their students.[1]

It is perhaps useful to remark upon the fact that the natural sciences became a generally accepted area of teaching and research at universities only after the reform of the German universities began in 1810 in Berlin according to the vision of Alexander von Humboldt, then Education Secretary of the Prussian government. In fact, a crucial feature of Humboldt's vision concerned the belief that knowledge ought to be pursued for its own sake, according to the internal logic of scientific inquiry and without regard for its practical relevance to social and economic problems. Far from adhering to the Humboldtian vision, research activities at universities became increasingly drawn to the investigation of problems that if not immediately dictated by practical needs were at least brought into focus as a result of the scientists' observation of related practical problems. More generally, through their teaching function, universities and similar institutions played a critical role in disseminating the scientific method, a scientific mentality and scientific culture, the three phenomena that Mokyr has characterized as 'the Industrial Enlightenment's debt to the scientific revolution' (2002, p. 36). The important point here is that an exclusive emphasis on the role of higher education institutions toward the diffusion of scientific knowledge would provide a distorted account of their contribution to economic development during the nineteenth century.

Novel institutions whose primary focus was to train engineers began to form in the mid-eighteenth century and proliferated during the nineteenth. The institutionalization of this form of training occurred according to different patterns in different countries. Thus, in Germany engineering education did not find acceptance in the universities and became the specialized focus of an alternative institution, the Technische Hochschulen. Things went differently elsewhere. Engineering colleges, formed in the USA since the second quarter of the century and in Japan since the 1870s, became part later on of fully fledged universities. A central purpose of the discussion that follows is to illustrate the emergence of national patterns and the pathways of cross-country influences in the nineteenth-century development of the academic systems in Germany, France, the USA and Japan.

2. SCIENTIFIC AND PRACTICAL KNOWLEDGE IN ENGINEERING EDUCATION

For most of the nineteenth century, engineering training focusing on the skills and knowledge useful in the industrial workplace continued to be the

province of vocational schools at the secondary level and otherwise transmitted through practical work experience. As is well known, Britain's
industrial leadership materialized at a time when industrial personnel
learned about relevant techniques on the job rather than through formal
schooling. Indeed, the transformation of the educational routes to industrial occupations in Britain lagged considerably behind those occurring in
countries whose economic development entered a catch-up phase during
the century.

An important distinction emerged early on between educational institutions aimed at training engineers for public service and those aimed at
training engineers for industry. In France, for example, the École des Ponts
et Chaussées (1775), the École des Mines (created in 1783, and moved to
Paris in 1816), and the École Polytechnique (1794) had been established.
The scope of their educational mandate (training civil engineers for the
public administration) limited their relevance for industrial development.
Only a few of the graduates from the École Polytechnique found employment in industrial enterprises. Industry-oriented technical education was
relegated since 1803 to the Écoles des Arts et Métiers, intermediate technical schools that emphasized vocational training and placed little emphasis
on mathematics and scientific learning. The perception of an emerging
industrial need for highly qualified technical personnel led in 1829 to the
establishment of the École Centrale des Arts et Manufactures (ECAM),
an institution privately funded by an industrialist, Alphonse Lavallée.
However, ECAM's curriculum drifted away from the emphasis on the
application of science to industrial processes that its founders envisaged.
While the graduates of the school were indeed predominantly employed in
industry, they were more likely to take on administrative and managerial
duties. Thus, around mid-century only fewer than a quarter of the graduates held jobs related to operations engineering or the development of new
products and processes (Shinn, 1980).

ECAM's experience illustrates a problem that plagued the development
of engineering educational institutions until at least the last quarter of the
nineteenth century: how to strike the right balance between teaching math
and natural sciences (a task that began to be picked up by universities
during that time period) and providing purely practical training in the education of industry engineers (Torstendahl, 1993). Indeed, the British policy
aimed at restricting the emigration of skilled workers (until 1824) and the
export of industrial machinery (until 1842) emphasizes the important fact
that industrial knowledge was believed to reside in the design of machines
and the tacit skills of the workforce, rather than in books. Thus, while many
educators acted upon the belief that a body of engineering science could be
taught at university-level institutions such as to promote the adoption of

British industrial technology by engineers and entrepreneurs, vocational schools continued to play a pivotal role in training personnel for the young industries of France and Germany.

This state of affairs reflected the difficulties in identifying the character of an engineering science that could actually prove useful in the practice of industrial production. These difficulties were most evident in the field of mechanical engineering that represented the technological core of the British industrial development. In Germany, the development of the field was heavily influenced by the educational objectives of a cadre of professors whose scientific work aimed at formulating general theories of machine building that could replace practical tinkering and empirically driven intuition in the design process.[2] The pursuit of this goal was also instrumental to elevating engineering education to the level of scientific education, as illustrated by the transformation of the reforming of the engineering educational system in Prussia during the 1870s.

Until then, two higher-level institutions, the Bau-Akademie (established in 1799) and the Gewerbe Institut (1821), reproduced in Prussia the differentiation between the École Polytechnique and the École Centrale in France. The former trained civil engineers for public service and the latter trained engineers for industry. The subordinate status of the Gewerbe Institut, whose graduates did not have access to the state exams for admission into the ranks of civil servants, was the focus of reform efforts at raising the Institut's admission standards and achieving for it academic standing equal to the Bau-Akademie. A reform plan formulated in 1864 proposed that the amount of training in pure science and mathematics be increased to the detriment of more applied and empirical aspects of the curriculum, and that workshops and laboratories be dismantled because they were unworthy of the pure science that engineering education was to become (Gispen, 1989, p. 79).

The reform of Prussian engineering education was accomplished under the leadership of Franz Reuleaux, a mechanical engineering professor who directed the Institut between 1868 and 1879.[3] The two engineering schools were merged into the Berlin Technische Hochschule in 1879 and the tension between science and practice as the focus of teaching was resolved by aligning the educational curricula to the model set by the French École Polytechnique, even if the latter's graduates were known to be poorly suited to work related to industrial technology. Accordingly, the engineering school placed a growing emphasis on providing students with a broad grounding in math and science that many educators perceived to be critical for understanding technology as something different from mere practical knowledge. This process has been referred to as the 'academization' of engineering (Manegold, 1978; Torstendahl, 1993).

Although such process helped the engineering schools to acquire a status similar to that of universities in the German educational system, it also exacerbated the mismatch between the engineers' formal training and the demands of their industrial employers. Ironically, it was Franz Reuleaux who brought into the focus of educational policy debates the problem represented by the weak relevance of the curriculum of the polytechnic schools to industrial practice. His *Letters from Philadelphia*, published in 1876 during a major economic crisis for the German economy, described German products presented at the World Exhibition as 'cheap and bad'.[4] Such poor showing reflected the industry's focus on the development of low-cost imitations of British machines. Reuleaux's proposed remedy was for industry to focus on quality and product value instead.

Many in the industrial community essentially agreed with the proposition that German machines lagged behind the British and American in technical merit. But at least a few believed that in addition to the 'cheap and bad', an even more important weakness of the German industry was that it developed products that were too expensive. These critics diagnosed the source of the German machinery firms' problems to be the engineering culture promoted in the national schools. According to their view, the German machine manufacturer was 'much too much a graduate from the Technische Hochschule,' approaching the task of designing machines without adequate consideration for costs. Indeed, the director of a machine-building firm in Mulheim, Joseph Schlink, commented in 1878 that the theoretical predilections of Germany's institutes of technical education had had very little success in promoting the advance of German machine building (Gispen, 1989, pp. 120–23).

In spite of his role in promoting the academization of engineering, Reuleaux's criticism of the German machinery firms provided the needed stimulus for the realization that the attempt to establish engineering education on purely theoretical and scientific grounds had proved fruitless. If the Technische Hochschule were to play an important role in supporting the catch-up of German firms with foreign machinery technology, the nearly exclusive pursuit of theoretical abstractions in their curricula had to give way to a wider reliance on students' training in laboratories and industrial workshops. This trend emerged at different times in different Hochschulen, but its beginnings can be set around 1868 when the first experimental technical laboratory was opened at the Hochschule in Munich (Weingart, 1978). This trend gained momentum in the 1890s when the technical schools acquired large-scale facilities for teaching and research where the study of technology could proceed through an understanding of the diversity of practical conditions based on experiments on machines of full scale under conditions which correspond to a realistic operation (Weingart, 1978, p. 272).

It should be noted that during the second half of the nineteenth century, industrial firms in Germany began to develop their own research and testing laboratories, and hence to recruit formally trained scientists and engineers. An important effect of the industrial development was likely that educators and policy-makers could assess the economic relevance of technological education at the Hochschulen on the basis of explicit demands from industry, rather than of latent demands as perceived by the faculty (Manegold, 1978). Indeed, it became increasingly common for professors to be recruited from the ranks of industrial engineers (especially in the case of the Privatdozenten), or to acquire first-hand knowledge of industrial processes and technologies through plant visits and by entertaining ongoing professional ties with industrial firms and personnel.

In a recent paper, Wolfgang König (1996) presents evidence documenting the importance of mechanisms enabling the flow of technical knowledge from industry to the Hochschulen in the field of electrical engineering, where courses were first offered in 1882 in Darmstadt. During the 1880s the professors appointed in the field were university physicists and instructors in mechanical engineering without any industry experience. Attempts to gain first-hand experience of industrial practice at electrical equipment firms such as Siemens-Schuckertwerkeit, Siemens & Halske, or AEG, were common among the early cohorts of professors. Over time, appointees at all ranks of the professoriate were likely to have an electrical engineering degree from a Technische Hochschule and had a growing amount of industrial experience. König concludes that whereas it has been common to refer to electrical equipment as a nineteenth-century science-based industry, it should *a fortiori* be said that electrical engineering was an industry-based science at least until World War I.

Whether or not the pattern of the knowledge flows in the field of electrical engineering is typical of other areas of engineering cannot be argued presently on empirical grounds. But König's work lends support to the claim that the ongoing industrial development enhanced the effectiveness of the engineering education at the Technische Hochschulen by providing teaching personnel, learning opportunities for professors, and equipment that could be used in laboratories. Along these lines, the growth in enrollments at the Technische Hochschule that began to pick up pace since the 1860s (Figure 3.1) may reflect the positive influence on the quality of education resulting from a more dynamic industrial environment.

The development of engineering education in France shared important features with the academization that occurred in Germany. Instead, both of these national experiences differed in important respects from the pattern observed in the USA, where utilitarian concerns regarding the goals of higher education dominated. The characteristics of professional education

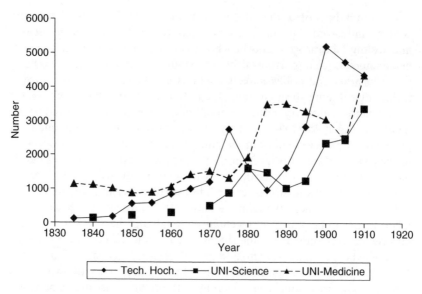

*Figure 3.1   Students at Prussian universities and technical institutes
            (1835–1900)*

in the curricula and the formation of new institutes reflected the US pen-
chant for the practical applications of science noted early in the nineteenth
century by Tocqueville (1876). The earliest program in engineering focused
on the training of members of the Corps of Engineers at the US Military
Academy in West Point (New York), established in 1802.[5] Training in the
mechanical arts and civil engineering was on the other hand the province
of secondary level and vocational schools, and was otherwise the result
of practical experience and of training abroad. As Sidney Pollard (1981)
notes with respect to Europe, an important contribution to the advance
of American technology came from skilled or educated immigrants, a flow
that continued throughout the nineteenth century and the early twentieth.
However, this mechanism was complemented and over time supplanted
in importance by the indigenous formation of a technically competent
workforce.

   An important milestone in the development of US technical education
was the creation of the Rensselaer College in 1823. Stephen Rensselaer
wished that the school would promote 'the application of science to the
common purposes of life.' The Institute's first president, Amos Eaton, drew
inspiration from the teaching of science in the Prussian universities and
polytechnics. During the early years of the institution, the curriculum was
strongly oriented to teaching in agricultural sciences, but already in 1835

a four-year degree program in civil engineering had been developed, the first of its kind in the USA. In 1846, a graduate from the college, B. Franklin Greene, was appointed director and proceeded to reorganize the curriculum along the lines of Paris's École Centrale. The college was renamed Rensselaer Polytechnic Institute in 1849 and engineering became the major field of study (Emmerson, 1973, pp. 144–6).

The diffusion of engineering education programs accelerated around mid-century. The central mechanism was the establishment of new colleges and schools with an explicit focus on engineering, such as Union College (established in 1845 in Schenectady, NY) and the Massachusetts Institute of Technology (1861). Although at a slower pace, courses in engineering, as well as in applied sciences, became common even at those colleges whose curriculum and degree programs followed more closely the model of the European universities. In some cases, elite colleges that considered engineering not to be a suitable discipline for their students' education established sister institutions aimed at providing scientific and engineering training. Thus the Lawrence Scientific School was established in 1847 as a branch of Harvard University thanks to the endowment provided by the merchant Abbott Lawrence, whose wish was to promote the application of scientific education to engineering, mining, and the invention and manufacture of machinery. Ultimately, the school program emphasized the teaching of the sciences, rather than engineering. Yale College followed in Harvard's footsteps with the creation of the Sheffield Scientific School in 1858, again thanks to a gift by a railroad entrepreneur. By the year 1880, 85 engineering schools were active at the college level.

Unlike in Germany, where the development of the polytechnic schools was supported by the public sector and heavily influenced by the requirements for the engineers' admission to public service, the development of the US colleges was largely the result of private investment.[6] Private institutions, dependent on tuition revenues for their financial viability, were naturally inclined to respond to the changing needs of a growing society by providing professional education in any field, with hardly any prejudice regarding the academic standing of the subject matter. But the practical value of higher education was not lost on the federal government either: it was central to the Morrill Act of 1862, legislation that Geiger (1986) credits with giving a crucial impulse to the reorientation of the US academic system toward utilitarian goals.

The Morrill Act authorized a grant of federal land to the states for the purpose of maintaining at least one college where the essential focus of learning would be agriculture and the mechanical arts. In a number of states the purposes of the Morrill Act were pursued at already existing colleges and schools. Thus private institutions like the Sheffield Scientific

School, MIT or the University of Michigan came to play the role of land grant colleges for their states. In others, the provisions of the Morrill Act were realized through the creation of altogether new academic institutions, either public (such as the University of Illinois (1867) and the University of California (1868)) or private. Among the latter, Cornell University (founded in 1868) was the first institution successfully providing educational programs in science, humanities and practical subjects. Indeed, by its third year of operation Cornell had the largest entering student class in the country's history.

In parallel with earlier developments in Europe, the 1850s witnessed the beginning of instruction in the field of mechanical engineering at US schools. Almost certainly the first bachelor degree program in mechanical engineering was offered at the Polytechnic College of Pennsylvania, an institution founded in 1853. Emmerson (1973) describes the design of the curriculum at this school as striking a balance between the educational and professional needs of prospective students and the director's desire to model the curricula on those of ECAM and the polytechnic school in Karlsruhe. The Worcester Polytechnic Institute established in 1865 in Massachusetts provided a degree in mechanical engineering whose curriculum involved a significant amount of workshop training. Indeed, the school awarded its degree to the students only after four years of honorable service in engineering practice beyond graduation.

These observations can be summarized in two points. First, the system of higher education in the USA was characterized by an enormous adaptive capacity. New schools formed in a relatively short time to fill niches that were poorly served by existing institutions. At the same time, the successful experience of innovative schools like Cornell University, or the spread of the elective system from Harvard College to other schools, signaled the value of a considerable degree of flexibility in the educational programs of individual institutions.[7] Second, the engineering curricula in the US colleges often represented an adaptation of European models to local conditions. Among the latter, differences in the standards of secondary education and the much greater emphasis given to practical work were of paramount importance.[8] As a result of these factors, the 'academization' of engineering that characterized developments in Germany and France was hardly a problem in the USA, in spite of the fact that many engineering schools drew inspiration from European institutions and very often adopted the same textbooks. European influences on US schools were partly the result of personal contacts among professors and of the fact that many US professors were trained in Europe.[9]

But in spite of the close interaction among scholars on the two sides of the Atlantic, the US engineering schools maintained a strong and distinctive orientation toward the empirical methods and a far greater reliance on extensive laboratory and workshop training in their curricula. The success of many industrial entrepreneurs lacking a formal education in sciences or engineering muted the kinds of status concerns that were partly responsible for the theoretical drift of European schools. Thicker interactions between engineering and the pure sciences developed over time in the areas of electrical and chemical engineering. With respect to the latter, the different institutionalization of engineering education in the USA and Germany has been argued by Rosenberg to be an important reason for the rise to leadership of the US firms in the chemical industry, an economic sector that had been dominated by German firms during the last third of the nineteenth century. But a proper discussion of this matter will be presented after a brief review of the history of education in the applied sciences in the next section.

3. UNIVERSITY-BASED SCIENTIFIC RESEARCH AND INDUSTRIAL DEVELOPMENT

The discussion of engineering education in the previous section indicates that the boundary between scientific and engineering education was rather blurred during the nineteenth century. But at least in Germany and France a persistent institutional separation existed between the universities – from which technology was excluded as a subject for teaching or research – and the engineering schools (Lundgreen, 1980).[10] While instruction in scientific subjects like chemistry and physics was ordinarily provided in the latter, it was mainly the development of applied scientific research in the former that turned out to have greater relevance to important aspects of industrial development.

It is useful to cast such development against the backdrop of the peculiar trajectory followed by the ideology of science at universities. While scientific societies and academies of the seventeenth and eighteenth centuries had been influenced by the Baconian utilitarian ideas about the study of science and technology (Emmerson, 1973; Stokes, 1997), the founding of the University of Berlin in 1810 – where science was taught in the faculty of philosophy – was inspired by the idea of education as an act of personal development associated with Alexander von Humboldt, then director of public education at the Prussian Ministry of the Interior. Thus, while science was accepted as a subject of teaching and research, laboratory research and empirical science were considered as lower-ranking activities and 'had to fight for emancipation from the domination of idealistic natural philosophy' (Keck, 1993, p. 118). As part of this fight, scientific work was often presented under the gloss of pure scientific investigations, even as it clearly addressed practical problems of agricultural and industrial production.

Among the most celebrated instances of work of this kind is that carried out by Louis Pasteur at Lille (Stokes, 1997). From his experiments on fermentation to his investigations and lectures on the manufacture of alcohol and sugar from beets, Pasteur's work was clearly focused on scientific problems dictated to his attention by the observation of industrial practice, even if he considered the idea of applied science to be an oxymoron (Böhme et al., 1978, p. 238). His lectures in chemistry were accompanied by visits to factories, and while he was dean of the faculty in 1854–57 he marked the end of the academic year by organizing trips to chemical and metallurgical establishments in the region (Paul, 1980). Pasteur's work was representative of the strong utilitarian bent that dominated the faculty of sciences at Lille at mid-century and spread to many other centers later on. The result of these trends was the formation of specialized technical institutes at faculties across the country.

The formation of institutes (or laboratory-based seminars) in medicine and the natural sciences at the German universities provides a useful perspective on the transformation of the standing of laboratory research. Their number at most universities inched up relatively slowly from 1820 to 1870, when their growth accelerated. For example, in Berlin the number of institutes and seminars went from 12 to 27, and then doubled by 1909. As their numbers grew, institutes went from being the personal creation of individual professors to being official and permanent parts of the university. Indeed, the chemist Justus von Liebig, who founded his laboratory at the University of Giessen in 1825, is known to have complained about the paucity of public funds provided for research. Like many other professors, he provided for the laboratory at least in part out of personal funds. Indeed, an important part of the struggle in the rise of applied science had to do with securing public funding for the expenses of institutes and their laboratories.

Such funding increased more or less across all the German universities, although there were differences among the various locations. In Berlin, the overall budget increased by 200 percent over the 1820–70 period, but the budget item related to institutes grew by 1000 percent. At the end of the period, expenses on institutes exceeded expenses on professorial salaries by a wide margin. In 1820 the former were only one-fourth as large as the latter. The increase in public support for the institutes signals both a growing recognition of the costs of conducting research in natural sciences and medicine and a response to the growing number of students pursuing doctoral degrees, largely involving laboratory research (McClelland, 1980).[11]

Developments associated with the research laboratory headed by Justus von Liebig at the University of Giessen in Germany are quite similar to those noted above regarding Pasteur's activities at Lille. Liebig professed his adherence to a conception of scientific research as independent from problems of industrial practice, although his research activities were very often inspired by and relevant to scientific questions emerging from practical problems (Weingart, 1978). According to Haber (1958), Liebig responded to critics of his teaching method, 'Once the principles and methods of pure chemistry had been absorbed, the practical utilization of this knowledge would follow as a matter of course' (p. 64). It is widely agreed among scholars that the catching up and forging ahead of the German chemical industry in the second half of the nineteenth century owed a great deal to the strength of the academic training in chemistry at German universities and the abundant supply of chemists who were accustomed to laboratory research of the kind that became common among the leading chemical firms of the period.

This last remark suggests that in fact the relevance of academic research to industrial needs and capabilities depended not so much on the institutional location of the research as on the nature of the research methods learned by students at both. University-based laboratory training in chemistry turned out to support the acquisition of technological capabilities for chemical firms whose activities included the first forms of systematic R&D in an industrial setting. Already in the 1830s, the University of Giessen had established itself as the leading center of research in organic chemistry. Even British students were likely to study in Germany if only to return home in order to practice their research at domestic academic institutions. Moreover, the growing number of chemists trained at the German universities exceeded the local industry demand for scientific talent. The result was a persistent underemployment among German chemists and their migration to other countries in search of suitable professional opportunities. German chemists represented an important source of scientific personnel for British firms and research institutions until developments in the German industry induced them to return to their home country (Haber, 1958; Murmann and Landau, 1998).

Among the Germans who moved to Britain, the experience of August Wilhelm Hofmann is particularly noteworthy. His arrival in London in 1845 was the result of the founding of the Royal College of Chemistry and a failed attempt by its promoters to lure Liebig himself to a professorship in organic chemistry. While Liebig declined the offer, he advised that the offer be extended to one of his students. Hofmann's research activities proved extremely valuable for the British dye industry until 1865 when he returned to Germany to head a new laboratory at the University of Berlin.

There, he took an active role in establishing ongoing collaborations with German chemical firms and acted as lead consultant to AGFA. As noted by Murmann (2003), Hofmann's involvement with industrial firms was not an exception. Furthermore, the pool of scientific and engineering talent that German chemical firms could draw upon extended beyond the university-trained chemists to the students from the Hochschulen, where chemistry was part of the curriculum.

Scholars more or less unanimously regard the university system of chemical research as the most important reason for the rise to leadership of the German chemical industry. Until the 1870s, Britain dominated the chemical industry, focusing on the production of inorganic chemicals. Its leadership however dissolved over the following decades as the growth of the industry focused on the production of synthetic organic chemicals. This field was dominated by the German industry.

But the German industry was not nearly as successful in the large-scale production of inorganic chemicals, a segment of the industry where competitive advantage rested primarily on the achievement of lower costs through large-scale production. Even in this respect, Rosenberg (1998, p. 198) has proposed that an important reason for the German industry's failure to dominate the production of inorganic chemicals was the separation between chemistry research, which was mostly carried out at universities, and engineering research, which was not. In contrast, such separation had all but disappeared in the US universities at the end of the century and the US industrial-academic complex had made considerably greater progress in the development of skills related to the design and engineering of large-scale industrial processes. Indeed, the USA (more specifically, the MIT) was the birthplace of chemical engineering as a specific field of academic instruction, and by the early twentieth century a rapid increase in the number of students attending chemical engineering courses had taken place.[12]

It should be noted that during the early development of the domestic chemical industry US students were likely to pursue advanced training in chemistry at German universities, predominantly, but also at French and British ones (Haber, 1958). A similar situation prevailed in the field of physics. This was the case in spite of the relatively strong US tradition of teaching in these fields and the adoption by US universities during the last quarter of the nineteenth century of the German model of the university based on the conduct of research and teaching. Thus, while the German experience illustrates an instance of catching up wherein the growth of the industry relied upon a strong pre-existing base of scientific research and training, the US case makes it clear that a considerable amount of technological progress can occur in a science-based industry even when national excellence in the science base has not been achieved (Rosenberg, 1998, p. 211).

This last remark suggests that the international movements of students of science and technology was also an important aspect of the diffusion of technology and science during the nineteenth century, one that has to be distinguished from the international movement of skilled industry personnel singled out by Pollard as the key transmission mechanism. Thus a significant fraction of the scientists working in the US chemical industry received their scientific education in Germany. British students accounted for about 12 percent of the students at Liebig's laboratory in Giessen between 1830 and 1850 (Murmann and Landau, 1998). The international character of academic education in the sciences was also an important factor in the development of national academic institutions.[13]

The influence of the German model on the evolution of US universities is quite remarkable. It is well known that the first incarnation of the modern graduate school in the USA at the Johns Hopkins University (founded in 1876) was heavily influenced by the German universities' emphasis on scientific research. Under the leadership of his first president, Daniel Coit Gilman, Johns Hopkins' faculty reached 53 units in 1884, '13 of whom had German doctorates and nearly all of whom had studied in Germany' (Emmerson, 1973, p. 288). As documented by other scholars (for example, Ben-David, 1977), the US universities quickly acquired original characteristics that will not be explored further in this chapter. It should be also noted that the German influence on US academic institutions was stronger in the organization of graduate programs in the sciences than it was in engineering, where in general the US universities held onto a curriculum that placed distinctly less emphasis on scientific training and more on practical learning.

4. KNOWLEDGE GATHERING AND INSTITUTION BUILDING IN JAPAN

The influences of foreign training and institutional developments are clearly visible and significant in Japan during the early phase of the Meiji restoration. After the long period of commercial isolation during the Tokugawa dynasty (1603–1868), when access to Western science and technology was seriously constrained, the acquisition of Western knowledge became an important focus of government policies aimed at promoting economic catch-up. The development of the resulting higher-level educational system was molded by the experiences brought home by Japanese educators and administrators who received their training abroad and by the recruitment of foreign scientists to teaching and research positions.

The development of the system occurred as the result of public and private initiatives, although the latter turned out to be short-lived and rather unsuccessful. In addition to schools focusing on the study of traditional Japanese culture, a number of private schools were founded in order to promote the study of medicine at Keio in 1874 and of engineering at Waseda in 1882. In 1889, a full-fledged science and engineering school was founded in Doshisha, called the Harris School of Science. All these programs failed within a few years for reasons ranging from financial difficulties, lack of formal university recognition, and outright opposition by the government to private initiative in the field of higher learning (Nagai, 1971). The survival of these institutions through their early years focused then on programs in the humanities, law and economics. An engineering department was established again in 1908 at Waseda, with a narrow focus on applied fields because faculties of pure science were already well established in the public universities. And a department of medicine was formed again in 1917 at Keio.[14]

While specialized schools were formed during the early years of the Meiji era, the public system had been organized since the 1870s around the concept of a general university. By the year 1918, when the government's University Ordinance gave formal university status to private colleges, the public university system included five centers including Tokyo (1886), Kyoto (1897), Sendai/Tohoku (1906), Fukuoka/Kyushu (1910), and Sapporo/Hokkaido (1918). The 1918 University Ordinance also promoted the creation of other public institutions at the prefectural and municipal level.

While early on teaching was the primary focus of the university system, during the 1880s a degree similar to the European doctoral degrees was defined (*hakushi*). During the following 30-year period, 1360 *hakushi* degrees were awarded. About half of the degrees were in medicine, a quarter in engineering. The number of degrees in mathematics and the sciences was rather small.[15]

One of the most important problems in the organization of a university system was the recruitment of teachers. Early on, appointments were typically offered to foreigners on the basis of recommendations provided by professors with whom Japanese students abroad had been in contact. Thus, a number of British chemists were appointed on the basis of the recommendation given by Alexander Williamson, Professor of Chemistry at the University of London, to his former pupil and government official, Ito Hirobumi. Williamson also conveyed his friend Lord Kelvin's recommendation that the British engineer Henry Dyer be invited to Japan. Within two years, in 1873, Dyer organized the Imperial College of Engineering for education in the sciences and engineering. Under Dyer's direction, a faculty of eight British professors offered instruction according to a four-year curriculum modeled after Zurich's ETH. The degree program included three years of practical experience that students could acquire at laboratory facilities of the university or at an industrial laboratory operated by the Ministry of Industries (Bartholomew, 1989; Odagiri and Goto, 1993). The College merged into the Tokyo University in 1886, where it became part of the Department of Engineering.

Established in 1877, Tokyo University was Japan's first and the only one for 20 years. The university was the result of a combination of three existing institutions, including a school of foreign languages, natural sciences, and engineering (*Kaisei Gakko*) and one of medicine (*Igakko*). According to initial plans, teaching was to be the only mission of the university and the laboratories for physics and chemistry were inadequate for the conduct of research. But the growing research aspirations of faculty and students were partially addressed by the completion of a new campus for the college of science in 1885. A year later the faculty of engineering was formed, including professors from the Imperial College of Engineering and engineering professors from the college of science of the university. Tokyo University was then renamed Imperial University.

The mid-1880s marked an important phase in the development of Japanese research institutions thanks to the government's commitment to use universities and research institutes in order to promote the catch-up of the Japanese economy with Europe and the USA. In addition to the upgrading of research facilities at Tokyo University, the government established a broad array of public research institutes and experiment stations spanning many areas of industry and agriculture.[16] Japan's minister of education at the time, Mori Arinori, intended these efforts to serve purely utilitarian goals, having little regard for people whose pursuit of knowledge was not useful to action. The course of Japanese government policy was influenced at least partly by the successes of the German system of universities and Hochschulen, both in terms of scientific production and in terms of supporting the rapid formation of a globally dominant national industry (organic chemicals) and the catch-up of others with the British leaders. But the organization of Japanese universities did not follow the German model all that closely.

In particular, questions as to whether or not universities should concern themselves with agricultural science or engineering did not play much of a role; nor did they lead to the same institutional separation that emerged in Germany. As for the internal organization of the faculties, the German chair system was rejected in favor of a departmental structure according to which any professor in an academic unit had responsibility for teaching any of the unit's courses. This arrangement was attacked for its inefficiency and its incompatibility with the specialization of the faculty. Thus, in 1893 a modified chair system was devised blending the system of multiple chairs typical of French universities in the fields where students' demand for courses was high and the hierarchical structure typical of the German universities with chair holders controlling junior faculty and students.

The Japanese colleges made extensive use of foreign personnel, whose compensation typically was several times over that provided to Japanese teachers. Indeed, the salaries paid to foreign teachers accounted for one-third of the Tokyo University budget in the late 1870s and even more during the following decade. The recruitment of foreign scientists followed a somewhat regular pattern, with Germans being the dominant group in medicine, British and US in mathematics, physics and chemistry. No one country dominated the ranks of engineering teachers, but according to Emmerson (1973), the 519 engineers who went to Japan on official visits between 1870 and 1885 were mostly from Britain, and then from France, Germany, the USA, Italy and other countries.

The recruitment cost of foreign teachers, some doubts about the quality and effectiveness of those actually recruited, and the growing demand for teachers to staff the expanding system of public universities, experiment stations and commissions, were the primary reasons for the government's continuing funding of a Ministry of Education program that since the late 1860s supported Japanese students' expenses at foreign schools. While the investment of public resources in order to send Japanese students abroad was at times a controversial issue, the program continued to operate at least until the eve of World War I. It is interesting to note that while in the 1870s Britain and the USA attracted comparable numbers of students to Germany, since then the latter became by far the most popular destination for the doctoral-level students abroad.[17] Nearly two-thirds of the roughly 3000 Japanese doctoral student-years spent abroad under this public program between 1869 and 1914 were spent in Germany. Other countries' shares were: 11 percent each in the USA and Britain, and only 7 percent in France (Bartholomew, 1989, p. 71).

While the official purpose of this program was best characterized as knowledge gathering and organized accordingly, the Japanese scientists considered traveling abroad to be an opportunity to participate in the research activities of professors at their host institutions, and to define collaborative or independent research projects. Occasionally, these two understandings collided and led to the abandonment of the program by at least a few Japanese scientists. But by and large, a persuasive case can be made to support the proposition that the study-abroad program provided the mechanism for establishing a tradition of research in the young academic institutions of the country and participation in the international network of scientists.

But there is hardly any doubt that the overseas tours of industrial and research facilities carried out by Japanese academics and other professionals were considered early on to be the most important form of domestic research. These knowledge-gathering activities pre-empted the commitment of resources to indigenous research in many fields. It should be noted that private firms did not engage in much research until the beginning of World War I, when the commercial ties to Germany had to be severed. Public funding of research was modest. Important programs were created in the medical field (largely thanks to Kitasato's Institute of Infectious Diseases), but hardly any in sciences and engineering until the end of the century. Research funding was very limited and no specific budgetary allocations were devoted to it within the universities.

Support for research aimed at industrial development increased as the access to foreign technology began to be restricted. Thus, in 1900 an Industrial Experiment Laboratory was established to conduct testing and analyses on a contract basis for national firms. From two divisions in industrial chemistry and chemical analysis staffed with technicians, the Laboratory was expanded in 1906 in the aftermath of the Russo-Japanese war to include divisions for ceramics, dyeing and electrochemistry in 1906. Similar pressures after the beginning of World War I created the conditions for establishing the Research Institute for Physics and Chemistry in 1917. This institute was patterned after the German Physicalische Technische Reichsanstalt established in 1887, and its research mission encompassed both basic research in the fields of chemistry and physics and applied research aimed at industrial technology. This institute grew considerably in size and range of scientific and technical fields from the mid-1920s when the current director Okochi Masatoshi addressed the financial constraints on the activities of the institute by making a push toward the commercialization of technologies patented by the Institute (Cusumano, 1989).

5. CONCLUSIONS

A preliminary assessment of the historical evidence reviewed in this chapter can be organized according to two criteria. The first focuses on the institutional mechanisms that were responsible for the international flows of knowledge across countries. The second focuses on the relationship between the factors that influenced the direction of development of the system of higher education and research and the emerging needs for knowledge and skills relevant for industrial development.

Several economic historians have argued that the diffusion of advanced British techniques to continental Europe and the USA was primarily stimulated by the migration of skilled personnel to these countries (Pollard,

1981; Landes, 1969). It is evident that a similar mechanism played an important role in the development of educational institutions. However, while British leadership in industrial technology made that country the origin of the relevant knowledge, the leadership in the development of higher education resided elsewhere and changed hands during the century. Accordingly, the French Écoles provided a template for the design of engineering schools in both Germany and the USA at the turn from the eighteenth to the nineteenth century. Later on, the German universities became identified as the premier scientific education centers because of the quality of their scientific research and training. Only after considerable changes in their organization and purpose were the German polytechnic schools in their Technische Hochschulen regarded as an important model for engineering education.

The historical record provides considerable evidence to the effect that the characteristics of the leading educational institutions influenced developments elsewhere through a variety of channels. A primary one was the agency of students and professors visiting foreign institutions, complemented by the diffusion of public knowledge about school curricula in various areas of science and engineering, and the diffusion of textbooks. The case of Japan in this respect is quite remarkable considering that the government gave financial support to the foreign studies undertaken by Japanese students and faculty, that early on a significant fraction of the faculty was recruited abroad and university courses in the scientific and engineering disciplines were taught in English, French, or German.

The flows of individuals occurring within the academic system provided a mechanism for diffusing not only institutional knowledge about curricula and the organization of teaching and research activities, but also scientific and technical knowledge originating from the host institutions. A prominent example is the diffusion of chemical scientific knowledge from Germany to Britain. This occurred in part through the return flow of British students taking seminars in Germany, and in part through the migration of German students in search of suitable professional opportunities. By the end of the century, US students in the fields of chemistry and physics would likely go to Germany for their advanced training. And around the same time, foreign students accounted for more than half of all students in electrical engineering at the Hochschule in Darmstadt.

Crucially, the diffusion of institutional knowledge related to higher education did not necessarily lead to the imitation of foreign institutions. Instead, a considerable amount of adaptation took place in different countries. Thus the US institutions of the early century, even when patterned after foreign schools like the École Polytechnique or any other, made provisions for the differences in the educational level of the prospective students. Innovative organizational forms resulted from these adaptive efforts. A short list of such innovations would include the US graduate school and the departmental organization of colleges, or the Japanese hybrid system of multiple chairs. The factors accounting for such adaptations are varied, almost certainly including a regard for the characteristics of the broader national educational system, the desire to address location-specific needs of students or other constituencies, the private or public nature of the educational programs, and so on.

This brings us to the second evaluative criterion proposed above, namely the relationship between the factors that influenced the direction of development of the system of higher education and research, and the emerging needs for knowledge and skills relevant for industrial development. At this preliminary stage of the investigation, it is useful to point out that neither the adaptations differentiating national systems nor the pattern of change within any given national system can be understood uniquely as motivated by the desire to make the universities and other schools more effective means for acquiring and disseminating knowledge relevant to industrial development. In fact, even if such an intent could be postulated, it would not be at all clear how a uniform set of prescriptions for the proper design of the system could have been derived from it by either government officers or educational entrepreneurs. On a positive note, the evidence indicates that a crucial distinction can be drawn according to the role of the state in organizing the educational institutions and its policies regarding the relation between access to certain jobs and educational attainment.

From this perspective, the USA appears to be the country where government intervention in the design of the educational institutions was most limited. When intervention at the level of the federal government occurred (through the Morrill Act), it came in the form of subsidizing state-based educational institutions (public or private) aimed at training students in those areas of technical knowledge where the science base for contemporary work practice was rather thin. Going back to Mokyr's definitions, the relevant propositional knowledge in these fields was characterized by a low scientific content. Furthermore, the government intervened in a market for higher education that already provided for a well-differentiated range of educational options, from the liberal arts programs of the elite school, to their scientific education spin-offs, to the specialized engineering schools. The emergence of a tradition of research-based education came only later and as a result of private initiative.

As argued by Nelson and Rosenberg (1994), the development of the US university system benefited from relatively open entry conditions in the market for higher education. Because schools were for the most part tuition-driven or dependent on donations and grants, the ability to provide students with valuable knowledge and skills was an important influence in institutional developments. Relationships with the economic environment and the feed-back loops from economic needs to the development of institutions were organized differently in the mostly publicly funded educational systems in Germany, France and Japan.

Important influences on the developments of the system came from the governments' desire to provide for the education of military and civil servants. By defining restrictive criteria for access to coveted positions in the public administration, they reduced the competition among institutions in terms of educating students for particular careers. Both in France and Germany, a hierarchy of social status formed relatively early that placed the industry-oriented polytechnic schools below the civil-service-oriented ones. The desire to gain equal status became a powerful influence on the development of the former, pulling in directions that were perhaps at odds with any short-term regard for industrial development needs. These pulls were also consistent with the intellectual orientation of the professors at the polytechnic schools, whose aspiration to establish a science of engineering gave short shrift to the value of practical workshop training. Indeed, most professors lacked industrial experience in this regard.

On the whole, it appears that the development of the system of higher education and research responded better to economic development needs when appropriate channels emerged for industrial practices and technical problems to play a role in the design of curricula and student activities. In the countries where the educational system was largely public, examples of such channels include the establishment of public experimental laboratories, recruitment of professors with industrial work experience, professors consulting with industrial firms and so on. Future work will investigate these processes more closely, and will broaden the focus to agricultural schools. There too, the development of curricula and other research activities was influenced by the conflict between practice and science that we have observed in the field of engineering.

NOTES

1. In his recent book, *The Gifts of Athena* (2002), Joel Mokyr argues that the rapid increase in prescriptive knowledge (knowledge about techniques) during the last three centuries was aided considerably by the concurrent growth and diffusion of a body of propositional knowledge (knowledge about natural phenomena and regularities, including but not limited to scientific knowledge). Mokyr's proposed distinction between propositional knowledge and scientific knowledge complements the characterization of technology provided by Nelson (1990), as including both generic technical knowledge and a localized body of practice.
2. Among the most influential figures of the time, Ferdinand Redtenbacher, Professor of Mechanical Engineering and Director of the Karlsruhe Polytechnical School, quipped

in 1854. 'For a long time now, I have been disgusted with the gobbledygook of the empiricists' (quoted in Gispen, 1989, p. 35). Redtenbacher, who moved to Karlsruhe from Zurich where he held a position in applied mathematics at the local industrial school, was one of the fathers of scientific mechanical engineering. Among his scientific contributions was an attempt to develop laws of construction of locomotives aimed at resolving problems of stability at high speed. While these laws are not known to have made a positive contribution to the practice of locomotive construction, Redtenbacher's ideas had a greater influence on the future of engineering education (Böhme et al., 1978).

3. One of Redtenbacher's students in Karlsruhe, Franz Reuleaux pursued similar scientific objectives to his teacher. His scientific work focused on developing a theory of machines based on the identification of fundamental mechanisms. Upon completing his studies in Karlsruhe, Reuleaux moved to Zurich's newly established Technical University (ETH), where he created a new program in mechanical engineering. His success there and the strong scientific reputation that he built over the years earned him an invitation to Berlin in 1864, where he developed the mechanical engineering program of the Gewerbe Institut.

4. Since 1862, Reuleaux had been traveling to World Exhibitions often as German ambassador (Moon, 2002).

5. Fifteen years later, the newly appointed director Sylvanus P. Thayer reorganized the curriculum after the model of the École Polytechnique (Emmerson, 1973).

6. Nelson and Rosenberg (1994) identify in the decentralization of the US academic system a key reason for its success in contributing to the economic development of the country.

7. Nelson and Rosenberg (1994) document how US universities distinguished themselves also in the twentieth century for the speed with which study programs are formed to support training and research in new fields of knowledge.

8. The differences in the approach to engineering typical of nineteenth-century US and French professors are illustrated by Kranakis's (1989) comparison of scientific work on essentially identical topics. Abstract mathematical formulation of engineering problems and solutions were typical of the French scientific literature, much as tables of data evinced from extensive laboratory testing were the hallmark of US engineering work. Workshop and laboratory experience was considered an essential, if not dominant, component of the training of the engineers. Around 1900, the hours of laboratory and workshop experience included in the mechanical engineering program at Cornell exceeded hours of lecture by 25 per cent.

9. Thus, Sylvanus Thayer spent four years at the École Polytechnique (1813–17) before becoming superintendent of the West Point Military Academy (Grattan-Guinness, 2005). The School of Mines at Columbia University was the creation of Thomas Egleston, a Yale graduate who studied at the École des Mines in Paris. At its founding in 1864, several of the engineers and scientists serving on the faculty of the school had received their training in France or Germany.

10. Another perspective on this phenomenon comes from the requirements for admission into the two kinds of schools. Since mid-century, access to the science faculties at universities was opened up to students graduating from the high schools that were conceived originally as preparing students for access to the Hochschulen. The academization of engineering is also relevant to the 1899 decision by Kaiser Wilhelm II to give the Hochschulen the right to grant doctoral degrees.

11. The number of doctorates increased from 851 during the 1820s to 1727 in the 1860s.

12. The emergence of chemical engineering in the USA as a body of specialized knowledge capable of broad applications to the design of continuous flow processes for the production of chemicals is regarded by Rosenberg (1998) to have been a critical factor influencing the strides made by the US chemical industry when it pioneered the use of petroleum as the dominant feedstock.

13. Thwing (1928) set at over 4600 the number of American students who had matriculated in German universities by the end of the nineteenth century.

14. This department directed itself to research in the area of contagious diseases under the deanship of Kitasato Shibasaburo. Kitasato is one of the leading scientists of the period. Upon returning from a period of foreign study with Robert Koch in Berlin, Kitasato pursued research in the area of contagious diseases. Highly critical of the research activities at Japanese universities, he headed the Institute of Infectious Diseases from 1894 to 1914 when the Institute was transferred to the Tokyo University. Because of his long-standing disputes with the university medical faculty, Kitasato abandoned the institute only to establish it as the Kitasato Institute with private funds.
15. Specifically, 56 degrees were awarded for research in biology, 54 in physics, 27 in chemistry, 22 in mathematics, and 18 in geology (Bartholomew, 1989, p. 52).
16. There were 15 non-academic laboratories in 1885. Another 15 were established before 1900. These laboratories included agricultural experiment stations, the Institute of Infectious Diseases, the Serological Institute, and in 1900 the Industrial Experiment Laboratory.
17. By Emmerson's estimate that 380 students were abroad in 1872 (1973, p. 229), it would appear that doctoral degree students accounted for only a small fraction of the phenomenon.

REFERENCES

Bartholomew, James R. (1989), *The Formation of Science in Japan*, New Haven, CT: Yale University Press.

Ben-David, Joseph (1977), *Centers of Learning*, New York: McGraw-Hill.

Böhme, Gernot et al. (1978), 'The "Scientification" of Technology,' in W. Krohn, E.T. Layton Jr and P. Weingart (eds), *The Dynamics of Science and Technology*, Dordrecht: D. Reidel Publishing Company, pp. 219–50.

Cohen, Wesley M., Richard R. Nelson and John P. Walsh (2002), 'The Influence of Public Research on Industrial R&D,' *Management Science*, **48** (1), 1–23.

Cusumano, Michael A. (1989), ' "Scientific Industry": Strategy, Technology, and Entrepreneurship in Prewar Japan,' in W.D. Wray (ed.), *Managing Industrial Enterprise*, Cambridge, MA: Harvard University Press, pp. 269–316.

Emmerson, George S. (1973), *Engineering Education: A Social History*, New York: Crane, Russak & Co.

Geiger, Roger L. (1986), *To Advance Knowledge*, Oxford: Oxford University Press.

Gerschenkron, Alexander (1962), *Economic Backwardness in Historical Perspective*, Cambridge, MA: Belknap Press.

Gispen, Kees (1989), *New Profession, Old Order*, Cambridge: Cambridge University Press.

Grattan-Guinness, Ivor (2005), 'The Ecole Polytechnique, 1794–1850: Differences over Educational Purpose and Teaching Practice,' *The American Mathematical Monthly*, **112** (3), 233–50.

Haber, Ludwig F. (1958), *The Chemical Industry During the Nineteenth Century*, Oxford: Oxford University Press.

Keck, Otto (1993), 'The National System for Technical Innovation in Germany,' in R.R. Nelson (ed.), *National Innovation Systems. A Comparative Analysis*, Oxford: Oxford University Press, pp. 115–57.

Klevorick, Alvin K., Richard C. Levin, Richard R. Nelson and Sidney C. Winter (1995), 'On the Sources and Significance of Interindustry Differences in Technological Opportunities,' *Research Policy*, **24**, 185–205.

König, Wolfgang (1996), 'Science-Based Industry or Industry-Based Science? Electrical Engineering in Germany before World War I,' *Technology and Culture*, **37** (1), 70–101.

Kranakis, Eda (1989), 'Social Determinants of Engineering Practice: A Comparative View of France and America in the Nineteenth Century,' *Social Studies of Science*, **19** (1), 5–70.

Landes, David S. (1969), *The Unbound Prometheus*, Cambridge: Cambridge University Press.

Lundgreen, Peter (1980), 'The Organization of Science and Technology in France: A German Perspective,' in R. Fox and G. Weisz (eds), *The Organization of Science and Technology in France, 1808–1914*, Cambridge: Cambridge University Press, pp. 311–32.

Manegold, Karl-Heinz (1978), 'Technology Academised: Education and Training of the Engineer in the 19th Century,' in W. Krohn, E.T. Layton Jr and P. Weingart (eds), *The Dynamics of Science and Technology*, Dordrecht: D. Reidel Publishing Company, pp. 137–58.

McClelland, Charles E. (1980), *State, Society, and University in Germany, 1700–1914*, Cambridge: Cambridge University Press.

Mokyr, Joel (2002), *The Gifts of Athena*, Princeton, NJ: Princeton University Press.

Moon, Francis C. (2002), 'Franz Reuleaux: Contributions to 19th Century Kinematics and Theory of Machines,' unpublished manuscript.

Murmann, Johann Peter (2003), *Knowledge and Competitive Advantage*, Cambridge: Cambridge University Press.

Murmann, Johann Peter and Ralph Landau (1998), 'On the Making of Competitive Advantage: The Development of the Chemical Industries of Britain and Germany Since 1850,' in A. Arora, R. Landau and N. Rosenberg (eds), *Chemicals and Long-Term Economic Growth: Insights from the Chemical Industry*, New York: John Wiley & Sons, pp. 27–70.

Nagai, Michio (1971), *Higher Education in Japan: Its Take-Off and Crash*, Tokyo: University of Tokyo Press.

Nelson, Richard R. (1990), 'Capitalism as an Engine of Progress,' *Research Policy*, **19**, 61–87.

Nelson, Richard R. and Nathan Rosenberg (1994), 'American Universities and Technical Advance in Industry,' *Research Policy*, **23**, 323–48.

Odagiri, Hiroyuki and Akira Goto (1993), 'The Japanese System of Innovation: Past, Present, and Future,' in R.R. Nelson (ed.), *National Innovation Systems. A Comparative Analysis*, Oxford: Oxford University Press, pp. 76–114.

Paul, Harry W. (1980), 'Apollo Courts the Vulcans: The Applied Science Institutes in Nineteenth Century French Science,' in R. Fox and G. Weisz (eds), *The Organization of Science and Technology in France, 1808–1914*, Cambridge: Cambridge University Press, pp. 155–82.

Pollard, Sidney (1981), *Peaceful Conquest*, Oxford: Oxford University Press.

Rosenberg, Nathan (1998), 'Technological Change in Chemicals: The Role of University-Industry Relations,' in A. Arora, R. Landau and N. Rosenberg (eds), *Chemicals and Long-Term Economic Growth: Insights from the Chemical Industry*, New York: John Wiley & Sons, pp. 193–230.

Shinn, Terry (1980), 'From "Corps" to "Profession": The Emergence and Definition of Industrial Engineering in Modern France,' in R. Fox and G. Weisz (eds), *The Organization of Science and Technology in France, 1808–1914*, Cambridge: Cambridge University Press, pp. 183–208.

Stokes, Donald E. (1997), *Pasteur's Quadrant: Basic Science and Technological Innovation*, Washington, DC: Brookings Institution.

Thwing, Charles F. (1928). *American and the German University; One Hundred Years of History*, New York: Macmillan Company.

Tocqueville, Alexis de (1876), *Democracy in America*, 6th edition, Boston, MA: John Allyn.

Torstendahl, Rolf (1993), 'The Transformation of Professional Education in the Nineteenth Century,' in S. Rothblatt and B. Wittrock (eds), *The European and American University since 1800: Historical and Sociological Essays*, Cambridge: Cambridge University Press, pp. 109–41.

Weingart, Peter (1978), 'The Relation between Science and Technology – A Sociological Explanation,' in W. Krohn, E.T. Layton Jr and P. Weingart (eds), *The Dynamics of Science and Technology*, Dordrecht: D. Reidel Publishing Company, pp. 251–86.

Wengenroth, Ulrich (2000), *Science, Technology, and Industry in the 19th Century*, Munich Center for the History of Science and Technology, Working Paper.

4. Patenting in public research. An evidence-based reflection on IPRs and the basic–applied research trade-off

Mario Calderini and Chiara Franzoni

1. INTRODUCTION

In recent years, extensive scientific literature has dealt with technology transfer and with the mechanisms that allow appropriability of social benefits from innovation (Martin and Scott, 2000). Much of this debate has focused on the capability of local innovation systems to provide coordination among the actors of technological change and empowered transfer mechanisms.

Related to the above-mentioned debate, policy makers have encouraged publicly funded research institutes to smooth the transfer of results from science to industry by means of joint research agreements, by creating spin-off firms, and by establishing intellectual property rights (IPRs) over results of research. Increasingly, legitimization of public research seems to be linked to the ability of national and local systems of innovation to directly benefit from science and to engage in positive exchanges with industry (Gibbons, 1999; Martin, 2001; Etzkowitz et al., 2000). The above trend has been guided in many countries by both political and regulatory actions, which overall resulted in an increase of technology transfer from public research (Mowery et al., 2002; Thursby and Kemp, 2002). However, this evidence of empowered commercialization of research reopened the debate in sociology and economics of science on the dangers of linking science to the market. On the one hand, it is not clear whether this increase has come at the expense of the economic value and quality of transferred technologies (Jensen et al., 2003b; Jaffe, 2000; Henderson et al., 1998; Gittelman and Kogut, 2003). On the other, there is the danger that we may jeopardize fundamental research and high-quality education for the sake of short-term development. Although all policies in support of technology transfer are clearly based on the assumption that scientific research and technological development are not inherently rival activities; that is, it is possible to extract technological applications without jeopardizing the quality of research, this position is not commonly accepted within the community of science. It is certainly acknowledged that virtuous interactions can occasionally arise between science and technology (Mansfield, 1995; Carraro et al., 2001; Fransman, 2001); however, it is doubtful that commercialization of research can be done at a negligible cost both in the short and in the long run.

However, it is only recently that empirical evidence has been provided to throw light on the positions of policy makers and scholars. The findings, apart from supporting the hypothesis of rivalry, have indicated that policy for technology transfer requires a richer interpretation of the relationship between science and the market, production of new knowledge and technological change.

In the present chapter we will summarize the position of the literature on the hypothesis of rivalry of science and technology, discuss the consequences for dynamic efficiency and present the findings of the empirical tests that have been recently made. Finally, we discuss the implications for political debate. The chapter is organized as follows: in Section 2 we summarize the hypothesis of rivalry; in Section 3 we describe recent findings of empirical tests; in Section 4 we discuss the implications for economics of science and innovation policy.

2. ARE SCIENCE AND TECHNOLOGY RIVALS OR MUTUALLY SUPPORTING?

To understand the question of rivalry between alternative scientific activities we must first refer to the problem of arranging a reward structure for science that is consistent with socially desirable goals. Productivity of science is crucial for long-term welfare, to the extent that it ensures the creation of new knowledge and fosters future technological change. An impressive body of literature has illustrated in recent decades that the market is unable to provide enough incentives for long-term-oriented research, due to the imperfect appropriability of knowledge and to strong uncertainty associated with discovery (Nelson, 1959; Dasgupta and David, 1994). This is why we cannot rely on the allocative efficiency of markets to arrange a reward structure that is socially desirable, particularly if we have to ensure the long-term growth of the economy. Recognition of market failures in knowledge productions on the one hand called for government intervention and public subsidies for research; on the other, it required the establishment of a reward structure other than the market to provide alignment of incentives and efficient allocation of resources. This is why, in all modern societies, policy for research was traditionally inspired by the principle that science had to be kept separated from the market in order to provide exogenous and unpredictable long-term trajectories of technological change for the benefit of the global economy (Martin and Scott, 2000).

Nevertheless, in recent decades, the expectations of society and policy makers of the goals of science have partially changed. Increasingly, scientists are required not only to ensure the long-term exploitable knowledge and up-to-date training of new generations, but also to assist the development and diffusion of technological applications to the market and support the competitive advantage of industry at the local and national level. Increasingly, scientists are asked to empower the link between discovery and economic exploitation and to be concerned with the returns on investments in research. At the same time, the composition of public subsidies given to research institutions is gradually shifting. Since the 1980s we have generally seen a global tendency to shrink public support to fundamental research and temporarily increase the funds devoted to transfer activities. Clearly, this shift in the goals given to science requires the emergence of a new equilibrium in the structure of incentives and rewards. This general trend, which underlies recent political and theoretical debate, is causing a parallel rearrangement of the design of tasks and incentives given to science. The most notable of these changes was the quest for the establishment of private rights over the results of publicly funded research (Geuna and Nesta, 2003) and the provision of institutional incentives for academic patenting (Lach and Shankerman, 2003), which signified the introduction of market-related incentives in the reward structure of scientists. This change was strongly opposed by many scholars, who argue that this new structure of incentives would increase development of applications at the expense of long-term trajectories of research. In order to understand more thoroughly the positions of scholars and policy makers on this matter, we need to refer to some general features in the design of incentives to discovery, which is a key issue in determining the productivity of research, and appreciate the coherence of the earlier system of rules. Scientists can potentially perform many alternative activities, namely research, teaching, consulting and development of applications for industrial use. Therefore, given that discovery is unpredictable and effort is subject to imperfect monitoring, individuals would choose to allocate their effort to the activities yielding the best marginal utilities; hence the arrangement of incentives given *ex ante* to scientists has crucial consequences *vis-à-vis* the potential of technological change (Gallini and Scotchmer, 2001; Levin and Stephan, 1991; Lach and Shankerman, 2003).

Modern societies traditionally relied on science to ensure the long-term exploitable knowledge and up-to-date training of new generations. These expectations were typically mirrored by (1) a combination of research and teaching in common research positions and (2) a reward structure of science based upon 'priority in discovery', as awarded by 'peer review' of the scientific community. The latter condition ensures that, regardless of the individual motivations leading scientists to discovery (motivated either by prize-seeking or puzzle-solving), recognition and merit could be gained only on the basis of the eminence and the centrality of the findings of previous works in the eyes of the scientific community (Levin and Stephan, 1991). A set of rules and institutions embedded in the scientific community strictly regulates the system of judgements and rewards, establishes what should be regarded as a success for research and what should be the prizes for the winners. Scientists that are first in discovery of a valuable piece of knowledge establish their 'priority' over it, that is, the right to be accountable for scientific advance, which gives recognition within the scientific community. Establishment of priority occurs as the scientist discloses the discovery by submitting his/her work to the validation of the 'peer review' of the scientific community, and publishes the work in open science (Dasgupta and David, 1985). Publication of results supports recognition within the scientific community and the best-recognized scientists are allowed to contribute more strongly to the peer review of science. That is, they gain legitimacy to affect judgements on what is to be counted as a success for science, and control over procedural rules within the community (Chubin and Hackett, 1990). This independent rationale to appraise the merits of research and to direct the best resources to the best scientists is ultimately the mechanism enabling the scientific community to foster inherently novel sources of knowledge (Polanyi, 1962; Merton, 1957; Chubin and Hackett, 1990). In this sense, the procedures of 'priority' and 'peer review' are able to align the behavior of scientists to a set of socially desired goals. First, they ensure that the recognition of merit and ultimately the allocation of the best resources to the best scientists is made by following inherently scientific criteria, which reduces the hazard of short-termism in lines of research (Dasgupta and David, 1994). Second, they ensure a widespread and immediate diffusion of results, which reduces the risk of duplication of effort. In fact, from the point of view of public welfare, once a new piece of knowledge has been discovered, the benefit of marginal discovery is null, whereas the social benefit increases with the rate and speed of its diffusion and application across the economic system.

Therefore, as we enlarge the goals of science to the development of applications for industrial use, we need to be concerned with the possible consequences of the effectiveness of the social and procedural rules regulating the scientific community (Dasgupta and David, 1985; David and Hall, 2000). In this respect, scholars have emphasized at least two different effects. First, a scientist who engages in frequent consulting activities and research agreements with industrial partners ultimately substitutes market goals for 'peer-review' judgement of his/her work. In the short run, since market incentives favor short-term research trajectories, this may result in a sub-optimal stock of fundamental research performed within the system and in an unbalanced mix of fundamental versus applied activities (David, 1998). In the long run, inclusion of market-related pay-offs in researchers' incentive structure may further weaken the rule of priority, thereby undermining the capability of the scientific community to provide a system of incentives aligned with long-term socially desirable growth (Dasgupta and David, 1985). Second, engaging in a relationship with industrial partners may require that scientists conform to the need to prevent the free circulation of findings by keeping the results of research confidential (Dasgupta and David, 1985). In this case, scientists may be tempted to postpone or even neglect publication in open science. Consequently, the problem of rivalry is likely to come about either at the level of research production or at the level of the disclosure of results. The former would cause a trade-off between fundamental and applied research and in the long run lead to a sub-optimal rate of technological change. The latter would reduce the capacity and pace of the diffusion of new knowledge within the system, and there is a danger that it would further weaken the system of rules and procedures that governs the scientific community. As we ask science to enlarge its mission, we need to take great care to arrange an appropriate structure of incentives supporting the new goals. This structure depends in turn on how we arrange the incentives for the individuals at a micro-level. As commercialization of results becomes part of the institutional objectives of research organizations, the latter create their internal units with dedicated personnel. These units, generally called technology transfer offices (TTOs), are likely to play a key role in the emerging equilibrium, because they will be the vehicles of market rewards on behalf of scientific community (Jensen et al., 2003a).

3. PATENTING AND PUBLISHING. THE EMPIRICAL EVIDENCE

The debate on the appropriate reward structure for science has been rich in contributions in recent decades. Nevertheless, only lately have we been able to support these views with some empirical evidence. First of all, some empirical analyses have been made to determine whether research institutions have the power to affect the effort devoted by their scientists to commercial activities by means of organizational variables. Although contract research and patents issued have no effect on a scientist's career, in the sense that the rank and eminence of a scientist typically do not depend on those activities, evidence has been found to indicate that scientists are likely to react to monetary incentives offered at the institutional level. Lach and Shankerman (2003) demonstrated that both the number of patents issued and the income from licenses are increasing in the percentage share of revenues guaranteed *ex ante* to the single researcher–inventor. Moreover, the institutional willingness to patent and the efficiency of internal TTOs were found to be able to increase the quantity of commercial activities performed (Thursby and Thursby, 2002). This evidence suggests that universities are reacting to the changing environment and that the shift in the system of incentives they create at the institutional level can produce a change in the behavior of scientists. The effect produced also depends on the principal–agent framework of relationships standing between academic administration, scientists and TTOs that belong to the same institution (Jensen et al., 2003a; Owen-Smith and Powell, 2001). Case study research has suggested that the technological applications submitted by the members of the faculties to the local TTO might have been adversely selected (Jensen et al., 2003b); that is, scientists may be tempted to rush to publication in open science for the most promising results of their research and consider patents as a second-best option. Furthermore, it may be the case that the policy push had the effect of inflating the number of patents issued for low-quality applications. This idea is further supported by the results of a comparative study by Mowery and Ziedonis (2002) on university patenting before and after the US Bayh–Dole Act. They found that patents held by those institutions that started patenting after the change in law were cited less than average patents issued by institutions that had an older tradition in patenting. These findings may be interpreted as evidence of decreasing marginal productivity of technology transfer and further suggest the need for a deeper understanding of the real benefits that can be obtained from academic patenting.

A number of recent empirical works have also investigated the potential for a trade-off at the level of the individual researchers. Interestingly, none of the works have found support for the hypothesis of the rivalry of basic and applied research, whereas most of them have found that patenting was likely to have some positive effect on the performances of scientists. Agrawal and Henderson (2002) studied a sample of 236 researchers from MIT that had both patented and published in the 15-year period 1983–97. The authors measured productivity in fundamental research by the number of papers published in scientific journals and eminence by the number of paper citations received. They assess the effect of having engaged in applied research as signaled by the number of patents issued.

Results indicated that the productivity in fundamental research was not significantly affected by the occurrence of a patent in previous years; furthermore the stock of patents accumulated by a researcher was likely to increase the number of article citations. A positive effect on citations was also suggested by Hicks and Hamilton (1999), who looked at the publications co-authored by scientists and practitioners and found that the latter have on average a higher impact compared to non-co-authored ones. Contrary to Agrawal and Henderson, a positive link was found between patenting and articles published in a number of recent studies, indicating that those scientists who have high scores in publications are also likely to have high scores in patents and vice versa. Van Looy et al. (2004) found that the scientists who were systematically involved in contract research at the Catholic University of Leuven (BE) published more than colleagues working in the faculties of the same university. Stephan et al. (2004) found a positive effect of publication counts on patent count by running a zero-inflated negative binomial regression in a sample of doctorate-recipients in computer sciences, life sciences, physical sciences and engineering. The same was also found in a recent work by Breschi et al. (2004), analyzing a sample of Italian public researchers who were former inventors in at least one EPO patent versus a control sample of researchers that never patented. They suggested the existence of a 'productivity fixed effect', inducing highly productive scientists to show comparatively better performances in both patenting and publishing. This can either be due to inherently individual heterogeneity with regard to productivity or to the effect of endogeneity of patenting versus publications, in the sense that private companies may be more willing to engage in contract research with scientists having the highest publication scores. The authors tend to separate the above effects from what they call a 'resource effect', namely a positive temporary increase in the availability of resources for research determined by licensing revenues or by contract research with industrial partners that accounts for a temporary increase of publications immediately after patent. Evidence of this effect was likewise found by Markiewicz and Di Minin (2004) in a broad sample of US researcher–inventors and by Calderini and Franzoni (2004), studying a population of Italian scientists in the field of chemistry for new materials across 30 years. Both these studies estimated a non-negligible increase in articles published in the years immediately after patenting. The latter study also indicated that the temporary increase in the number of publications is not likely to alter the expected quality of the publication. Furthermore, it indicated that the average impact factor of publications is likely to increase in the two years preceding the patent priority date, which can be interpreted as evidence of endogenous patenting. Some findings also gave support to the claim that patenting produces a delay in the publication of results. Calderini and Franzoni (2004) found that a temporary increase in publications of the 'resource-effect' type is likely to emerge with a one to three years' delay, meaning that additional publications are allowed as a by-product of contract research with no decrease in quality, but a slow-down in the pace of publication is likely to occur in the case of patenting. Besides, the practice of industry in obtaining delays in publication of results until the filing of a patent is complete has been documented in a number of case studies and surveys across various disciplines (see Van Looy et al., 2004).

Summarizing, a consistent body of evidence is now available that denies the existence of a trade-off between patenting and publishing at least in terms of the number of publications produced, due to both a 'resource effect' and a 'productivity fixed effect'. Hence we can reasonably argue that scientists who publish a great deal can also patent without worsening their scientific performances and that contract research is likely to generate an additional stream of results that is still of interest in the eyes of the scientific community, although with a delay in publication. Certainly we need to be aware that all the previous studies judge the impact of development activities by looking at publication-related measures of scientific performance; consequently, they all share the same potential for misrepresentation of related figures. The advantages and limitations of this kind of analysis have been widely discussed in the literature (see Moed et al., 1985; Seglen, 1992; De Solla Price, 1963; Martin and Irvine, 1983; Narin and Hamilton, 1996; Peritz et al., 1992). For the purposes of inquiring into the trade-off between science and technology, the drawback of these methods is that it is especially hard to appraise the long-term orientation of research content in order to check for possible effects of contract research on the definition of the scientist's research agenda. However, even our notion of fundamental research and long-term orientation is ambiguous. Further reflections are probably needed in order to sharpen our understanding on this matter. However, the evidence collected so far certainly allows us to delineate some findings on the features of the underlying phenomena and to derive implications for policy of science and technology.

4.   IMPLICATIONS FOR POLICY OF SCIENCE AND TECHNOLOGY

As previously explained, society is increasingly concerned with social returns on public investments in research. To empower the transfer of results to industry, policy makers in recent decades have strengthened the incentives given to scientists for the development of application and the commercialization of technology. These measures have raised the concern of a potential shift in the allocation of resources from long- to short-term research, which would have negative consequences for technological change. However, what has emerged so far clearly shows that we have absolutely no evidence of a crowd-out of fundamental research versus development of technological applications for scientists working in public research institutions. On the contrary, in nearly all cases, an additional flow of results suitable for publication in scientific journals was obtained by giving scientists additional resources, for instance by means of contract research. This suggests that the sample of scientists analyzed did not have to renounce scientific research for the sake of doing more commercial exploitation, meaning that they were still operating in the upward-sloping portion of their productivity functions. In such conditions, every policy measure that increases the quantity of funds made available to research is likely to produce sensible benefits for social welfare, including measures that claim external support to science. However, it should be recognized that an increase of commercialization activities sooner or later should yield decreasing marginal returns. Besides, in many of the cited cases, transfer of results from science to the market was effected with no or very little political and institutional support. Therefore, every observed transaction was Pareto-efficient within the strict market incentive framework. However, as we inflate the incentives for scientists to patent by means of policy intervention, less-promising technologies are likely to be developed and we will potentially obtain fewer and lower-quality applications. Besides, in the many advanced experiments, universities have reported difficulties in selling their technologies and excess expenses of patent portfolios have become a major concern (Jensen et al., 2003b). Therefore policy makers and research institutions should take care that an excess emphasis on commercialization might result in extra expenses for universities in the form of increased operating costs, rather than in additional funds made available to research.

A second major result of empirical analyses was to show that patent applications come from high-quality scientists and highly rated results. Although high-quality research tends to be long-term-oriented, the evidence indicates that it also has the potential to produce more technological applications. Private companies choose star scientists to engage in contract research and most probably use scientific excellence as assessed by the scientific community to detect eminence. This indicates that they look at research institutions as potential providers of high-impact applications, rather than as partners for the outsourcing of trivial development activities. Consequently, because top-quality research is likely be more productive in every respect and vice versa, policy measures cannot aim at separating performers of top-quality research and providers of shorter-term applications in the allocation of resources. They also cannot expect the private sector to provide additional funds to low-quality research institutions. Therefore public subsidies to fundamental research are needed even for the goal of obtaining more exploitation from research and every reduction of funds to fundamental research is likely to result also in a lower transfer of results. A side implication is that every shift of funds from research to development would produce a decrease in both.

A notable result of the empirical findings is that, although no crowding out of science and technology would arise at the level of production, an empowered link with the private sector is likely to be problematic as regards the disclosure of results. Private companies tend to ask for confidentiality of findings and delays in publication in open science, to protect their competitive advantage and to obtain longer-term Schumpeterian rents. Of course this tendency is stronger the weaker the level of protection guaranteed by patents and the longer the non-disclosure period required in the patent procedure. Therefore a wise policy for technology transfer should include additional measures to lower the possible negative effect of delays in the diffusion of new knowledge. As long as the behavior of researchers strictly depends on the rules of the scientific community there is no need to impose publication, since the latter is strongly embedded in the incentive structure offered to individuals. However, as we link scientists' rewards to the market, disclosure of results may need to be enforced by means of a proper disclosure policy. This concern is especially important for all the results that have been originated at least partially by public funds either in the form of state and charity grants or through the use of publicly funded labs and facilities, in order to ensure the maximum public support. In those cases, the government may consider imposing a prompt disclosure of research results by law on all cases of joint and contract research agreements. Furthermore, some parallel adjustments in the IPR legislation are probably needed to smooth the potential for conflicting incentives to disclosure by contracting parties. A possible revision would include a clause of the type in force in the USA, which deems an inventor's divulgation in open science not to represent previous disclosure if a patent application is filed in the following 12 months. Besides, attention should be given to shorten the delay occurring between the file of a patent and its publication.

Finally, further implications of the empirical results can be derived concerning the issue of establishing private rights over inventions of public scientists and over results of publicly funded research. In the presence of positive marginal productivity of technology development, no prescription can be made against the law that allocates IPRs to universities or to individuals. To the extent that establishing private rights allows the emergence of a market for technology that would not arise otherwise, enabling private appropriation of results of public investments in research may be a Pareto-optimal solution. In this respect, research institutions may be better at tolerating the risk involved with patenting, given that they can diversify their portfolio of investments. This is true to the extent that private companies see the benefits of bargaining with a unique partner and generally as long as no slow-down of negotiations and patent procedures is caused by the introduction of a third party. Therefore allocation of IPRs to universities is advisable, provided that the latter minimize the bureaucracy and give to the local TTO a set of incentives aligned with the social good. A socially desirable set of incentives for the TTO should include not only the maximization of rents from transfer of knowledge, but also the minimization of time-to-disclosure. Additionally, universities probably give priority to non-exclusive as compared to exclusive licensing, at least in all those cases where non-exclusive licensing does not impede transactions. On the contrary, if universities cannot be an efficient counterpart, it is probably preferable to leave the IPRs to individual scientists and allow private negotiations with industrial partners. Furthermore, allocation of IPRs to institutions would bring the comparative advantage of facilitating the task of enforcing a possible clause of compulsory disclosure and allowing for non-exclusive licensing to industry. However, while licensing to industry, research institutions should be aware that they might encounter a potential trade-off depending on the way they exert their bargaining power in the negotiations. If universities go for the top dollar, they may extract high revenues from licensing invention in the short run, but this may reduce the investments in research in the following periods. Therefore universities may consider allowing greater appropriation of rents in order to obtain higher investments later.

REFERENCES

Agrawal, A. and Henderson, R. (2002), 'Putting patents in context: exploring knowledge transfer from MIT', *Management Science*, **48** (1), 44–60.
Breschi, S., Lissoni, F. and Montobbio, F. (2004), 'Open science and university patenting: a bibliometric analysis of the Italian case', paper presented at tenth International J.S. Schumpeter Society Conference on Innovation, Industrial Dynamics and Structural Transformation Schumpeterian Legacies, Milan, 9–12 June.
Calderini, M. and Franzoni, C. (2004), 'Is academic patenting detrimental to high quality research? An empirical analysis of the relationship between scientific careers and patent applications', Working Paper no. 162, CESPRI, University Bocconi.

Carraro, F., Pomè, A. and Siniscalco, D. (2001), 'Science versus profit in research: lessons from the human genome project', CEPR Discussion Paper no. 2890, London, Centre for Economic Policy Research, www.cepr.org/pubs/dps/DP2890.asp.

Chubin, D.E. and Hackett, E.J. (1990), 'Peerless science: peer review and US science policy', Albany: State University of New York Press.

Dasgupta, P. and David, P.A. (1985), 'Information disclosure and the economics of science and technology', CEPR Discussion Paper no. 73, London, Centre for Economic Policy Research, www.cepr.org/pubs/dps/DP73.asp.

Dasgupta, P. and David, P.A. (1994), 'Towards a new economy of science', *Research Policy*, **23**, 487–521.

David, P.A. (1998), 'The political economy of public science', in Helen Lawton Smith (ed.), *The Regulation of Science and Technology*, London: Macmillan.

David, P.A. and Hall, B.H. (2000), 'Heart of darkness: modeling public–private funding interactions inside the R&D black box', *NBER Working Paper 7538*, Cambridge, MA, National Bureau of Economic Research.

De Solla Price, D.J. (1963), *Little Science, Big Science*, New York: Columbia University Press.

Etzkowitz, H., Webster, A., Gebhardt, C. and Cantisano Terra, B.R. (2000), 'The future of the university and the university of the future: evolution of ivory tower to entrepreneurial paradigm', *Research Policy*, **29**, 313–30.

Fransman, M. (2001), 'Designing Dolly: interactions between economics, technology and science in the evolution of hybrid institutions', *Research Policy*, **30**, 263–73.

Gallini, N. and Scotchmer, S. (2001), 'Intellectual property: when is it the best incentive system?', Working Paper no. E01-303, Department of Economics, University of California, Berkeley, USA.

Geuna, A. and Nesta, L. (2003), 'University patenting and its effects on academic research', SPRU Electronic Working Paper Series no. 99.

Gibbons, M. (1999), 'Science's new social contract with society', *Nature*, **402**, 81–4.

Gittelman, M. and Kogut, B. (2003), 'Does good science lead to valuable knowledge? Biotechnology firms and the evolutionary logic of citation patterns', *Management Science*, **49** (4), 366–82.

Henderson, R., Jaffe, A.B. and Trajtenberg, M. (1998), 'Universities as a source of commercial technology: a detailed analysis of university patenting 1965–1988', *The Review of Economics and Statistics*, **80**, 119–27.

Hicks, D. and Hamilton, K. (1999), 'Does university–industry collaboration adversely affect university research?', *Issues in Science and Technology Online*, 74–75, Summer 1999, www.issues.org/15.4/realnumbers.htm.

Jaffe, A.B. (2000), 'The U.S. patent system in transition: policy innovation and the innovation process', *Research Policy*, **29**, 531–57.

Jensen, R., Thursby, J.G. and Thursby, M.C. (2003a), The disclosure and licensing of university inventions, NBER Working Paper no. 9734.

Jensen, R., Thursby, J.G. and Thursby, M.C. (2003b), 'The best we can do with the s**t we get to work with', *International Journal of Industrial Organization*, **21**, 1271–300.

Lach, S. and Shankerman, M. (2003), 'Incentives and invention in universities', CEPR Discussion Paper no. 3916, London, Centre for Economic Policy Research.

Levin, S.G. and Stephan, P.E. (1991), 'Research productivity over the life cycle: Evidence for academic scientists', *American Economic Review*, **81** (1), 114–32.

Mansfield, Edwin (1995), 'Academic research underlying industrial innovations: sources, characteristics, and financing', *Review of Economics and Statistics*, **77** (1), 55–65.

Markiewicz, K.R. and Di Minin, A. (2004), 'Commercializing the laboratory: the relationship between faculty patenting and publishing', Working Paper, Haas School of Business.

Martin, B.R. (2001), 'The changing social contract for science and the evolution of the university', in Geuna, A., Salter, A.J., Steinmueller, W.E. and Hoffman Y.E. (eds), *Science and Innovation: Rethinking the Rationales for Funding and Governance*, Cheltenham, UK and Northampton, MA, USA: Edward Elgar.

Martin, B.R. and Irvine, J. (1983), 'Assessing basic research. Some partial indicators of scientific progress in radio astronomy', *Research Policy*, **12**, 61–90.

Martin, S. and Scott, J.T. (2000), 'The nature of innovation market failure and the design of public support for private innovation', *Research Policy*, **29**, 437–47.

Merton, R.K. (1957), 'Priorities in scientific discovery: a chapter in the sociology of science', *American Sociological Review*, **22** (6), 635–59.

Moed, H.F., Burger, W.J.M., Frankfort, J.G. and Van Raan, A.F.J. (1985), 'The use of bibliometric data for the measurement of university research performance', *Research Policy*, **14**, 131–49.

Mowery, D.C., Nelson, R.R., Sampat, B.N. and Ziedonis, A.A. (2002), 'The growth of patenting and licensing by U.S. universities: an assessment of the effects of the Bayh–Dole act of 1980', *Research Policy*, **30**, 99–119.

Mowery, D.C. and Ziedonis, A.A. (2002), 'Academic patent quality and quantity before and after the Bayh–Dole act in the United States', *Research Policy*, **31**, 399–418.

Narin, F. and Hamilton, K.S. (1996), 'Bibliometric performance measures', *Scientometrics*, **36** (3), 293–310.

Nelson, R. (1959), 'The simple economics of basic scientific research', *Journal of Political Economy*, **67** (3), 297–306.

Owen-Smith, J. and Powell, W.W. (2001), 'To patent or not: faculty decisions and institutional success at technology transfer', *Journal of Technology Transfer*, **26**, 99–114.

Polanyi, M. (1962), 'The republic of science. Its political and economic theory', *Minerva*, **I** (1), 54–73.

Peritz, B.C. (1992), 'On the objectives of citation analysis: problems of theory and method', *Journal of the American Society for Information Science*, **43** (6), 448–51.

Seglen, P.O. (1992), 'How representative is the journal impact factor?', *Research Evaluation*, **2**, 143–9.

Stephan, P.E., Gurmu, S., Sumell, A.J. and Black, G. (2004), 'Who's patenting in the university? Evidence from a Survey of Doctorate Recipients', draft.

Thursby, J.G. and Kemp, S. (2002), 'Growth and productive efficiency of university intellectual property licensing', *Research Policy*, **31**, 109–24.

Thursby, J.G. and Thursby, M.C. (2002), 'Who is selling the ivory tower? Sources of growth in university licensing', *Management Science*, **48** (1), 90–104.

Van Looy, B., Ramga, M., Callaert, J., Debackere, K. and Zimmermann, E. (2004), 'Combining entrepreneurial and scientific performance in academia: towards a compounded and reciprocal Matthew-effect?', *Research Policy*, **33** (3), 425–41.

PART II

International Business Linkages
between Foreign-owned Multinationals
and Local Actors

5. MNCs, local clustering and science–technology relationships

John Cantwell

BACKGROUND

Since the 1960s, when location was central to discussions such as those on the product cycle model (Vernon, 1966) and the role of US direct investment in Europe (Dunning, 1970), interest in it as a critical factor in international business has experienced first a decline and recently a revival. The lessening of interest in the 1970s was largely due to the shift in emphasis in the international business literature from macro-level questions about countries and their trade and balance-of-payments positions towards micro-level questions to do with the organization of cross-border operations within firms. So the focus of investigation shifted from location to the firm.

However, the international company itself has gradually come to be perceived in a wider context. The revival of concern with location has been in part based on major changes in the economic environment, such as the increasing importance of intellectual capital as the key wealth-creating asset, increasing globalization in the form of a closer integration of activity between countries, but at the same time an increasing concentration of some specialized knowledge-based functions within selected sub-national regions, and the rise of alliance capitalism (Dunning, 1998). Alliance capitalism involves both strategic alliances and acquisition exchange deals between leading firms, but it also incorporates extended local networks in many vicinities that entail new and often closer relationships not merely between firms themselves but between firms and other local actors (such as universities), in what have sometimes been referred to as regional and national systems of innovation.

The notion of the internationally networked multinational corporation (MNC) and its corollary, the geographical dispersal of sources of creativity within the MNC, has revived the interest in the location of competence-creating subsidiaries and the use of location as a source of competitive advantage for the firm. From the perspective of developing locations that wish to catch up economically and technologically, the dispersion of knowledge-creating functions within the MNC and to partner companies that form part of its international network (of suppliers, sub-contractors etc.), together with the fragmentation of production systems associated with a growth in outsourcing (Feenstra, 1998), have presented new opportunities. While knowledge spillovers between MNCs and indigenous firms in regions in Europe and North America most often involve foreign-owned subsidiaries operating locally, in countries such as Korea and Taiwan the dispersion of the knowledge-creating nodes of an international MNC system to suitably capable new centres has often relied on cross-border sub-contracting and independent outsourcing linkages within global production networks (Hobday, 1995; Ernst, 2001).

Elsewhere trade economists have rediscovered economic geography, economies of agglomeration and path-dependency, while industrial economists have become interested once more in clusters. Historically the location of economic activity was mainly a concern of economic geographers and locational economists. Due to the changes in the economic environment, however, there was a relaxation in some of the restrictive assumptions that had formed the independent foundation of the theory of international trade (notably that of perfect factor mobility across space within countries, but high factor immobility between countries) and had precluded the cross-fertilization between locational studies and the work of the international trade economists. The more recent work in the industrial geography area considers external economies, the importance of technology and innovative activity, and the way they may be transferred across space. Trade economists have likewise begun to recognize the role of technology spillovers as a location-specific externality, rather than treating technology as readily transferable and internationally available, unlike factors of production. Thus a dialogue between these once historically separate streams of research has emerged in the recent past. As a result a better picture of the allocation of economic activity exists and forms the basis for a clearer understanding of how locational factors influence MNC activity (Dunning, 1998).

This chapter is intended to provide an overview of the relationship between MNCs and local economic systems, from both a theoretical and empirical point of view. The chapter first discusses the origins of clusters as seen through theory and statistics, before turning to some empirical evidence on cluster origins and dynamics. The second section introduces the principal types of spillovers and associated cluster types that have been observed, and subsequently Section 3 explores the science–technology linkages found in clusters. The chapter concludes with a section on the interaction between locational hierarchies and the investments of MNCs, and the effects of such hierarchies on the strategy of MNCs.

1. ORIGINS OF CLUSTERS – THEORY, STATISTICS AND EMPIRICAL EVIDENCE

Economic activities of a common kind show a strong tendency to agglomerate in certain locations, giving rise to patterns of national and regional specialization (Caniëls, 2000). The performance and the growth of firms depend to a large extent on the conditions of the environment in which they operate, and particularly on those in the immediate proximity (Malmberg et al., 1996). The phenomenon of concentration of economic activities in space, and its persistence over time, was first observed by Marshall (1891), who listed three fundamental advantages (or externalities) which cause firms to agglomerate:

- a pooled market for skilled workers with industry-specific competencies;
- the availability of non-tradable and intermediate inputs provided by local suppliers;
- the easy transmission of new ideas, which increases productivity through technical, organizational and production improvements.

A common location offers cultural similarities which improve the ease and the speed of knowledge diffusion, providing the right environment for the development of a common language, shared codes of communication and interaction, collective values and institutions. Therefore, more recent approaches to the analysis of the benefits of agglomeration have shifted attention away from traditional purely economic factors – such as distance and non-linearity of transport costs identified by orthodox location theory (Hotelling, 1929; Lösch, 1954; Weber, 1929) – to the characteristics of the social and institutional localized systems, supposing that they can provide a better understanding of the geographical concentration of economic and innovative activity, as well as of the dynamics of technological specialization patterns.

The literature on the advantages of the geographical agglomeration of technological and productive activities has developed along a twofold perspective. The first, and antecedent approach, has followed the Marshallian tradition in trying to identify such advantages and their implications for overall economic growth. Within this approach the spatial dimension represents a factor characterizing economic development, in relation to which the local innovation potential is assumed to be only one variable among others. The second and more recent line of research has instead addressed the localized structural factors, which shape the innovation capacity of specific geographical contexts. This has given rise to heterogeneous subnational typologies of innovative activity – all coming back to a broadly defined form of spatial organization, that is, the innovative cluster.

Inter-organizational network relationships – between firms and science infrastructure, between producers and users at inter-firm level, between firms and the institutional environment – are strongly influenced by spatial proximity mechanisms that favour processes of polarization and cumulativeness (De Bresson, 1987; Lundvall, 1992; Von Hippel, 1989). Furthermore, the use of informal channels for knowledge diffusion (so-called tacit or uncodified knowledge) provides another argument for the tendency of knowledge-based activities to be geographically confined. Ellison and Glaeser (1997) offer some evidence on the geographic concentration of US manufacturing industry, which applies in a wide variety of industries. They suggest that the explanation for geographic concentration varies by industry and that natural advantage may often play a role as industries co-agglomerate both with upstream suppliers and with downstream customers. Developing the industry specificity of clustering further, Steinle and Schiele (2002) set out the conditions under which an industry is more likely to cluster. They distinguish between necessary conditions, which are divisibility of the process and transportability of the product, and sufficient conditions, which consist of a long value chain, multiple competencies, network innovation and volatility of the market.

A useful distinction is usually made between two different types of agglomeration forces which shape spatial organization, pushing related firms and industries to cluster spatially in one of two ways that may lead to patterns of uneven regional development, that is, the emergence of centres and peripheries at the global and national level. There has been a debate as to which type of clustering predominates in a given setting and how the reasons for clustering have changed over time (Porter, 2000). On the one hand, there are general external economies and spillover effects – so-called 'urbanization economies' – which attract all kinds of economic activities into certain areas. This provokes the emergence of regional cores with broad sectoral specializations varying across different locations. These might be termed all-round centres of excellence, or higher-order centres. For an economic model of the differentiation into an industrial core and agricultural periphery under consideration of simple pecuniary externalities see Krugman (1991).

On the other hand, 'localization economies' are fostered in spatial clusters of firms undertaking similar or related activities. These kinds of forces are likely to be industry-specific and to produce cumulative mechanisms, which enable host locations to increase their production, technological and organizational competence over time (Dicken and Lloyd, 1990; Richardson, 1969). These might be termed specialized centres, or intermediate centres (by comparison with lower-order sites that lack locational attractiveness to most MNCs). As shown by Baptista and Swann (1998), agglomeration spillovers may operate for intra-industry clustering, whilst instead congestion effects may tend to dominate, offsetting positive spillovers, in the inter-industry case. For this reason general centres of excellence tend to be more geographically dispersed (spread out over larger areas) than are specialized centres.

Local interaction follows patterns of both collaboration and competition, which can produce stable mechanisms of collective knowledge accumulation. On the one hand, as suggested by Porter's (1990) 'diamond approach', competitive pressures and the associated push to innovation provide the dynamics of the advantage that firms derive in this virtuous circle. The competitive advantage of a regional system is thus created and sustained through highly localized processes of rivalry, which in turn are reinforced by their own capacity to attract resources from outside. On the other hand, spatial concentration boosts the intensity of interchanges and demonstration effects within the regional system, thus increasing the extent of collaboration and fostering a common attitude towards innovation (a localized system helps reduce the elements of dynamic uncertainty).

A variety of empirical and descriptive studies have examined evidence on the cluster phenomenon *per se*, focusing on different issues, such as initial cluster formation and growth (De Vet and Scott, 1992; Dorfman, 1983; Feldman, 2001; Kenney and Von Burg, 1999). In their work on initial cluster formation Feldman and Schreuder (1996) for example focus on the pharmaceutical industry in the Mid-Atlantic region and on the very early historical origins of this cluster. They identified the basic factors that shaped the development of the industry and anchored the industry in the region as a series of historical circumstances, the influence of government actions and legislation, and the development of unique capabilities.

A slightly different, and more general, perspective on cluster formation is adopted by Audretsch and Feldman (1996a). Their study of US innovation data examines the clustering of innovative activity and focuses on the propensity to cluster controlling for the effects of agglomeration of production. The results indicate that the agglomeration of production remains constant over the life cycle and is more concentrated where new technology is important. Innovative activity, however, tends to cluster more when tacit knowledge plays an important role, which is greatest in the early stages of the life cycle. In addition, the concentration of production has a bigger influence on the agglomeration of innovation in the mature and declining life cycle stages.

Other studies have placed emphasis on dynamic aspects such as the entry of firms into the cluster and firm growth or performance in clusters (Appold,

1995; Baptista and Swann, 1999; Maggioni, 2002; Pandit et al., 2001; Prevezer, 1997; Stuart and Sorenson, 2002). In this area Swann and Prevezer (1996) began a series of research investigations into cluster dynamics, specifically the impact of cluster strength and the strength of the science base on entry into the cluster and firm growth. They show that the factors attracting entry into a cluster are different for the biotech and computing industry, and that there is also a difference between entrants and incumbents in absorbing different kinds of spillovers.

Taking a narrower focus on cluster dynamics, Malmberg et al. (1996) examine the impact of geographical location on the innovation process, firm competitiveness and the impact of MNC presence in the clusters on the knowledge accumulation process. In drawing on a variety of empirical studies as well as the relevant theoretical work on the process of local knowledge accumulation and the different agglomeration forces that lead to spatial clustering, they provide a very comprehensive overview of the topic.

2. TYPES OF SPILLOVERS AND CLUSTERS

The literature usually distinguishes between three different categories of location-specific knowledge spillovers:

- intra-industry spillovers and specialization externalities (classical clustering), which can be offset by gravitational pull and congestion effects;
- inter-industry spillovers and diversity externalities (urbanization economies in all-round centres);
- external sources of knowledge, and science–technology spillovers.

Intra-industry spillovers are associated with the presence of a wide range of technologically active firms within a given sector, all in the same geographical area. The geographical concentration of firms engaged in similar activities leads to further local clustering of related firms and the local accumulation of relevant knowledge (Braunerhjelm et al., 2000). The link between knowledge spillovers and clustering has been clearly established empirically. Not only do industries in which new knowledge plays an important part in production tend to cluster more (Audretsch and Feldman, 1996b), but firms in clusters with strong ties between similar firms tend also to innovate more than firms outside these regions (Baptista and Swann, 1998). Intra-industry spillovers relate to specialization externalities, as in Marshall's early contribution. They materialize as an appropriate agglomeration pattern that facilitates asset sharing. The firms of each country tend to embark on a path of technological accumulation that has certain unique characteristics and sustains a distinct profile of national technological specialization (Rosenberg, 1976; Cantwell, 2000b). The kinds of linkages that grow up between competitors, suppliers and customers in any region or country are also, to some extent, peculiar to that location, and imbue the technology creation of its firms with distinctive features (Mariotti and Piscitello, 2001). For these reasons, other MNCs often need to be on site with their own production and their innovatory capacity if they are to properly benefit from the latest advances in geographically local-ized technological development, to feed their innovation (Cantwell, 1989; Kogut and Chang, 1991). In addition to the more intangible effects of knowledge spillovers, Bernstein and Nadiri (1989) also find evidence for more quantifiable effects. In their empirical study of four industries they find that costs decline for the knowledge-receiving firm while the rate of R&D investment and capital accumulation increases. Overall the social rates of return to R&D exceed the private returns.

However, such beneficial local clustering effects require a sufficient initial cross-firm diversity of activity in a location to start the process. If a local innovative system is dominated by a single major player or strong leader company, then this leader may exercise a forceful gravitational pull of the best resources, implying a particular kind of congestion effect for any other entrant. There may also be a more active competitive deterrence and government policies that favour a local champion in such cases.

Diversity externalities, or urbanization economies, can be related to general purpose technologies (GPTs), entailing inter-industry spillovers (Lipsey et al., 1998) associated with the existence of firms working in several different fields of productive and technological endeavour. Indeed, the more diverse the learning activities conducted in the region, the wider the range of potential cross-overs from which the firm could potentially benefit. Such spillovers relate to diversity externalities, which favour the creation of new ideas across sectors, as originally suggested by Jacobs (1961). They are more likely to occur in an all-round 'higher-order' centre of excellence, which attracts the research-based investments of a wide variety of foreign-owned MNCs and facilitates a more favourable interac-tion with indigenous firms. In the absence of strong competitive forces among the firms in the cluster, the milieu is particularly conducive to interaction between MNCs and local firms and thus offers greater oppor-tunities for inter-company alliances for the purposes of technological col-laboration and exchange (Cantwell et al., 2001; Cantwell and Mudambi, 2000). An analysis of data from 170 US cities focusing on industry growth through knowledge spillovers in cities by Glaeser et al. (1992) confirms Jacobs's ideas empirically. It shows that growth is mostly supported by diversity of industry and competition (which partly also supports Porter's view) and thus suggests that diversity may promote innovation and knowledge spillovers to a greater extent. Further empirical evidence of urbanization economies is offered by Ciccone and Hall (1996), who develop a model to analyse the impact of employment density on labour productivity and subsequently estimate the parameters using gross state product and employment data across US states for 1988. Their results indicate that a doubling of employment density increases average labour productivity by around 6 per cent.

In addition to these types of spillovers, there are usually localized connections to outside sources of knowledge. This is especially likely to be true of foreign-owned firms in an economy, which tend to have a greater degree of locational mobility when siting their corporate research, and so pay greater attention to being close to relevant public research facilities. These specific types of spillover will be further discussed in the next section.

3.   SCIENCE–TECHNOLOGY LINKAGES

Firms' efforts to advance technology do not generally proceed in isolation but are strongly supported by various external sources of knowledge: public research centres, universities, industry associations, an adequate educational system and science base (Breschi, 2000; Kline and Rosenberg, 1986; Nelson, 1993; Nelson and Rosenberg, 1999; Rosenberg and Nelson, 1996). There is growing evidence, so far mainly from the USA, that these science–technology or university–industry linkages tend to be geographically localized (Acs et al., 2000; Audretsch and Feldman, 1996b; Audretsch and Stephan, 1996; Jaffe, 1989; Jaffe, et al., 1993).

The more that an industry is research-driven (like pharmaceuticals) and the more that technological knowledge can be assimilated to scientific knowledge, the closer the links between firms and universities. The role of science in technological development has been appreciated since at least the time of the industrial revolution. In chapter 1 of *The Wealth of Nations*, Adam Smith identifies science as one source of new technology, together with producers of machinery, and 'learning by doing' in production linked to the inventiveness associated with greater specialization. In *Democracy in America*, De Tocqueville predicted the growing importance of basic research in industrializing society, in providing training for (future) industrial problem-solvers, and advances in basic understanding necessary to solve practical problems. Karl Marx emphasized the linkages running in the opposite direction, arguing that technological development in the capitalist system stimulates basic science by generating the resources, problems, data and instruments for scientific activities. Practical problem-solving has occasionally led to new branches of science. Marx also stressed the way in which mechanization (the major line of technological development of the nineteenth century) facilitated the application of scientific knowledge to production. These historical differences have persisted to the present day, and are reflected in the varying intensity of R&D activities in different industries. R&D intensity is high in chemicals, electrical products and in aerospace; it is medium in mechanical engineering and in motor vehicles; and low in most other industries.

Recent work summarised by Pavitt (1991) suggests that the main technological and economic benefits of basic research are not in the (easy) transfer of codified information, but in the (complex) support of a technological problem-solving capacity. In various fields there is now a greater awareness of the mathematical result that non-linear models involving interactions between three or more variables generate complex and non-predictable systems, understanding the properties of which requires trial and error and simulation, rather than deduction from the application of scientific knowledge by using local axioms.

Instead, basic research provides training for researchers who go on to work in industry and elsewhere. Background tacit knowledge and know-how is acquired through actively engaging in basic research, and improves the effectiveness of technological search activities. Furthermore, basic research provides instrumentation that is developed into industrial applications and it also enables membership of national and international networks of professional scientists and engineers. These networks are useful, not so much for the transmission of received information and results, as for interactions that improve the learning activities of each participant.

The common assumption in economics (and in many policy circles) is that the economic benefits of basic research are widely and freely available, because they take the form of easily reproducible and transmissible information. If so, globalization would undermine the case for the national public subsidization of basic research (for a critique of which view see Cantwell, 1999). Instead, recent research suggests that the economic benefits of basic research take the form of a contribution to (and an interaction with) the tacit problem-solving capability of firms (Zucker et al., 1998). Hence these benefits are for the most part geographically and linguistically localized, since they are embodied in institutions and individuals and are transmitted principally through personal (face-to-face) contacts. Most interactions (and the more effective interactions) between the realms of science and technology – for example through the training of individuals, or in the corporate development of scientific instruments – take place locally.

Recent work has focused on the actual type of the science–technology link, that is, whether the knowledge is transferred through market mechanisms or through spillover mechanisms, or externalities. Initial empirical results have not been conclusive as to whether market mechanisms show the same geographical mediation as spillovers. Audretsch and Stephan (1996), for example, find that the influence of proximity between researchers and firms is largest when establishing ties and when the exchanges are informal; it also depends on the role played by the scientist within the particular firm receiving the knowledge. When the exchange of knowledge is formalized, however, the location factor did not seem to matter. The opposite results were obtained by Zucker et al. (1998), who found that the local exchange between universities and firms is mostly a market exchange, and the benefits for performance through knowledge transfer are not due to generalized spillovers. The most recent work by Mowery and Ziedonis (2001) bridges these two perspectives and compares the importance of location for market exchanges with that for generalized spillovers and thus offers an even more detailed picture of the actual science–technology interaction. They distinguish between different types of knowledge, that is, whether their transfer requires complementary know-how or rather constitutes research tools, and show that the formalized exchanges of the former are more localized than the latter because of the required close interaction between the inventor and the receiving firms. The results of their study also suggest that the formalized exchanges are somewhat more geographically localized than spillovers. The three studies indicate that the science–technology link is not uniform and equally geographically mediated but rather depends on a variety of factors, such as the role of the scientist in the interaction, the type of knowledge transferred and to some extent also the industry under consideration.

4.   LOCATIONAL HIERARCHIES AND MNCS

The changes in economic activity, that is, the greater importance of knowledge as a key asset, the role of alliance capitalism and increased globalization, have forced MNCs to consider the implications of locating in a specific area as an integral part of their overall strategies: where to locate key activities such as R&D, how to distribute the charters across subsidiary networks based on the constraints and opportunities of the local markets (Birkinshaw and Hood, 1998), and how to manage the independence and simultaneous integration of the parts of the network.

The notion that the geographical dispersion of technological development enhances innovation in the network of the MNC as a whole is founded on the belief that innovation is location-specific as well as firm-specific (Cantwell, 1989). The scientific and technological traditions of each country, the shared experience of its researchers and production engineers, and the communication between them across companies, the nature of its educational system, and its common business practices all contribute to the distinctiveness of the path of technology development undertaken in each location (Cantwell, 2000b; Pavitt, 1987; Rosenberg, 1976). By drawing on innovations of various kinds depending upon the conditions prevailing in the relevant local research centre, MNCs develop a more complex technological system and by accessing differentiated streams of knowledge have an important source of competitive advantage (Almeida, 1996; Dunning, 1996; Dunning and Wymbs, 1999; Fors and Zejan, 1996; Kümmerle, 1999a; Pearce, 1999). The attractiveness of locations for other research-related investments may well be strengthened in the process. The involvement of foreign-owned MNCs in research in centres of innovation has a direct effect on broadening the scope of local technological capability, and an indirect effect through its competitive stimulus, encouraging other firms to extend their local research programmes. The process helps to establish locational poles of attraction for research-related activity. According to Storper (1992), the characteristics of the increasing technological dynamism, which requires both the minimization of cost in production and avoidance of lock-in at the same time, further support the creation of the so-called technology districts, because this geographical form is the most effective way of managing the trade-off between cost minimization and technological flexibility.

The increased role of locationally dispersed sourcing of technology from the major centres of excellence through the international networks of more globally integrated MNCs (Cantwell, 1995) has led to a growing interest in the asset-acquiring motive for foreign direct investment (FDI) (Cantwell, 1989; Cantwell and Janne, 1999; Cantwell and Piscitello, 2000), and in the greater decentralization in the management of international R&D to capture 'home-base-augmenting' benefits (Kümmerle, 1999a, 1999b).

Internationalization has supported corporate technological diversification since the form of technological development varies between locations as well as between firms (Cantwell and Janne, 1999; Cantwell and Piscitello, 2000; Zander, 1997). By locating production in an alternative centre of innovation in its industry the MNC gains access to a new but complementary avenue of technological development, which it integrates with its existing lines. By increasing the overlap between the technological profiles of firms, competition between MNCs is raised in each international industry, but so also are cooperative agreements as the numbers of knowledge spillovers between firms increases as well. Apart from the rise in technological interrelatedness, the potential opportunities for cross-border learning within MNCs have been enhanced by an increased take-up of information and communication technologies (ICT). ICT specialization seems to amplify the firm's technological flexibility by enabling it to fuse together a wider range of formerly separate technologies.

However, the creation of technology may be locationally concentrated or dispersed according to the degree of complexity embedded in it. Some kinds of technologies are geographically easily dispersed, whilst the uncodified character of others makes cross-border learning within and across organizations much more difficult. Thus, although multinationals have shown a greater internationalization of their R&D facilities recently, it depends upon the type of technological activity involved. The development of science-based fields of activity (e.g. ICT, biotechnology and new materials) and an industry's core technologies appears to require a greater intensity of face-to-face interaction (Cantwell and Santangelo, 2000). None the less, it may sometimes still be the case that science-based and firm- and industry-specific core technologies are dispersed internationally. The main factors driving the occasional geographical dispersion of the creation of these kinds of otherwise highly localized technologies are either locally embedded specialization which cannot be accessed elsewhere, or company-specific global strategies that utilize the development of an organizationally complex international network for technological learning (Cantwell and Santangelo, 1999).

The more typical pattern of international specialization in innovative activity within the MNC is for the development of technologies that are core to the firm's industry to be concentrated at home, while other fields of technological activity may be located abroad, and in this sense the internationalization of research tends to be complementary to the home base (Cantwell and Kosmopoulou, 2002). Thus, when science-based technology creation is internationally dispersed it is most often attributable to foreign technology acquisition by the firms of 'other' industries – for example, chemical industry MNCs developing electrical technologies abroad, or electrical equipment MNCs developing specialized chemical processes outside their home countries (Cantwell and Santangelo, 1999, 2000). From the point of view of host countries as opposed to investing MNCs, a local centre of excellence for some specialized field of innovation (say in chemicals) will tend to attract investments in local chemical research not so much by foreign-owned MNCs in the chemical industry, but to a greater extent by MNCs from other industries, whose objective is to tap into the resources of the centre in order to diversify their own technological base (Cantwell and Kosmopoulou, 2002).

Evidence has now emerged that the choice of foreign location for technological development in support of what is done in the home base of the

MNC depends upon whether host regions within countries are either major centres for innovation or not. The sectoral composition of technological strengths differs across regional centres, while the technological specialization of foreign-owned affiliates depends upon the rank of the regional location in the geographical hierarchy and upon its gradual change over time (Cantwell and Janne, 1999).

It is possible to distinguish between higher-order and intermediate regional centres of technological excellence (Cantwell et al., 2001). Such centres arise as a consequence of the interaction and the intensity of general external economies and localization economies, which in turn depend upon the characteristics of the regional innovation system considered. Clearly, the other extreme is that of lower-order regions, that is, technologically weak and backward regions that have an inadequate innovative base in order to compete with other locations and to be attractive for external flows of knowledge and technology. This differentiation has enabled us to distinguish between the form of potential knowledge spillovers and technological networks in operation between foreign-owned firms and their indigenous counterparts in different locations. These interactions are more likely to further upgrade higher-order regional locations, in which the local-for-local strategy of subsidiaries aims at exploring local knowledge and expertise, which will be integrated to widen technological competence at the corporate level through the intra-firm network (local-for-global) (Cantwell and Iammarino, 1998). Indeed, when foreign research has a more pronounced exploratory nature, it is likely to be attracted by higher-order cores, treating them as a source of general expertise and skills (Cantwell et al., 2001).

Intermediate locations, with a narrower scope of technological advantages, are seen as sources of specific capabilities in some particular field and thus they might be negatively affected due to the local-for-local strategy of foreign affiliates, which follows a logic of exploitation of indigenous expertise. In other words, if the position of the region in the hierarchy falls as it becomes more narrowly focused, so the profile of technological specialization of foreign-owned firms in that region becomes more closely related to the equivalent pattern of specialization of indigenous firms in the same region.

Even in the case of higher-order regions, the broadening of specialization is just one of the possible forms of incremental change in the composition of local innovation, since regional profiles may, in other cases, be reinforced and concentrated in their established areas of technological expertise. Only some higher-order cores are able to adjust their profiles of specialization to the highest technological opportunities over time, whilst others – which experience a slower process of convergence between old and new technologies – may end up by losing gradually their competitiveness (Cantwell and Iammarino, 2001).

Core systems appear to be rooted in GPTs – for example background engineering, mechanical methods, electronics and information and communication technologies (ICTs) – in which foreign-owned and indigenous firms' technological advantages appear to overlap in these higher-order centres. MNC subsidiaries account for an increasing share of all new technologies that are introduced in the multinational networks and are associated with a significantly higher probability of entry into new and more distantly related fields of technology (especially GPTs), creating a long-term drift into new technological competence.

There is evidence that, for example, in chemicals the affiliates of German MNCs are technologically specialized in other European centres in accordance with the local strengths of the centre in question, and the same is true of British chemical MNCs apart from in Germany. However, British MNCs in chemicals when operating in Germany follow a pattern of technological specialization that accords with their own comparative advantages in the industry and those of their home centre, the UK. They do not appear to be especially prone to try to tap into the areas in which German expertise is relatively greatest, but rather treat Germany as a general reservoir of skills that can be used principally to extend those lines of operation on which they are already focused (and can themselves contribute most to the German system) (Cantwell and Sanna-Randaccio, 1992).

In other words, firms based in higher-order centres are more likely to establish a locationally specialized network of technological activity in support of corporate innovation than are firms that originate from lower-order centres (Cantwell and Janne, 1999). Thus, at least until recently, patterns of technological specialization within an industry seem to have been strengthened mainly by the networks of MNCs from the leading centres. This may also be partly attributable to gravitational pull and competitive deterrence effects when (local areas within) the leading centres are dominated by specific MNCs, thereby excluding these locations from the networks of other MNCs at least for diversification purposes.

Whereas most regions are not major centres and tend to be highly specialized in their profile of technological development, and hence attract foreign-owned activity in the same narrow range of fields; in the major centres much of the locally sited innovation of foreign-owned MNCs does not match very well the specific fields of local specialization, but is rather geared towards the development of technologies that are core to the current techno-economic paradigm (notably ICT) or earlier paradigms (notably mechanical technologies) (Cantwell et al., 2001). The need to develop these latter technologies is shared by the firms of all industries, and the knowledge spillovers between MNCs and local firms in this case may be inter-industry in character.

While there is now ample evidence that MNCs do tap into local knowledge networks (Kümmerle, 1999a; Zander, 1999), recent research explores in more detail under which conditions MNCs source knowledge from the centres they are located in. In his study of US patent data, Frost (2001) finds that a subsidiary is most likely to source knowledge locally if it follows an exploration strategy, first, if the sourcing is related to a technical field in which the home country is relatively disadvantaged and the host country is relatively advantaged; and second, if the technological capabilities of the subsidiary are strong; third, if the subsidiary is large, and last, if the firm has a wide overall presence in the host country and its membership in technical networks. Cantwell and Mudambi (2003) report similarly interesting findings. An analysis of US patents granted to UK subsidiaries of non-UK MNCs and survey data indicates that local industry concentration and resource scarcity negatively affects the likelihood of a subsidiary receiving a competence-creating mandate and thus for sourcing knowledge locally. The degree to which a competence-creating subsidiary sources knowledge locally also is positively affected by whether the subsidiary was acquired, whereas for competence-exploiting subsidiaries acquisition affects local knowledge sourcing negatively.

5. CONCLUSION

The economic landscape has undergone many significant changes in the last few decades, the most extensive of which is globalization. In its wake certain kinds of economic activity have become more and more easily dispersed across space and distance matters less in the transfer of goods and people. However, at the same time 'sticky places within such slippery space' (Markusen, 1996) are emerging especially with respect to knowledge-intensive activities. Thus the location decision is an increasingly important issue for the multinational firm and more and more closely interacts with and is inseparable from the analysis and strategic planning of internalization and ownership-specific advantages (Cantwell, 2000a; Dunning, 1998, 2000), through the efficient management of cross-border transactions and the creative development of in-house corporate competence. With the rising awareness by MNCs of locational advantages as a competitiveness-enhancing and -sustaining factor, the understanding of the very specific processes and phenomena involved in a variety of locational types has become fundamental, and they are no longer just something that is 'in the air', as Marshall had once noted over 100 years ago.

REFERENCES

Acs, Z.J., De La Mothe, J. and Paquet, G. (2000), 'Regional innovation: in search of an enabling strategy', in Z.J. Acs (ed.), *Regional Innovation, Knowledge and Global Change*, London: Pinter.

Almeida, P. (1996), 'Knowledge sourcing by foreign multinationals: patent citation analysis in the US semiconductor industry', *Strategic Management Journal*, **17**, 155–65.

Appold, S.J. (1995), 'Agglomeration, interorganizational networks, and competitive performance in the US metalworking sector', *Economic Geography*, **71** (1), 27–54.

Audretsch, D.B. and Feldman, M.P. (1996a), 'Innovative clusters and the industry life cycle', *Review of Industrial Organization*, **11**, 253–73.

Audretsch, D.B. and Feldman, M.P. (1996b), 'R&D spillovers and the geography of innovation and production', *American Economic Review*, **86** (3), 630–40.

Audretsch, D.B. and Stephan, P.E. (1996), 'Company–scientist locational links: the case of biotechnology', *American Economic Review*, **86** (3), 641–52.

Baptista, R. and Swann, G.M.P. (1998), 'Do firms in clusters innovate more?' *Research Policy*, **27**, 525–40.

Baptista, R. and Swann, G.M.P. (1999), 'A comparison of clustering dynamics in the US and UK computer industries', *Journal of Evolutionary Economics*, **9**, 373–99.

Bernstein, J.I. and Nadiri, M.I. (1989), 'Research and development and intra-industry spillovers: an empirical application of dynamic duality', *Review of Economic Studies*, **56** (2), 249–67.

Birkinshaw, J. and Hood, N. (1998), 'Multinational subsidiary development: capability evolution and charter change in foreign-owned subsidiary companies', *Academy of Management Review*, **23** (4), 773–95.

Braunerhjelm, P., Faini, R., Norman, V., Ruane, F. and Seabright, P. (eds) (2000), *Integration and the Regions of Europe: How the Right Policies can Prevent Polarization*, London: Centre for Economic Policy Research.

Breschi, S. (2000), 'The geography of innovation: a cross sector analysis', *Regional Studies*, **34**, 213–29.

Caniëls, M.C.J. (2000), *Knowledge Spillovers and Economic Growth: Regional Growth Differentials across Europe*, Cheltenham, UK and Northampton, MA, USA: Edward Elgar.

Cantwell, J.A. (1989), *Technological Innovation and Multinational Corporations*, Oxford: Basil Blackwell.

Cantwell, J.A. (1995), 'The globalisation of technology: what remains of the product cycle model?' *Cambridge Journal of Economics*, **19** (1), 155–74.

Cantwell, J.A. (1999), 'Innovation as the principal source of growth in the global economy', in D. Archibugi, J. Howells and J. Michie (eds), *Innovation Policy in a Global Economy*, Cambridge and New York: Cambridge University Press.

Cantwell, J.A. (2000a), 'A survey of theories of international production', in C.N. Pitelis and R. Sugden (eds), *The Nature of the Transnational Firm*, London and New York: Routledge.

Cantwell, J.A. (2000b), 'Technological lock-in of large firms since the interwar period', *European Review of Economic History*, **4** (2), 147–74.

Cantwell, J.A. and Iammarino, S. (1998), 'MNCs, technological innovation and regional systems in the EU: some evidence in the Italian case', *International Journal of the Economics of Business*, **5** (3), 383–408.

Cantwell, J.A. and Iammarino, S. (2001), 'EU regions and multinational corporations: change, stability and strengthening of technological comparative advantages', *Industrial and Corporate Change*, **10** (4), 1007–37.

Cantwell, J.A., Iammarino, S. and Noonan, C.A. (2001), 'Sticky places in slippery space – the location of innovation by MNCs in the European regions', in N. Pain (ed.), *Inward Investment, Technological Change and Growth: The Impact of MNCs on the UK Economy*, London and New York: Palgrave Macmillan.

Cantwell, J.A. and Janne, O.E.M. (1999), 'Technological globalisation and innovative centres: the role of corporate technological leadership and locational hierarchy', *Research Policy*, **28** (2–3), 119–44.

Cantwell, J.A. and Kosmopoulou, E. (2002), 'What determines the internationalization of corporate technology?', in M. Forsgren, H. Håkanson and V. Havila (eds), *Critical Perspectives on Internationalisation*, Oxford: Pergamon.

Cantwell, J.A. and Mudambi, R. (2000), 'The location of MNE R&D activity: the role of investment incentives', *Management International Review*, **39** (Special Issue 1), 123–47.

Cantwell, J.A. and Mudambi, R. (2003), 'On the nature of knowledge creation in MNE subsidiaries: an empirical analysis using patent data', paper presented at the DRUID Summer Conference, www.druid.dk/conferences/summer 2003.

Cantwell, J.A. and Piscitello, L. (2000), 'Accumulating technological competence – its changing impact on corporate diversification and internationalization', *Industrial and Corporate Change*, **9** (1), 21–51.

Cantwell, J.A. and Sanna-Randaccio, F. (1992), 'Intra-industry direct investment in the European Community: oligopolistic rivalry and technological competition', in J.A. Cantwell (ed.), *Multinational Investment in Modern Europe: Strategic Interaction in The Integrated Community*, Aldershot, UK and Brookfield, USA: Edward Elgar.

Cantwell, J.A. and Santangelo, G.D. (1999), 'The frontier of international technology networks: sourcing abroad the most highly tacit capabilities', *Information Economics and Policy*, **11** (1), 101–23.

Cantwell, J.A. and Santangelo, G.D. (2000), 'Capitalism, profits and innovation in the new techno-economic paradigm', *Journal of Evolutionary Economics*, **10** (1–2), 131–57.

Ciccone, A. and Hall, R.E. (1996), 'Productivity and the density of economic activity', *American Economic Review*, **86** (1), 54–70.

De Bresson, C. (1987), 'I poli tecnologici dello sviluppo', *L'Industria*, **3**, 301–408.

De Vet, J.M. and Scott, A.J. (1992), 'The Southern California medical device industry: Innovation, new firm formation and location', *Research Policy*, **21**, 145–61.

Dicken, P. and Lloyd, P.E. (eds) (1990), *Location in Space: Theoretical Perspectives in Economic Geography*, New York: HarperCollins.

Dorfman, N.S. (1983), 'Route 128: The development of a regional high technology economy', *Research Policy*, **12**, 299–316.

Dunning, J.H. (1970), *Studies in International Investment*, London: Allen and Unwin.

Dunning, J.H. (1996), 'The geographical sources of competitiveness of firms. Some results of a new survey', *Transnational Corporations*, **5** (3), 1–21.

Dunning, J.H. (1998), 'Location and the multinational enterprise: a neglected factor?', *Journal of International Business Studies*, **29** (1), 45–66.

Dunning, J.H. (2000), 'Regions, globalization, and the knowledge economy: the issues stated', in J.H. Dunning (ed.), *Regions, Globalization, and the Knowledge-Based Economy*, Oxford and New York: Oxford University Press.

Dunning, J.H. and Wymbs, C. (1999), 'The geographical sourcing of technology-based assets by multinational enterprises', in D. Archibugi, J. Howells and J. Michie (eds), *Innovation Policy in a Global Economy*, Cambridge and New York: Cambridge University Press.

Ellison, G. and Glaeser, E.L. (1997), 'Geographic concentration in US manufacturing industries: a dartboard approach', *Journal of Political Economy*, **105** (5), 889–927.

Ernst, D. (2001), 'Small firms competing in globalized high-tech industries: the co-evolution of domestic and international knowledge linkages in Taiwan's computer industry', in P. Guerrieri, S. Iammarino and C. Pietrobelli (eds), *The Global Challenge to Industrial Districts: SMEs in Italy and Taiwan*, Cheltenham, UK and Northampton, MA, USA: Edward Elgar.

Feenstra, R. (1998), 'Integration of trade and disintegration of production in the global economy', *Journal of Economic Perspectives*, **12**, 31–50.

Feldman, M.P. (2001), 'The entrepreneurial event revisited: firm formation in a regional context', *Industrial and Corporate Change*, **10** (4), 861–91.

Feldman, M.P. and Schreuder, Y. (1996), 'Initial advantage: the origins of the geographic concentration of the pharmaceutical industry in the mid-Atlantic region', *Industrial and Corporate Change*, **5** (3), 839–62.

Fors, G. and Zejan, M. (1996), 'Overseas R&D by multinationals in foreign centers of excellence', Industrial Institute for Economics and Social Research Working Paper, no. 458, www.iui.se/wp/wp458/wp458.htm.

Frost, T.S. (2001), 'The geographic sources of foreign subsidiaries' innovations', *Strategic Management Journal*, **22** (2), 101–23.

Glaeser, E.L., Kallal, H.D., Scheinkman, J.A. and Shleifer, A. (1992), 'Growth in cities', *Journal of Political Economy*, **100** (6), 1126–52.

Hobday, M. (1995), *Innovation in East Asia: The Challenge to Japan*, Aldershot, UK and Brookfield, USA: Edward Elgar.

Hotelling, H. (1929), 'Stability in competition', *Economic Journal*, **39** (153), 41–57.

Jacobs, J. (1961), *The Death and Life of Great American Cities*, New York: Random House.

Jaffe, A.B. (1989), 'Real effects of academic research', *American Economic Review*, **79** (5), 957–70.

Jaffe, A.B., Trajtenberg, M. and Henderson, R. (1993), 'Geographic localization of knowledge spillovers as evidenced by patent citations', *Quarterly Journal of Economics*, **108** (3), 577–98.

Kenney, M. and Von Burg, U. (1999), 'Technology, entrepreneurship and path dependence: industrial clustering in Silicon Valley and Route 128', *Industrial and Corporate Change*, **8** (1), 67–193.

Kline, S.J. and Rosenberg, N. (1986), 'An overview of innovation', in R. Landau and N. Rosenberg (eds), *The Positive Sum Strategy*, New York: National Academy Press.

Kogut, B. and Chang, S.J. (1991), 'Technological capabilities and Japanese foreign direct investment in the United States', *Review of Economics and Statistics*, **73**, 401–13.

Krugman, P.R. (1991), 'Increasing returns and economic geography', *Journal of Political Economy*, **99** (3), 483–99.

Kümmerle, W. (1999a), 'The drivers of foreign direct investment into research and development: an empirical investigation', *Journal of International Business Studies*, **30** (1), 1–24.

Kümmerle, W. (1999b), 'Foreign direct investment in industrial research in the pharmaceutical and electronic industries – results from a survey of multinational firms', *Research Policy*, **28** (2–3), 179–93.

Lipsey, R.G., Bekar, C. and Carlaw, K. (1998), 'What requires explanation?' in E. Helpman (ed.), *General Purpose Technologies and Economic Growth*, Cambridge, MA: MIT Press.

Lösch, A. (1954), *The Economics of Location*, New Haven, CT: Yale University Press.

Lundvall, B.Å. (1992), *National Systems of Innovation*, London: Pinter.

Maggioni, M.A. (2002), 'Empirical analyses of the location of high-tech firms and of cluster development', in *Clustering Dynamics and the Location of High Tech Firms*, Heidelberg and New York: Physica-Verlag.

Malmberg, A., Sölvell, Ö. and Zander, I. (1996), 'Spatial clustering, local accumulation of knowledge and firm competitiveness', *Geografiska Annaler Series B: Human Geography*, **78** (2), 85–97.

Mariotti, S. and Piscitello, L. (2001), 'The role of territorial externalities in affecting internationalisation of production by SMEs', *Entrepreneurship and Regional Development*, **13**, 65–80.

Markusen, A. (1996), 'Sticky places in slippery space: a typology of industrial districts', *Economic Geography*, **72** (3), 293–313.

Marshall, A. (1891), *Principles of Economics*, London: Macmillan.

Mowery, D.C. and Ziedonis, A.A. (2001), 'The geographic reach of market and non-market channels of technology transfer: comparing citations and licenses of university patents', NBER Working Paper, no. 8568.

Nelson, R.R. (ed.) (1993), *National Systems of Innovation*, London: Frances Pinter.

Nelson, R.R. and Rosenberg, N. (1999), 'Science, technological advance and economic growth', in A.D. Chandler, P. Hagström and Ö. Sölvell (eds), *The Dynamic Firm: The Role of Technology, Strategy, Organization, and Regions*, Oxford and New York: Oxford University Press.

Pandit, N.R., Cook, G.A.S. and Swann, G.M.P. (2001), 'The dynamics of industrial clustering in British financial services', *Service Industries Journal*, **21** (4), 33–61.

Pavitt, K.L.R. (1987), 'International patterns of technological accumulation', in N. Hood and J.E. Vahlne (eds), *Strategies in Global Competition*, London: Croom Helm.

Pavitt, K.L.R. (1991), 'What makes basic research economically useful?' *Research Policy*, **20** (2), 109–20.

Pearce, R.D. (1999), 'Decentralized R&D and strategic competitiveness: globalised approaches to generation and use of technology in MNEs', *Research Policy*, **28** (2–3), 157–78.

Porter, M.E. (1990), *The Competitive Advantage of Nations*, New York: Free Press.

Porter, M.E. (2000), 'Location, competition and economic development: local clusters in a global economy', *Economic Development Quarterly*, **14** (1), 15–34.

Prevezer, M. (1997), 'The dynamics of industrial clustering in biotechnology', *Small Business Economics*, **9** (3), 255–71.

Richardson, H.W. (ed.) (1969), *Elements of Regional Economics*, Harmondsworth: Penguin.

Rosenberg, N. (1976), *Perspectives on Technology*, Cambridge and New York: Cambridge University Press.

Rosenberg, N. and Nelson, R.R. (1996), 'The roles of universities in the advance of industrial technology', in R.S. Rosenbloom and W.J. Spencer (eds), *Engines of Innovation: US Industrial Research at the End of an Era*, Boston, MA: Harvard Business School Press.

Steinle, C. and Schiele, H. (2002), 'When do industries cluster? A proposal on how to assess an industry's propensity to concentrate at a single region or nation', *Research Policy*, **31**, 849–58.

Storper, M. (1992), 'The limits to globalization: technology districts and international trade', *Economic Geography*, **68**, 60–93.

Stuart, T. and Sorenson, O. (2002), 'The geography of opportunity: spatial heterogeneity in founding rates and the performance of biotechnology firms', *Research Policy*, **36**, 1–25.

Swann, G.M.P. and Prevezer, M. (1996), 'A comparison of the dynamics of industrial clustering in computing and biotechnology', *Research Policy*, **25**, 1139–57.

Vernon, R. (1966), 'International investment and international trade in the product cycle', *Quarterly Journal of Economics*, **80** (2), 190–207.

Von Hippel, E. (1989), *The Sources of Innovation*, Oxford: Oxford University Press.

Weber, A. (1929), *Theory of the Location of Industries*, Chicago: University of Chicago Press.

Zander, I. (1997), 'Technological diversification in the multinational corporation: historical evolution and future prospects', *Research Policy*, **26** (2), 209–28.

Zander, I. (1999), 'How do you mean "global"? An empirical investigation of innovation networks in the multinational corporation', *Research Policy*, **28** (2–3), 195–213.

Zucker, L.G., Darby, M.R. and Armstrong, J. (1998), 'Geographically localized knowledge: spillovers or markets?', *Economic Inquiry*, **36**, 65–86.

6. Creating, importing and losing competitive advantage: evidence from the Austrian manufacturing sector

Christian Bellak

1. INTRODUCTION

There is considerable interest from governments in policies to boost the competitiveness of firms within their jurisdiction. Designing the 'right' policies, which effectively stimulate the firms' competitive position in markets, requires not only information on the present competitiveness of a country's firms, but also some prediction about the behaviour of domestic and foreign firms in different industries in the future. The possibility exists that policy measures become ineffective if they counteract or do not affect the firms' strategies at all.

Governments have several options in maintaining the competitiveness of their countries and regions: domestic firms create competitive advantage; foreign firms investing in the country transfer ('import') competitive advantage from their parent; and the linkages which exist between these two groups of firms may lead to new advantages that could not be developed by either group of firms alone. A similar argument about the creation of competitive advantage applies to the loss of competitive advantage. It has been argued in various studies that the response of a multinational enterprise (MNE) to a deterioration of its market share or the discovery of new market opportunities (e.g. new markets, new product or process technologies) depends on the current sources of competitiveness, but empirical evidence is still scarce. The configuration of these sources first determines whether the firm will choose to produce in the same location or shift production to a new location; and/or second, whether domestic firms will supply the good/service or whether this is done by foreign firms (either via trade links or via local production).

The resulting international production patterns (IPPs) and international trade patterns (ITPs) are determined by two sources, namely location advantages on the one hand and firm-specific advantages (FSAs) on the other hand (Hirsch and Meshulach, 1991). While the first source, the comparative advantage (CA), and consequently the location of production have been widely researched, the interaction between foreign and domestic firms, which enters our measure of firm specific advantage below, has gained less attention.

This chapter discusses the possible strategies of firms depending on four different combinations of the sources of competitiveness. Also, we look at the changes in these sources in a sample of manufacturing firms over a policy-relevant time span (ten years) and the firms' responses to such changes.

The analysis also shows the difficulties arising in the analysis of international firms, despite many improvements with respect to data, reporting systems and so on. Although many problems remain, it is hoped that the approach will be used in other countries as well. This type of analysis has also been fruitfully applied in such fields as strategic alliances (e.g. Sleuwaegen et al., 1998), outward investment of Japanese firms (e.g. Kimura and Pugel, 2001), entry/exit of firms (e.g. Audretsch, 1994), economic geography (Dunning, 1996) and the technological competitiveness of firms (e.g. Patel and Vega, 1997; Herrera, 1992). The approach chosen here may also be viewed as an analysis of the underlying forces of the investment development path (Dunning and Narula, 1996).

The chapter is organized as follows: first, we discuss location advantage and firm-specific advantage as the main sources of competitiveness and resulting location strategies of firms. Six propositions follow from the theoretical discussion. The subsequent section introduces the data and the operationalization of both types of advantages. The results are presented. Using the 1990 advantage combinations as the basis for the future strategies (here: 1995 and 2000), the changes of employment, value added and exports turn out to be in line with our expectation. A short concluding section argues for a differentiated industrial policy approach, yet the revealed empirical dynamics of gains and losses of competitiveness increase the risk of policy failure.

2.   ASSUMPTIONS AND DEFINITIONS

Assume two countries, home (H) and foreign (F), and two parent firms, domestic (pd) and abroad (pa) as well as their affiliates abroad (aa, aa^*). Firms may invest or trade (see Figure 6.1). An important assumption is that firm-specific advantages (FSAs) are developed at the location of the parent company.

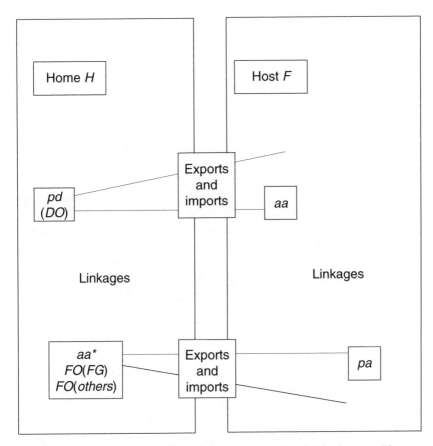

Note: *pd*: parent domestic; *aa*: affiliate abroad; *pa*: parent abroad; * foreign-owned from the viewpoint of the home country.

Figure 6.1   The setting

Throughout the chapter we distinguish three types of home-country (*H*) firms: (i) fragmentators (*FO(FG)*) are those manufacturing firms which are foreign-owned (i.e. which are affiliates) and where the share of exports in total sales is arbitrarily chosen above 90 per cent.[1] In this way, we try to account for the increasing fragmentation of production, suggesting that fragmentators react differently to changes in the advantage combination. (ii) The rest of the foreign-owned firms (including sales affiliates, holding companies, production for the local market etc.) are termed '*FO*(others)'. (iii) Domestically owned firms (*DO*) are those MNEs where the parent company is located in home country *H*.

An early appearance of the concept of the separation of the sources of competitiveness is Kogut's article (1985) where different types of firm integration are derived from the various combinations of comparative and firm-specific advantages and disadvantages. Hirsch and Meshulach (1991) further extend the concept to include MNEs explicitly. Before we discuss the interaction between both types of advantages, they are described separately.

Important Aspects of Firm-specific Advantages (FSAs)

A variety of terms is used in the literature synonymously to describe 'firm-specific advantages', namely 'monopolistic advantages', 'ownership advantages' (Erramilli et al., 1997, p. 736) or 'proprietary assets' (Caves, 1996). Economists like Caves stress (a) technological advantages, (b) entrepreneurial excess capacity and (c) multi-plant economies. Similarly, international business scholars like Dunning (1996) identify three main kinds of firm-specific advantage: (a) monopoly power, (b) scarce, unusual and sustainable resources and capabilities, and (c) managerial capabilities.

The common characteristic of firm-specific advantages is that they are mobile between national markets (Anand and Delios, 1997) and they differ in productivity from comparable assets possessed by competing firms (Caves, 1996, p. 3). FSAs are 'produced' or created by the foreign or the domestic firm, not obtained in the marketplace. Mobility of FSAs is an important distinctive characteristic of the firm-specific advantage compared to the location-specific advantage. What is relevant for a firm to become an MNE is therefore not just the possession of a superior FSA, but the fact that most FSAs are mobile. (This reflects the difference between a necessary and a sufficient condition.) Rugman and Verbeke (1992) distinguish location-bound (e.g. cooperation with local institutions) and non-location-bound (e.g. technological) FSAs as core sources of a firm's competitiveness and maintain that these are managerial-decision variables, while location-specific advantages are largely exogenous to the firm.

The *specific-advantage hypothesis* (Koutsoyiannis, 1982) explains why firms possessing FSAs become MNEs, since FSAs may compensate for disadvantages arising when entering a foreign market. Thus FSAs determine whether a market is served by domestic or foreign firms (i.e. the 'who' question). This points to the relative nature of FSAs compared to comparative advantage.

FSAs are thus a source of *integration* of activities (e.g. horizontally or vertically) which requires mobility; through their mobility they enable firms to follow *fragmentation* strategies, taking advantage of location–factor cost differentials.

Also, FSAs can be exploited without additional costs within the affiliates of the MNE. This public-good nature of FSAs provides an important motive for international production.

Besides the asset view of the *exploitation* of FSA (static approach) is the ability of a firm to *learn* what constitutes a FSA (dynamic approach). In addition, the global network of an MNE itself brings 'significant performance benefits to organisations (. . .), such as the ability to leverage scale economies, the potential to take advantage of arbitrage opportunities in factor cost differentials across multiple locations and the ability to hasten new product development and introduction' (Gomes and Ramaswamy, 1999, p. 174). Dunning (1999, p. 8) points to the path-dependence in upgrading a firm's core competencies. Anand and Kogut (1997) argue that the path-dependence of FSAs *inter alia* suggests their *creation* is related to geography.

Important Aspects of Location-specific Advantages (LSAs)

LSAs are available to all firms in the same manner ('common basis'), regardless of whether they are owned by domestic or foreign firms, but not all firms make the same use of it. These factors are termed universal production factors (like cheap labour) by Hirsch and Meshulach (1991). Anand and Kogut also argue that location advantages are shared among firms from the same locality (1997, p. 449f.), which is a clear distinction from firm-specific advantages.

Comparative advantage is location-bound, that is, immobile. Several authors stress the importance of location factors in determining the competitiveness of similar firms in the same industry but different locations.

The LSAs are specific to nations or regions, because they are created and changed by governments that have monopoly position within their jurisdiction in shaping these factors (e.g. labour market regulations). Moreover, as long as positive externalities arise, governments do not want to exclude firms from using location factors as inputs.

Dunning uses the term 'location advantages', which comprises resources (tangible, intangible) as well as the institutional environment. Examples are not only the physical infrastructure of a country, the national innovation system or the general institutional environment, but also factors such as distance-related transaction costs, interactive learning, spatially related innovation and technological standards (Dunning 1999, p. 18f.). According to Anand and Kogut (1997), a particularly important location factor is the attractiveness of a location as a source of technology in order to tap into local knowledge (p. 446).

A Note on the Interplay between the Two Types of Advantage

LSAs are not only important for the *creation* of FSAs (which is bound mostly to the home country), but also determine the way that FSAs are *exploited* (which is not bound to the home country). Many authors point to the mutual dependence between LSA and FSA, for example Kravis (1985): 'Country-specific advantages [. . .] may also determine the nature of the firm-specific advantage (FSA) that enables the MNE to produce competitively in a foreign country' (p. 61). Pavitt and Patel (1999) and Barré (1996) for example discuss the relationship between MNEs' technology strategies and national systems of innovation. The fact that MNEs may tap into various fields of innovation in different locations may also make them more independent of the location advantage of a certain region or nation. For example, Abd-el-Rahmen (1991) suggests that under a given comparative advantage, firm performance with identical products will differ, resulting from a firm-based, individual, differentiated exploitation of conditions of imperfect competition.

From Conceptual to Empirical Aspects

In empirical analysis measuring comparative advantage (CA) would be sufficient in a world without factor mobility, where FSAs and CA coincide and only national firms exist. Yet there are several reasons for the need to consider FSAs and LSAs separately in empirical analysis, rooted in the modern theory of international trade and deriving from the concept of nationality.

While in 'traditional trade theory, the nation comparative advantage and the firm competitive advantage are synonymous' (Mucchielli, 1998, p. xiii), factor proportion theories based on comparative advantage alone fail to explain IPPs, once factor mobility is introduced. This is best expressed by Caves (1996), who states that 'in general, the more mobile are factors of production, the less does comparative advantage have to do with patterns of production' (p. 43). Thus the existence of MNEs leads to specialization patterns, which deviate from those predicted on the basis of pure trade theory (e.g. Helpman, 1984). 'The failure of the RCA methodology to deliver accurate predictions in the Irish case is accounted for by its inability to take into account the size and nature of the FDI inflows that accession triggered. Most of the jobs in foreign-owned industry were in sectors in which Ireland had a revealed comparative *dis-advantage*' (Barry, 2002, emphasis added). Also, trade motivated by other factors than comparative advantage (Krugman, 1980) is not accounted for in a pure factor endowments view (Helpman, 1984; Markusen, 1998). Moreover, the firm-specific nature of FSAs implies that comparative advantage analysis neglects firm-to-firm differences.

Introducing MNEs also implies relevance of the territorial dimension, since 'their capabilities become largely independent of a single country's factor endowment' (Ietto-Gillies, 2002, p. 181). The resulting 'non-coincidence between ownership and territoriality' (ibid., p. 179) means that only FSAs of purely domestic firms and LSAs of their home country coincide. FSAs of affiliates abroad are developed by the parent firm at home and are transferred to rather than created in the host country. Part of FSAs used by foreign firms in the host country are based on LSAs abroad (in their home country). Examining samples of firms on a nation-based concept without taking the territorial aspect into account would therefore wrongly attribute a comparative advantage to all firms in a region/country, not allowing for the fact that part of the FSAs were transferred from abroad. In other words, not all FSAs actually *used* in a region/country have been *created* there. Therefore it is necessary to treat domestic firms and foreign affiliates as two distinct subgroups. Ietto-Gillies concludes that 'for this reason it is useful to keep the demarcation between competitive (of companies) and comparative (of countries) advantages' (ibid., p. 181).

It has been argued that the interplay of FSAs and LSAs determines the nature of production, of trade and FDI flows. The next section explains how the firm strategies are linked to these advantages.

3. FIRM STRATEGIES ON THE BASIS OF COMPETITIVE AND COMPARATIVE ADVANTAGE

We start with a description of each cell in the matrix (Figure 6.2), developing six propositions. The location of a certain industry in a specific cell is a result of the interaction between domestic and foreign firms and their relative firm-specific advantages (see 'operationalization' below). Interaction may take the form of competition or of various linkages (upstream, downstream) between domestic and foreign firms. The interactions may be cause or effect of the existence of FSAs; causality cannot be established here.

Cell A

Cell A is characterized by the lack of CA, combined with FSAs. Consequently, we expect few exporting activities and primarily defensive outward FDI, since firms exploit their FSAs abroad via horizontal integration. Since CA is less than 1, this points to a high import penetration.

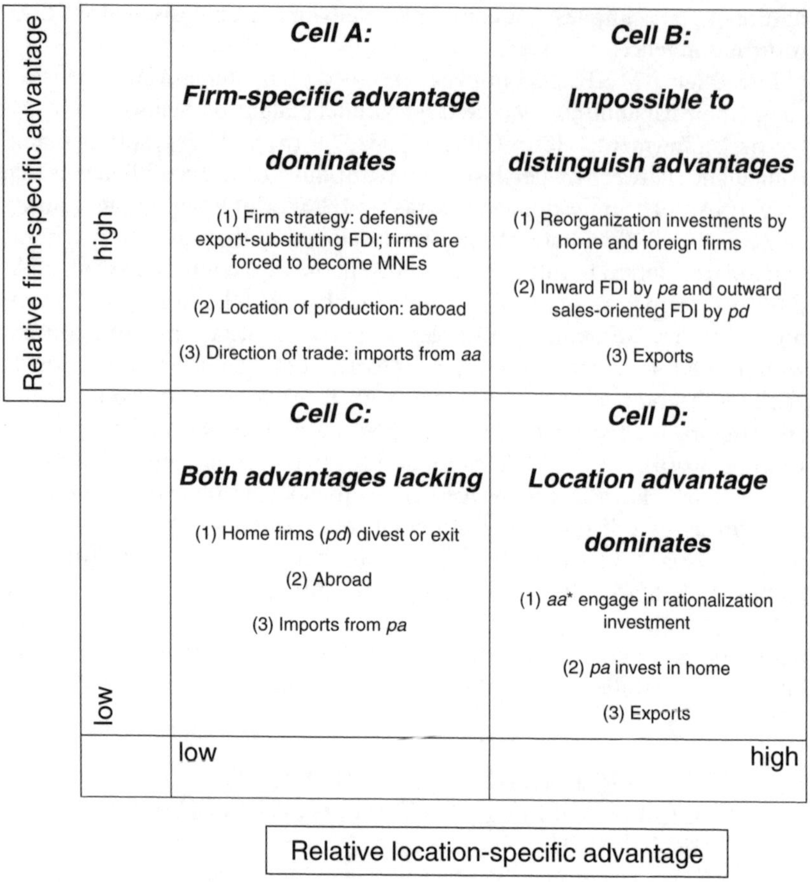

		Cell A: **Firm-specific advantage** **dominates** (1) Firm strategy: defensive export-substituting FDI; firms are forced to become MNEs (2) Location of production: abroad (3) Direction of trade: imports from *aa*	Cell B: **Impossible to** **distinguish advantages** (1) Reorganization investments by home and foreign firms (2) Inward FDI by *pa* and outward sales-oriented FDI by *pd* (3) Exports
Relative firm-specific advantage	high		
	low	Cell C: **Both advantages lacking** (1) Home firms (*pd*) divest or exit (2) Abroad (3) Imports from *pa*	Cell D: **Location advantage** **dominates** (1) *aa** engage in rationalization investment (2) *pa* invest in home (3) Exports
		low	high

Relative location-specific advantage

Figure 6.2   Dynamic matrix (home-country view)

Also, the lack of CA must be due to the lack of LSAs, since FSAs are given. Therefore, we expect primarily domestic firms, yet with relatively low sales volumes.

Proposition 1. Home country *H* firms in cell A engage in defensive *export-substituting FDI*. They locate production abroad and re-import part of it.

Cell B

Cell B includes domestic firms which are strong exporters, based on their FSAs; at the same time the favourable location advantages will attract some foreign firms. Here we expect typical multinational industries, characterized by vertical and horizontal integration. In this cell, foreign and domestic firms interact through the forces of competition and oligopolistic reactions. Technological cooperation with the competitive domestic firms will enable the foreign firms to profit not only from location advantage, but from direct know-how and technology exchange (absolute advantage); this will be a main reason why foreign-owned firms are present in cell B despite their relative firm-specific disadvantage.

Proposition 2. Home and foreign firms in cell B invest in reorganization and rationalization FDI in home country H and set up sales-oriented FDI in host country F.

Cell C

Trade and production occur despite a lack of comparative advantage. As we will see below, a substantial part of value-added and employment is located there, similarly to the scenario of Belgium reported in Sleuwaegen et al. (1998). Firms in cell C contain relatively weak domestic firms with firm-specific disadvantages. Therefore, exports and outward FDI should be low and import penetration high (comparative disadvantage). The pure comparative advantage hypothesis ('HOS') suggests that there are no firms and no trade in cell C. Thus, if firms are located in cell C, they are either producing at a comparative disadvantage and will be outcompeted, for example by imports, or the production is based on other factors such as transport costs, home market effect etc.

Proposition 3. Firms in cell C exit or divest. Home-country H's markets will be served by foreign firms from abroad (*pa*). Presence of firms in cell C may be due to sunk costs, high transaction costs of disinvestment, the immobility of their FSAs or other factors referred to above.

Cell D

Cell D is predominantly populated by strong foreign firms, taking advantage of the location advantages and the absence of FSAs with domestic firms. Foreign penetration via inward FDI should therefore be high and primarily fragmentators (from the argument of comparative advantage) should be located here. While pure fragmentators take advantage of low labour or energy costs and the like, the more sophisticated foreign firms will benefit from the linkages with local actors. Yet these will not be primarily domestic firms as they have a relative firm-specific disadvantage,[2] but those domestic institutions that constitute the intangible location advantage (e.g., local system of innovation, education system, labour market institutions).

Proposition 4. Foreign firms (*aa**) in cell D will expand their production in country *H*, partly by takeover, and export part of their output to their home country *F*.

In addition to the propositions related directly to the cells in the matrix, we derive additional propositions, which are thought to be relevant for the loss or the gain of advantages of firms and industries:

Proposition 5. Shifts of firms between advantage combinations are explained partly by new firms and partly by existing firms.

Proposition 6. Given the heterogeneity of firms within industries and the large variety of possible linkages between firms and public institutions, the location of an industry in one of the four cells is a firm-specific rather than an industry-specific phenomenon.

4. DATA AND OPERATIONALIZATION

Data

Two data sets, one on Austrian trade (exports and imports), the other on Austrian manufacturing firms, are merged on a three-digit NACE level (see Appendix table). According to the conceptual discussion, the first is used to calculate CA, while value-added, taken from the firms' balance-sheet data, is used to calculate relative FSAs. All firm data are measured in Austrian Schillings (ATS); all trade data are measured in million ATS.

The degree of representation is shown in Tables 6.1 and 6.2. Since multi-nationality is positively related to size, we think we cover a large share of foreign and Austrian MNEs. By two-digit industry, the degree of representation is over 30 per cent and in only two is it below 10 per cent, by employment.

While the first data set is standard, the second data set requires more detailed discussion, since it is the limiting factor in the merging process. In order to classify the firms by industry (according to the *Systematik der Wirtschaftstätigkeiten*), we used the *Firmenbuch* and also checked for changes of the most important industry for each firm in 1990, 1995 and 2000. Since the calculation of relative FSAs requires the availability of foreign and domestic firms in an industry, we lose several industries. Further, we follow the same firms over ten years and compare these to changes in the total sample.

Operationalization

Earlier studies using the concept described above and represented in the matrix in Figure 6.2 reveal that there is considerable disagreement about the

Table 6.1   Degree of representation, 2000

2-digit industry	Employees in total population*	Sample employees	Employees (%)
15	74 993	17 106	22.81
17	20 436	6607	32.33
18	10 427	6002	57.56
19	6177	2119	34.30
20	34 829	1599	4.59
21	17 547	14 643	83.45
22	25 726	3072	11.94
24	26 994	12 550	46.49
25	29 340	7513	25.61
26	34 113	4712	13.81
27	32 724	6744	20.61
28	62 583	8439	13.48
29	74 308	30 275	40.74
31	28 799	16 264	56.47
32	30 320	19 919	65.70
33	13 490	2397	17.77
34	28 991	16 988	58.60
36	45 679	2958	6.48
Total	597 476	179 907	30.11

* *Source:*   Table 23.06, *Statistisches Jahrbuch* 2003 and own calculations.

Table 6.2   Degree of representation by size class

Size classes	Total population	Sample	Sample in % of total population
20–49	71 691	337	0.47
50–99	59 265	2041	3.44
100–249	111 033	24 718	22.26
250–499	94 760	43 529	45.94
500–999	78 982	56 746	71.85
1000+	102 609	48 852	47.61
Total	518 340	176 223	34.00

operationalization of the FSA and LSA as the two sources of the 'kalei-doscope comparative advantage' (Feenstra, 1998, p. 31).

LSA in this study is therefore not measured directly, but results from the combination of FSA and CA, which are measured in the following way. For comparative advantage we use a standard formula:

$$RCA = (X_i/M_i) / (X/M)$$

where i is industry i, X is exports and M is imports.

The operationalization of the FSA is controversial. Hirsch and Cherniawski (1997) use an export ratio in order to measure FSA, but state that the ideal measure would include overseas value-added as well. Sleuwaegen et al. (1998) use a measure where both domestic and foreign firms are included. This measure, which is also adopted in this chapter, relates to the relative nature of FSAs, which is the core of the specific-advantage hypothesis referred to above.

$$RFSA_i = (AF_i/FF_i) / (AF/FF)$$

(Ratio of value-added[3] by Austrian firms (AF) to value-added by foreign based firms (FF) in industry i relative to total value-added by Austrian firms to value-added by foreign firms in Austria)

Ideally, FSA should be calculated 'by function' (R&D, production, marketing etc.) in order to be consistent with RCA and LSA.[4] This suggests that using the firm as the unit of analysis is not fully appropriate; yet it can be interpreted as an 'average' FSA.

5. RESULTS

Figure 6.3 uses data on the two-digit industry level contained in Tables 6.7a–c and shows the actual distribution of industries across cells during 1990, 1995 and 2000. It is thus an empirical representation of the matrix presented in Figure 6.2, plotting the RFSA and the RCA for the three observation years. We chose to show only two-digit values, because at the three-digit level, the observations would be too crowded, especially at low values. Figure 6.3a shows the advantage combinations of cells A and B, where RFSA equals or is larger than 3.0. Figure 6.3b shows the distribution of advantage combinations across all four cells for RFSA values smaller than 3.0, using a stretched Y axis. Let us look at each cell in turn.

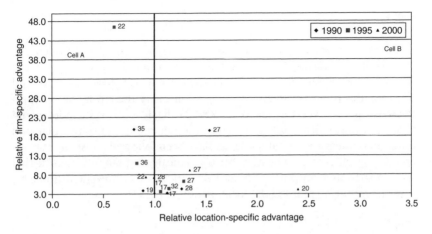

Figure 6.3a   Dynamics 1990–1995–2000 (values for FSA > 3.0)

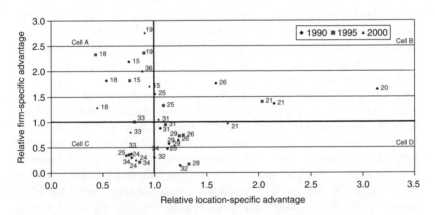

*Figure 6.3b   Dynamics 1990–1995–2000 (values for FSA < 3.0; wider
scale for Y axis)*

Cell A

The fact that firms located in cell A lose value-added at home as well as in their exports not unexpectedly points to re-location of production abroad (vertical integration). The firms 'escaped' a set of location factors which did not meet their demand for the exploitation of their FSAs. Since relative FSA dominates here, this has been a defensive strategy in order to secure overall competitiveness.

Cell B

Firms show strong employment losses, yet they also lose value-added and exports, despite having both advantages, which would suggest a growth of the industries located in cell B. While the employment loss may be bound to rationalization investment, an indication being the strong labour productivity gains over the ten-year period, the loss of value-added and exports could be the result of reorganization investment. Both vertical and horizontal integration strategies may have been followed by Austrian firms abroad as well as foreign firms in Austria. Another explanation may be that factors such as transport costs and distant markets prevented domestic firms from fully exploiting the location advantages.

Cell C

Firms in cell C show a strong loss of employment in 1995–2000, yet value-added and export gains, mainly owing to the fact that six firms/industries from other cells shift to cell C, rather than gains of existing firms over time (distributional effect). The importance of cell C, both in terms of industries as well as in employment and value-added share, is apparent. The fact that both advantages are lacking either did not prevent foreign firms from acquiring Austrian firms, five out of six being fragmentators. This is not easy to explain, since foreign fragmentators are especially dependent on location factors (particularly cost-related factors at least in mature sectors): firms shifting from cells A and B to cell C may not have yet exited, since exit or divestment takes time and does not occur immediately. On the other hand, firms may try to shift back to one of the other cells. Also, it points to a parallel deterioration of relative location advantages, particularly used by those industries that move from cell B to cell C, which makes it harder to develop new FSAs. Another explanation would be that even if the domestic firms did not have any advantage, the takeover may have led to the 'injection' of FSAs from the new parent abroad, which may explain that the firms have not divested so far.

Cell D

Here, firms show the strongest value-added, export and employment gain. This points to an improvement of relative location factors which has obviously attracted *new* foreign firms to exploit their transferred FSAs or *existing* firms even to develop or improve their FSAs.

The resulting employment, value-added and export effects of the strategies followed by domestic and foreign firms are presented in Table 6.3.

Table 6.3   Change of various indicators by cell 1990–1995–2000

Cell	Number of firms		Employment		Value-added		Exports	
	1995–2000	1990–2000	1995–2000	1990–2000	1995–2000	1990–2000	1995–2000	1990–2000
A	−11	−7	−7740	−7167	−6 876 161.00	−5 777 586.00	−15 719 180.00	−11 121 478.00
B	−9	−3	−8778	−11 690	−6 059 881.00	−5 822 062.00	−3 039 209.00	−8 498 448.00
C	−1	6	−4838	413	1 832 623.00	9 479 849.00	15 943 486.00	21 538 207.00
D	21	4	15 819	1 837	28 812 329.00	11 857 796.00	68 868 623.00	33 264 606.00
Total	0	0	−5 537	−16 607	17 708 910.00	9 737 997.00	66 053 720.00	35 182 887.00

In absolute terms, cell D reflects the largest changes in employment, value-added and exports for both subperiods, which shows that the foreign-owned firms have been a particularly dynamic group. The primarily domestically owned firms in cells A and B experienced a decrease in all measures used, thus suggesting a decreasing competitiveness relative to foreign-owned firms. Not surprisingly, firms in cell C show dramatic employment losses during the second half of the period, while value-added increased slightly. This is a sign of strong and successful restructuring activity since it led to a net increase in all measures over the whole period.

The differences between the overall sample development and the balanced panel are shown in Tables 6.4a and 6.4b, and in Table 6.5. This type of comparison is important, because changes in the firm aggregated in each cell over time may be prompted by the shift of firms across cells (i.e. the overall shift effect) or by a change in the activity of firms that were present in the cell at the beginning and at the end of the period (i.e. the balanced panel effect). Tables 6.4a and 6.4b show the latter effect, while Table 6.5 compares both effects, presenting clear evidence that the larger part of changing employment and value-added in each cell can be attributed to shifting firms and industries across cells, rather than the existing firms' activities (i.e. the overall shift effect is much larger than the balanced panel effect). This evidence is also an indication that the dynamics of the sources of competitiveness make it difficult to predict industry evolution.

Further, Table 6.6 shows the subgroup of industries and firms that change cells, divided by the shift of industries across cells caused by changes in the sample firms, while the balanced panel firms are remarkably stable, even at the three-digit level. Interestingly, seven industries gained advantages, while only three lost advantages at the three-digit level, while at the two-digit level, all industries lost advantages, which points to the diversity of firms within industries. In terms of proportion of firms, 30 per cent of balanced panel firms are included in the industries changing cells between 1995 and 2000 (19 per cent). This is a remarkable increase in the second half compared to the first half of the period 1990–2000. It seems that even during short periods, gain or loss of competitiveness across cells in addition to intra-cell shifts affects a high proportion of the firm population. Appropriate policies will therefore be difficult to develop in such a dynamic environment. The risk of policy failure will be high.

Table 6.6a shows several trade-related indicators. The net trade index varies between -1 and $+1$: 1 indicates pure exports and the highest comparative advantage, -1 indicates pure imports and the highest disadvantage; and 0 indicates balanced trade. The net trade index by definition is negative for cells A and C and reflects relatively balanced trade across cells on an industry level. This result is somewhat surprising as pure

Table 6.4a Balanced panel effect 1995–2000

	N			Employment			Value-added		
	1995	2000	Change	1995	2000	Change	1995	2000	Change
Total	141	141	0	97 228	91 691	−5537	86 724 310.00	104 433 220.00	17 708 910.00
DO	74	64	−10	45 448	40 093	−5355	38 087 116.00	39 645 124.00	1 558 008.00
FO(FG)	11	21	10	8 696	15 055	6359	7 243 542.00	19 530 105.00	12 286 563.00
FO(other)	56	56	0	43 084	36 543	−6541	41 393 652.00	45 257 991.00	3 864 339.00

Table 6.4b Balanced panel effect 1990–2000

	N			Employment			Value-added		
	1990	2000	Change	1990	2000	Change	1990	2000	Change
Total	58	58	0	66 433	49 826	−16 607	48 155 499.00	57 893 496.00	9 737 997.00
DO	31	25	−6	31 817	19 621	−12 196	22 636 646.00	20 063 990.00	−2 572 656.00
FO(FG)	3	8	5	1834	4842	3008	1 134 525.00	5 196 704.00	4 062 179.00
FO(other)	24	25	1	32 782	25 363	−7419	24 384 328.00	32 632 802.00	8 248 474.00

Table 6.5   *Overall shift (OS) effect versus balanced panel (BP) effect (firms with exports only)*

Change in	1995–2000 (N=141)		1990–2000 (N=58)	
	OS	BP	OS	BP
Number of firms	78	0	207	0
Employment	28 061	−5 537	62 167	−16 607
Value-added	55 815 926	17 708 910	99 889 164	9 737 997

comparative advantage analysis would have suggested a clear distinction of industries into net exporters and net importers. This underlines the importance of also looking at the FSA.

Table 6.7 sheds light on the question of firm- or industry-specific causes of clustering of firms in cells of the matrix. We check whether the three-digit industries are mainly located in the same cell as the respective two-digit industry in order to answer this question. The evidence clearly suggests that it is a firm-specific phenomenon, if we compare the three-digit and the two-digit clustering across cells (cf. cols 4 and 8).

Overall, the results are plausible, yet the descriptive evidence does not enable us to draw causal interpretations. Nevertheless, some policy conclusions are suggested on the basis of the firms' strategies during 1990–2000.

6.   CONCLUSIONS

It has been argued throughout the chapter that two types of information are crucial in order to design efficient policies for stimulating the competitiveness of firms: first, the locational strategies of firms on the basis of their existing FSA; and second, a proper assessment of the comparative location quality. While the latter is more often found in economic analysis, only the first approach can clarify the question of whether FSAs have been 'imported' via foreign MNEs or developed locally. In addition, the importance of the linkages between domestic and foreign firms has been stressed as determinants of FSAs.

The chapter presented a simple approach to deliver information on the two sources of competitiveness and should thus contribute to a rational location policy (Murtha and Lenway, 1994). The revealed strategies of the firms across the cells of the matrix suggest a differentiated policy approach, taking into account the four possible advantage combinations. From an efficiency viewpoint domestic firms in industries where both advantages are

Table 6.6   Industries and firms changing cells

Number of industries, 3-digit	Industries changing cells 1995–2000	Industries changing cells 1990–2000	Number of industries, 2-digit	Industries changing cells 1995–2000	Industries changing cells 1990–2000
153	C to A		17	B to A	
211	B to D		21	B to D	
241	A to C				
244	C to D				
251	C to A				
274	A to B				
294	B to C				
295		D to B	26		B to D
321		D to B	28		B to A
341		C to D			
Sum of number of firms changing cells	42	11	Sum of number of firms changing cells	22	7
Sum of number of industries changing cells	7	3	Sum of number of industries changing cells	2	2
Sample *n*	141	58		141	58

Table 6.6a   Import and export ratio and net trade index across cells in 2000

	Import ratio	Export ratio	Net trade index
Cell A	0.226	0.153	−0.173
Cell B	0.232	0.311	0.163
Cell C	0.239	0.167	−0.160
Cell D	0.304	0.369	0.114

Notes:
Import ratio is defined as: M_i/M.
Export ratio is defined as: X_i/X.
Net trade index is defined as: $(X_{t,i} - M_{t,i})/(X_{t,i} + M_{t,i})$.

lacking (cell C) should probably not be addressed by policy measures, since they will be lost despite policy intervention. Firms in cell B, on the other hand, may not be the primary concern of policy makers, unless their level of activity deteriorates in the home country, as was the case in Austria. Yet firms and industries where either advantage is given (cell A or cell D) may be policy targets due to the complementary nature of both advantages in some fields (e.g. national systems of innovation mentioned above and firms'

Table 6.7a   Clustering of 3-digit industries at 2-digit level in 1990

3-digit industries	FSA	LSA	Cell in matrix	2-digit industries	FSA	LSA	Cell in matrix
153	0.342	0.533	C	15	2.191	0.750	A
158	1.325	0.709	A				
159	1691.492	1.346	B				
177	0.204	0.609	C	17	3.238	1.125	B
182	1.821	0.560	A	18	1.821	0.536	A
193	3.921	0.832	A	19	3.921	0.887	A
202	1.347	3.704	B	20	1.638	3.137	B
211	1.204	2.149	B	21	1.356	2.149	B
212	2.431	2.149	B				
241	1.226	0.810	A	24	0.296	0.776	C
246	0.189	0.509	C				
251	0.323	1.259	D	25	0.477	1.120	D
252	1.146	1.057	B				
262	0.538	2.986	D	26	1.758	1.590	B
268	2.240	1.938	B				
272	1.110	2.147	B	27	19.485	1.537	B
281	0.555	1.545	D	28	4.322	1.265	B
282	0.996	1.346	D				
287	3.532	0.873	A				
291	0.754	0.939	C	29	0.571	1.139	D
292	0.465	1.168	D				
295	1.176	1.438	B				
311	2.442	1.226	B	31	0.875	1.054	D
312	0.682	0.834	C				
313	0.024	1.387	D				
315	1.038	0.901	A				
321	0.487	1.086	D	32	0.146	1.243	D
322	0.156	0.582	C				
334	0.396	1.213	D	33	0.374	0.775	C
341	0.288	0.692	C	34	0.339	0.724	C
352	17.528	3.248	B	35	19.778	0.800	A

Table 6.7b   Clustering of 3-digit industries at 2-digit level in 1995

3-digit industries	FSA	LSA	Cell in matrix	2-digit industries	FSA	LSA	Cell in matrix
151	0.724	0.912	C	15	1.8204	0.7600	A
153	0.506	0.707	C				
158	0.961	0.577	C				
159	26.447	1.861	B				
171	1.954	1.217	B	17	3.6641	1.0616	B
177	0.728	0.567	C				
182	2.329	0.443	A	18	2.3290	0.4322	A
193	2.365	0.779	A	19	2.3655	0.8954	A
211	1.454	2.119	B	21	1.4012	2.0318	B
212	1.166	1.810	B				
221	22.811	0.540	A	22	46.4784	0.6094	A
241	1.048	0.806	A	24	0.3575	0.7517	C
243	0.274	0.664	C				
244	0.125	0.835	C				
246	1.789	0.546	A				
251	0.411	0.920	C	25	1.3254	1.0848	B
252	3.046	1.166	B				
261	0.305	1.445	D	26	0.7427	1.2743	D
262	0.702	2.039	D				
265	1.052	0.201	A				
266	0.151	2.929	D				
268	0.752	1.491	D				
272	0.739	1.508	D	27	6.3038	1.2849	B
274	1.264	0.808	A				
281	1.354	1.480	B	28	4.3784	1.1391	B
282	4.684	1.080	B				
286	7.610	1.406	B				
287	1.494	0.831	A				
291	0.688	0.987	C	29	0.7213	1.2358	D
292	0.263	1.233	D				
293	7.070	1.027	B				
294	3.243	1.035	B				
295	1.724	1.864	B				
311	2.399	1.526	B	31	0.9528	1.1047	D
312	0.434	0.889	C				
313	0.306	1.519	D				
315	1.337	0.862	A				
321	1.994	1.476	B	32	0.1702	1.3292	D
322	0.122	0.856	C				
331	1.517	0.714	A	33	1.0075	0.8052	A

Table 6.7b   (continued)

3-digit industries	FSA	LSA	Cell in matrix	2-digit industries	FSA	LSA	Cell in matrix
332	0.257	0.897	C				
334	2.185	1.069	B				
341	0.157	0.843	C	34	0.2056	0.8555	C
343	0.300	0.875	C				
361	23.411	0.631	A	36	10.9740	0.8266	A
364	3.799	3.131	B				

Table 6.7c   *Clustering of 3-digit industries at 2-digit level in 2000*

3-digit industries	FSA	LSA	Cell in matrix	2-digit industries	FSA	LSA	Cell in matrix
151	4.023	0.927	A	15	1.7065	0.9493	A
153	2.144	0.830	A				
158	0.785	0.788	C				
159	3.381	2.502	B				
171	3.166	1.201	B	17	3.2941	0.9990	A
172	7.365	1.407	B				
175	2.489	1.224	B				
177	0.618	0.371	C				
182	1.285	0.458	A	18	1.2852	0.4490	A
193	2.760	0.724	A	19	2.7602	0.9047	A
201	0.950	3.606	D	20	4.0939	2.4004	B
211	0.729	1.716	D	21	0.9760	1.7055	D
212	2.508	1.679	B				
221	3.453	0.851	A	22	7.3578	0.9161	A
241	0.433	0.803	C	24	0.2500	0.8191	C
243	1.587	0.707	A				
244	0.082	1.006	D				
246	2.889	0.555	A				
251	0.840	0.691	C	25	1.5565	1.0035	B
252	2.525	1.143	B				
262	1.434	1.863	B	26	0.6499	1.2266	D
265	2.078	0.283	A				
266	0.674	1.096	D				
268	0.175	1.698	D				
272	1.132	1.934	B	27	9.1539	1.3447	B
274	2.939	1.076	B				
281	1.422	1.035	B	28	7.2501	0.9969	A

International business linkages

Table 6.7c   (continued)

3-digit industries	FSA	LSA	Cell in matrix	2-digit industries	FSA	LSA	Cell in matrix
286	12.991	1.451	B				
287	3.816	0.758	A				
291	0.371	0.846	C	29	0.6455	1.2287	D
292	0.647	1.214	D				
293	2.935	1.335	B				
294	1.055	0.992	A				
295	1.412	1.787	B				
297	0.056	0.913	C				
311	2.509	1.633	B	31	1.0506	1.0376	B
312	0.513	0.882	C				
313	0.938	1.057	D				
315	11.719	0.886	A				
316	1.829	0.830	A				
321	0.837	1.269	D	32	0.3064	1.0012	D
322	0.190	0.469	C				
331	0.768	0.713	C	33	0.7979	0.7658	C
334	1.786	0.888	A				
341	0.360	1.142	D	34	0.3180	0.9956	C
342	0.691	0.805	C				
364	0.380	1.737	D	36	1.9995	0.8790	A

technology strategies and cooperation). Domestic firms in cell A may be *indirectly* supported by supplying specific infrastructure or affecting cost conditions via (the abolition of) regulations. A higher flexibility of the labour market and the deregulation of important intermediate-input industries like the electricity sector were high on the agenda in Austria during the surveyed period. Domestic firms in cell D may be *directly* supported by R&D grants, a better local integration into the national system of innovation and so on.

However, the dynamics described for the period 1990–2000 make it difficult to introduce efficient policies successfully (see Bellak, 2005). The main policy failure may derive from the fact that the wrong firms benefit from certain policy measures, because firms shift across and within cells rather quickly.

The advantages of this type of analytical approach are its easy application; its simplicity in that the four advantage combinations are relevant for policy strategies and thus can be easily communicated to decision makers; the limited demand concerning data; the use of value-added instead of sales data; the derivation from the theory of the MNE and trade theory; and the fact that it allows for other factors than just factor endowment to motivate trade. The major limitation in this type of analysis is the unit of analysis, the firm. Classification at the three-digit level is almost impossible with large firms, which are typically diversified at least across similar three-digit industries. Therefore we did not choose the corporate level (holding company) but the operative level, which is closer to the plant level and thus can be classified more accurately.

NOTES

1. (gross sales: include VAT – net sales: exclude VAT – total sales: domestic sales + exports)
2. Yet some linkages may be important in the downstream value-added stages such as distribution and marketing.
3. Value-added is defined as *Betriebsleistung + Ertragszinsen − Materialaufwand − Aufwand für bezogene Leistungen − ordentlicher Betriebsaufwand*.
4. I would like to thank Mark Casson for pointing out to me this important limitation.

REFERENCES

Abd-el-Rahmen, K. (1991), 'Firms' Competitive and National Comparative Advantage as Joint Determinants of Trade Composition', *Weltwirtschaftliches Archiv*, **127**(1), 83–97.

Anand, J. and Delios, A. (1997), 'Location Specificity and the Transferability of Downstream Assets to Foreign Subsidiaries', *Journal of International Business Studies*, **28**(3), 579–604.

Anand, J. and Kogut, B. (1997), 'Technological Capabilities of Countries, Firm Rivalry and Foreign Direct Investment', *Journal of International Business Studies*, **28**(3), 445–65.

Audretsch, D.B. (1994), 'Business Survival and the Decision to Exit', *Journal of the Economics of Business*, **1**(1), 125–38.

Barré, R. (1996), 'Relationships Between Multinational Firms' Technology Strategies and National Innovation Systems: A Model and an Empirical Analysis', in OECD (ed.), *Innovation, Patents and Technological Strategies*, Paris: OECD, pp. 201–22.

Barry, F. (2002), 'EU Accession and FDI flows to CEE-Countries: Lessons from the Irish Experience', in R. Lipsey (ed.), *Foreign Direct Investment in the Real and the Financial Sector of Industrial Countries*, Deutsche Bundesbank.

Bellak, C. (2005), 'Adjustment Strategies of Multinational Enterprises to Changing International Competitiveness', *International Journal of the Economics of Business*, **12**(1), February, 139–62.

Caves, R.E. (1996), *Multinational Enterprise and Economic Analysis – Cambridge Surveys of Economic Literature*, Cambridge: Cambridge University Press.

Dunning, J.H. (1996), 'The Geographical Sources of Competitiveness of Firms: The Results of a New Survey', *Transnational Corporations*, **5**(3), 1–30.

International business linkages

Dunning, J.H. (1999), *The Eclectic Paradigm as an Envelope for Economic and Business Theories of MNE Activity*, Discussion Papers in International Investment & Business Studies, 263, University of Reading, UK.
Dunning, J.H. and Narula, R. (1996), *Foreign Direct Investment and Governments*, London: Routledge.
Erramilli, M.K., Agarwal, S. and Kim, S. (1997), 'Are Firm-specific Advantages Location-specific Too?', *Journal of International Business Studies*, **28**(4), 735–57.
Feenstra, R.C. (1998), 'Integration of Trade and Disintegration of Production in the Global Economy', *Journal of Economic Perspectives*, **12**(4), 31–50.
Gomes, L. and Ramaswamy, K. (1999), 'An Empirical Examination of the Form of Relationship Between Multinationality and Performance', *Journal of International Business Studies*, **30**(1), 173–88.
Helpman, E. (1984), 'A Simple Theory of International Trade with Multinational Corporations', *Journal of Political Economy*, **92**(3), 451–71.
Herrera, J.J.D. (1992), 'Cross-Direct Investment and Technological Capability of Spanish Domestic Firms', in J. Cantwell (ed.), *Multinational investment in modern Europe*, Aldershot, UK and Brookfield, USA: Edward Elgar, pp. 214–55.
Hirsch, S. and Cherniawski, A. (1997), *Comparative Advantage, Competitive Advantage and Foreign Direct Investment: a Conceptual Scheme and Empirical Evidence*, Discussion Paper 97.13, presented at EIBA, Stuttgart.
Hirsch, S. and Meshulach, A. (1991), 'Towards a Unified Theory of Internationalization', WP 10–91, *Business and Economic Studies on European Integration*, Copenhagen.
Ietto-Gillies, G. (2002), *Transnational Corporations*, London: Routledge.
Kimura, Y. and Pugel, T.A. (2001), 'Competitive and Comparative Advantages: The Determinants of Japanese Direct Investment Activity in Manufacturing', in Narula, R. (ed.), *Trade and Investment in a Globalising World*, Amsterdam: Pergamon, pp. 69–85.
Kogut, B. (1985), 'Designing Global Strategies: Comparative and Competitive Value-added Chains', *Sloan Management Review*, Summer, 15–28.
Koutsoyiannis, A. (1982), *Non-price Decisions: The Firm in a Modern Context*, London: Macmillan.
Kravis, I.B. (1985), 'Comment on Rugman', in Erdelik, A. (ed.), *Multinationals as Mutual Invaders*, New York: St Martin's Press, pp. 60–64.
Krugman, P. (1980), 'Scale Economies, Product Differentiation, and the Pattern of Trade', *American Economic Review*, **70**, 950–59.
Markusen, J.R. (1998), 'Multinational Enterprises, and the Theories of Trade and Location', in Braunerhjelm, P. and Ekholm, K. (eds), *The Geography of Multinationals*, Boston: Kluwer Academic Publishers, pp. 9–32.
Mucchielli, J.-L. (1998), *Multinational Location Strategy*, Greenwich, CT: JAI Press.
Murtha, T.P. and Lenway, S.A. (1994), 'Country Capabilities and the Strategic State: How National Political Institutions Affect Multinational Corporations' Strategies', *Strategic Management Journal*, **15**, 113–29.
Patel, P. and Vega, M. (1997), 'Patterns of Internationalisation of Corporate Technology: Location vs. Home Country Advantages', *SPRU Electronic Working Paper Series*, 8, Brighton, University of Sussex.
Pavitt, K. and Patel, P. (1999), 'Global Corporations and National Systems of Innovation: Who Dominates Whom?', in D. Archibugi, J. Howells and J. Mitchie

(eds), *Innovation Policy in a Global Economy*, Cambridge: Cambridge University Press, pp. 94–119.

Rugman, A.M. and Verbeke, A. (1992), 'Multinational Enterprise and National Economic Policy', in Buckley, P.J. and M. Casson (eds), *Multinational Enterprises in the World Economy*, Aldershot, UK and Brookfield, USA: Edward Elgar, pp. 194–211.

Sleuwaegen, L., Veugelers, R. and Yamawaki, H. (1998), 'Comparative and Competitive Advantages: The Performance of the EU in a Global Context', *Research in Global Strategic Management*, **6**, 141–63.

APPENDIX

1990

A	B
Manufacture of other fruit products Manufacture of other wearing apparel and accessories Manufacture of footwear Manufacture of basic chemicals Manufacture of other fabricated metal products Manufacture of lighting equipment and electric lamps	Manufacture of beverages Manufacture of veneer sheets Manufacture of pulp, paper and paperboard Manufacture of electric motors, generators and transformers Manufacture of railway and tramway locomotives and rolling stock Manufacture of articles of paper and paperboard Manufacture of plastic products Manufacture of other non-metallic mineral products Manufacture of other special purpose machinery
C	D
Processing and preserving of fruit and vegetables Manufacture of knitted and crochetted articles Manufacture of other chemical products Manufacture of machinery for the production and use of mechanical power Manufacture of electricity distribution and control apparatus Manufacture of television and radio transmitters	Manufacture of rubber products Manufacture of non-refractory ceramic goods other than for construction purposes Manufacture of structural metal products Manufacture of tanks, reservoirs, and containers of metal Manufacture of other general purpose machinery Manufacture of insulated wire and cable Manufacture of electronic valves and tubes and other electronic components Manufacture of optical instruments and photographic equipment

1995

A	B
Manufacture of other wearing apparel and accessories Manufacture of footwear Publishing Manufacture of basic chemicals	Manufacture of beverages Preparation and spinning of textile fibres Manufacture of pulp, paper and paperboard

Manufacture of other chemical products Manufacture of cement, lime and plaster Manufacture of basic precious and non-ferrous metals Manufacture of other fabricated metal products Manufacture of lighting equipment and electronic lamps Manufacture of medical and surgical equipment and orthopaedic appliances	Manufacture of articles of paper and paperboard Manufacture of plastic products Manufacture of structural metal products Manufacture of cutlery, tools and general hardware Manufacture of agricultural and forestry machinery Manufacture of machine tools Manufacture of other special-purpose machinery Manufacture of sports goods Manufacture of electric motors, generators and transformers Manufacture of electronic valves and tubes and other electronic components Manufacture of optical instruments and photographic equipment
C	D
Production, processing and preserving of meat and meat products Processing and preserving of fruit and vegetables Manufacture of other fruit products Manufacture of knitted and crochetted articles Manufacture of paints, varnishes and similar coatings, printing ink and mastics Manufacture of machinery for the production and use of mechanical power Manufacture of pharmaceuticals, medicinal and botanical products Manufacture of rubber products Manufacture of electricity distribution and control apparatus Manufacture of TV and radio transmitters and apparatus for line telephony Manufacture of instruments and appliances for measuring, checking, testing . . . except industrial process control equipment Manufacture of motor vehicles Manufacture of parts and accessories for motor vehicles and their engines	Manufacture of glass and glass products Manufacture of non-refractory ceramic goods Manufacture of articles of concrete, plaster and cement Manufacture of other non-metallic mineral products Manufacture of tubes Manufacture of other general-purpose machinery Manufacture of insulated wire and cable

2000

A	B
Production, processing and preserving of meat and meat products Processing and preserving of fruit and vegetables Manufacture of other wearing apparel and accessories Manufacture of footwear Publishing Manufacture of paints, varnishes and similar coatings Manufacture of other chemical products Manufacture of cement, lime and plaster Manufacture of other fabricated metal products Manufacture of machine-tools Manufacture of lighting equipment and electric lamps Manufacture of electrical equipment n.e.c. Manufacture of optical instruments and photographic equipment	Manufacture of beverages Preparation and spinning of textile fibres Textile weaving Manufacture of other textiles Manufacture of articles of paper and paperboard Manufacture of plastic products Manufacture of non-refractory ceramic goods Manufacture of tubes Manufacture of basic precious and non-ferrous metals Manufacture of structural metal products Manufacture of cutlery, tools, and general hardware Manufacture of agricultural and forestry machinery Manufacture of other special-purpose machinery Manufacture of electric motors, generators and transformers
C	D
Manufacture of other food products Manufacture of knitted and crochetted materials Manufacture of basic chemicals Manufacture of rubber products Manufacture of machinery for the production and use of mechanical power Manufacture of domestic appliances n.e.c. Manufacture of electricity distribution and control apparatus Manufacture of TV and radio transmitters . . . Manufacture of medical and surgical equipment . . . Manufacture of bodies for motor vehicles	Saw milling and planing of wood, impregnation of wood Manufacture of pulp, paper and paperboard Manufacture of pharmaceuticals, medicinal and botanical products Manufacture of articles of concrete, plaster and cement Manufacture of other non-metallic mineral products Manufacture of other general purpose machinery Manufacture of insulated wire and cable Manufacture of electronic valves and tubes and other electronic components Manufacture of motor vehicles Manufacture of sports goods

7. Dynamic capability, innovation networks and foreign firms: the Turkish case*

Aykut Lenger and Erol Taymaz

1. INTRODUCTION

The conventional understanding of technical change as a linear process relating to invention in science, introduction into the market and consequent diffusion has been replaced by a more complex one in the last couple of decades. When Mansfield proposed, in the early 1970s, that the innovation process is not simply the outcome of basic R&D expenditures, he was referring to the nonlinear character of the process itself, which is also responsive to feedbacks from production and marketing problems and needs as well as technological opportunities (Mansfield, 1994). More recently, a comprehensive effort to describe and understand technological change has led to the theoretical conceptualization of the process as a system. The idea in this perspective is that the innovation process is of a nonlinear character such that each stage of the process is deeply affected by the interaction of the institutions at work, which together constitute a system (Freeman, 1987, 1988, 2002; Lundvall, 1988, 1992; Nelson, 1988, 1993; Kim, 2000). This approach, the so-called national innovation system,[1] is defined by Freeman (1987), who first introduced the concept into the theoretical discussion as the network of institutions, both public and private, which produce, import, adapt and diffuse new technologies by their activities and interactions. The main focus in this literature is the institutions, whether R&D laboratories, universities, administrative government bodies, financial intermediaries, or firms. Technology policy can be used to achieve a greater connectivity between these institutions, which is a precondition for pushing the innovation possibility frontier further ahead (Metcalfe, 1994).

The literature on technological change in developing countries has traditionally dealt with the issue of 'technology transfer' by disregarding the systemic aspects of the process. Does the systems view offer a better analytical tool to understand the experience of developing countries? This question is the main motivation in this study. Freeman (2002) argues that the Gerschenkronian type of technology transfer should be complemented by a systems approach of national innovation to better explain some successful catch-up cases. Dosi (1999) argues that the systems approach should take into account some micro-thinking at the aggregated level of system approach. In what follows, we try to link the systems approach to innovation to the micro-founded dynamic capability argument. Our study will be focused on innovation networks and the role of foreign firms in these networks because both the conventional and evolutionary approaches emphasize that foreign firms are instrumental in transferring technology and/or raising technological capabilities of developing countries.

The outline of the study is as follows. The next section discusses the conventional (developmentalism/modernism) and evolutionary (dynamic capabilities) approaches and their implications. In the third section, we set out the legal framework and present a brief overview of multinational corporations' (MNCs) activity in Turkey. The fourth section provides new evidence on the interactions between domestic and foreign firms within innovation networks in Turkish manufacturing industries. The aim of this empirical analysis is two-fold: (i) to analyze differences in innovative performance of domestic and foreign firms, and (ii) to investigate the types of interaction in which domestic and foreign firms are engaged. The determinants of innovativeness, including the effects of spillovers from foreign firms, are analyzed by using econometric techniques in the fifth section. The last section summarizes our main findings.

2. DEVELOPMENTALISM/MODERNISM VERSUS DYNAMIC CAPABILITIES

The motto 'There is no need to reinvent the wheel' best summarizes the discussion in the literature of development economics on technological change in backward/developing countries. Under Gerschenkron's hypothesis, relative backwardness has been taken for granted as an advantage since, unlike developed countries, countries that are backward do not need to make such an effort to gain access to new technologies. 'New' technologies are already there, and backward countries have free access to this open source that Bell (1989) calls the 'book of blueprints'. These new technologies have a public-good and non-rival nature, and backward countries therefore acquire tacit knowledge without worrying about generating it or adapting to it (Lall, 1992), with licensing, foreign direct investment and so on at much lower cost than that of developed countries (Freeman, 2002). Gerschenkron attributes these advantages to the backwardness of these countries (Bell, 1989; Radosevic, 1999). Furthermore, these countries would enjoy economies of scale because of the expanded market in developed countries. The only thing that backward countries have to sacrifice is the relatively high cost of production, which would be driven down by the learning-by-doing effect as a function of accumulated output over time. Eventually, these countries will catch up with the developed ones. It is obvious that this explanation is theoretically grounded on the Solovian neoclassical model in which convergence of countries' income level is directly implied.

Plenty of issues can be raised and discussed here. First, the modernist understanding of the catch-up process might be compatible with the linear representation of the innovation process. Backward countries do not necessarily commit themselves to basic research in science, and they can simply transfer new technologies produced in developed countries.

Second, technology is viewed as a pure public good and can be fully transferred in blueprints; that is, it has no tacit component. The drawback of this characterization is well discussed and criticized in evolutionary theory (Nelson and Winter, 1982; Rosenberg, 1982; Dosi, 2000b).

Third, the adoption and diffusion of new technologies by backward countries follows a linear process which fits well into the three-stage linear model of *innovation* mentioned at the outset. Relatedly, the developmentalist/modernist approach gives rise to the linear process of technological capability building. Technological capability, mainly drawing on the works of Dahlman et al. (1987) and Lall (1992), was defined as the ability to identify, acquire, absorb, adapt technologies to local conditions, and finally improve them. Building technological capability in a country, or in a firm, was deemed to follow these linear/sequential steps. However, recent literature on this issue points to the invalidity of linear capability building, and instead emphasizes the nonlinear and complex nature of technological learning (see Chen and Qu, 2003, for the Chinese case).

Fourth, this approach can explain only lagging-behind and catching-up, but not forging-ahead, dynamics. The developmentalist/modernist approach is associated with the neoclassical type of growth model in which the engine of growth is capital accumulation. However, capital accumulation alone cannot explain why, for example, Japan has outperformed other countries.

The developmentalist/modernist approach is plagued by two major problems. First, the idea that relative backwardness might work positively for a developing country (firm) is problematic. As Dosi (2000c) explains, a major technological opportunity may act as a powerful incentive to innovate for a firm near the technological frontier, whereas it may act as a disincentive for a firm with insufficient technological capability. Tacitness of knowledge, lack of capability, deficient understanding of new technologies, and the complex and interdependent nature of technological change could make developing-country firms lag behind, rather than catch up, developed-country firms. Second, the developmentalist/modernist approach implicitly assumes that developing countries should follow the same pattern as developed countries. So this approach is purely a replication approach. In a static world, this replication is not a problem; however, in a rapidly changing environment the replication approach poses some difficulties: while the developing countries try to replicate the same success by limiting themselves to mastering transferred technologies, the world changes, and they never reach the frontier.

The salient feature of the evolutionary approach distinguishing it from developmentalism/modernism is the recognition of the fact that the environment within which the firm operates changes continuously. No firm can ever have full information about its environment. Moreover, the complex and ever-changing nature of the environment implies that firms make use of routines or 'rules of thumb' in their decisions (Nelson and Winter, 1982). The developmentalist/modernist approach considers the optimum use of resources for a given stock of knowledge (for developing countries, transfer of *existing* technology) as the main problem. Therefore, as emphasized by Teece (2000), it is inherently static. However, what matters in reality is the ability for unceasing learning and adaptation, that is, dynamic capability. Dynamic capability can be defined as the ability of an organization to adapt its activity and thus renew its competence as required by the changing environment in which the organization operates through interaction with a set of agents (see, for example, Dosi and Marengo, 2000; Teece et al. 2000; Teece, 2000).

Firms differ from each other in terms of the knowledge set they acquire, the decision rules they use, and the dynamic capabilities they control. Diversity forms the basis for competition: those that are adaptable to the environment are more likely to survive. However, competition among firms, in turn, generates diversity because firms continuously transform the environment through learning and innovation activities. Diversity has another important implication: interaction among firms (and other institutions that make up the national system of innovation) becomes crucial to carry on effective learning and innovation activities because firms are endowed with complementary assets (knowledge, rules and capabilities).

The evolutionary view suggests that technology acquisition, even in the simplest case of technology transfer, requires active involvement of both the recipient and supplier firms. Knowledge is partly tacit and has to be regenerated by the recipient, usually by interacting with the supplier. The effectiveness of this process depends on dynamic capabilities and the form of interaction between the supplier/user firms (and other supporting institutions).

Developmentalist/modernist and evolutionary conceptualizations lead to different policy recommendations. The former approach deals mainly with the costs (and benefits) of transferred technology whereas the evolutionary approach emphasizes the importance of enhancing capabilities at the firm level (dynamic capabilities), and at the national level (connectivity between institutions) (see Metcalfe, 1994).

Innovation (the development of new products, processes and organizations) is basically an interactive process. Recent advances in science and technology have led to, on the one hand, an increase in knowledge content of products and processes, and, on the other hand, the importance of generic technologies that can be used in various products and processes. These two processes, which form two sides of the same coin, have increased the need to extend the knowledge base of industrial firms. As Rosenberg (1982) suggested, the process of innovation cannot fit into the boundaries of a single firm. Therefore, firms can now innovate only within an intensive web of interactions with other firms (suppliers, buyers, and even competitors), consumers, research institutions, and so on; that is, they can be innovative and, thus, competitive, only if they can form and be part of *innovation networks* (for a small group of studies, see Lundvall, 1988; Nelson and Rosenberg, 1993; Smith, 1995; OECD 1999, 2000).

Multinational corporations (MNCs), in spite of their gigantic size and possibilities to tap into knowledge sources all around the world, are not immune from this trend, and tend to establish and be part of international innovation networks. As Cantwell (1994) explains, international networks of MNCs have become a major source for technological accumulation and diffusion. It is thus not surprising to observe that MNCs have received considerable attention in development economics literature. They have been considered as an important channel for transfer of technology to developing countries. They bring advanced technologies and practices to developing countries, and these technologies and practices can diffuse to domestic firms through spillovers (imitation, demonstration effects, training local labor, etc.). Moreover, MNCs are embedded into the production and innovation systems of developing countries, and by taking part in these systems, they may help to raise the dynamic capabilities of domestic firms, especially those that are vertically related with MNCs (suppliers and users). Moreover, MNCs possess a different body of knowledge, which could provide a new source of exploration of new opportunities by domestic firms (for a detailed analysis, see Pavitt and Patel, 1999).[2]

Before discussing the Turkish case, we would like to recapitulate the empirical evidence on the complementarity/substitutiability of domestic effort and foreign technologies. The complementarity-substitutiability discussion flourished in the context of protectionist/import-substitution policies in developing countries. Any evidence confirming complementarity between foreign technology and in-house effort can be taken as counter-evidence to the protectionist view. If we extend the insight provided by Rosenberg (1982) about technical change, which cannot be limited to the boundaries of a single firm, to country level, we can easily understand that developing countries should exploit foreign knowledge sources. Otherwise, without this exploitation, the contribution of purely domestic technological activity would not be sufficient, and would be wasteful, as in the case of 'reinventing the wheel'. In that sense, foreign knowledge sources complement domestic activities. Thus the mounting empirical evidence on complementarity between foreign technological activities and in-house technological effort remains totally unsurprising (Lall, 1980; Braga and Willmore, 1991; Katrak, 1997; Veugelers, 1997; Veugelers and Cassiman, 1999, Radosevic, 1999). In our view, there is a critical distinction in the nature of domestic activity in a complementary relation. The domestic technological effort can be quite weak in the face of the foreign one; it might simply understand and adapt the foreign technology to local conditions, without any improvement in capability. We regard this process as a purely know-how transfer (a purely codified knowledge transfer). However, the know-why element (Teece, 1994) in the activity, which is associated with the tacit character of knowledge, is one of the driving forces for localized technology creation.

To recap, the catch-up explanation that draws on the convergence hypothesis cannot be taken as complementary to the systems approach to innovation since the former is characterized by a static developmentalist/modernist approach whereas the latter is characterized in terms of dynamic capabilities. Therefore, these two are substitute explanations for the experience of developing countries. Given the insights provided by the discussion above, the systems approach to innovation seems to be the appropriate tool for understanding the innovation process in developing countries. In the following sections, we will analyze the extent to which MNCs are involved in domestic networks, and their impact on developing technological capabilities in Turkish manufacturing industries.

3. MULTINATIONAL CORPORATIONS AND LEGAL FRAMEWORK IN TURKEY

The legal infrastructure for foreign investment was established in Turkey soon after World War II. The Foreign Capital Law was enacted in 1954 and the related Decree of the Council of Ministers remained in force until the late 1980s. The Law and the Decree provided a quite liberal framework of general principles designed to create a favorable environment for foreign direct investment (FDI). However, it is suggested by some researchers that the government institutions, and most importantly the State Planning Organization, which were suspicious of foreign capital, had effectively kept inward foreign investment at low levels with various restrictive bureaucratic practices (Erdilek, 1982). Thus the *cumulative* total of FDI authorized from 1950 to 1980 had reached only US$229 million (Öniş, 1994).

The import substitution industrialization strategy followed by the Turkish governments in the 1960s and 1970s had to be abandoned as a result of a severe balance-of-payments crisis in the late 1970s. On 24 January 1980, the Turkish government announced a stabilization program that was fully implemented under the military regime after September 1980. The new program was based on outward-oriented trade strategy and foreign trade and, later, capital markets have been liberalized to a large extent (for a comprehensive overview, see Kepenek and Yentürk, 2000).

The administrative system regulating FDI was reorganized in the early 1980s to simplify investment procedures and to eliminate ambiguities arising from the fragmented bureaucratic structure. Moreover, all the discriminatory treatment that foreign investors were subject to and the conditions on local equity participation were gradually eliminated (Erdilek, 1986). The complete liberalization of capital accounts in 1989 provided an additional impetus for foreign investment. As a result, the number of firms with foreign participation increased from 78 in 1980 to 1856 in 1990 and to 5328 in 2000, whereas the total value of inflow of FDI reached US$6 billion in the 1980–89 period and US$11.8 billion in the 1990–2000 period.[3] Manufacturing industry alone accounted for 55 percent of cumulative authorized FDI in the post-1980 period.[4]

Annual FDI was about US$1billion in the 1990s. The share of foreign firms[5] in the total number of private firms in manufacturing industry was about 1 percent in 1983, but it increased continuously up to 2 percent in 1999, and 3.5 percent in 2000 through acquisitions and entry.[6] The share of foreign firms in private manufacturing employment was about 6 percent, with 50 000 people employed by foreign firms in 1983. The employment share of foreign firms increased gradually, especially after 1988, and reached 11 percent in 2000.

Foreign firms are on average more productive than domestic firms. Consequently, their share in manufacturing value-added is quite substantial. They produced about 11–14 percent of value-added in the mid-1980s, and increased their share continuously until 2000 (24 percent). The value-added share of majority-owned foreign firms follows a similar pattern. Majority-owned foreign firms did not increase significantly their share in value-added until 1987. However, after the elimination of local equity participation and minimum export requirements in 1986 (Öniş, 1994, p. 96), majority-owned foreign firms realized a rapid growth in their valued-added share throughout the period under consideration. In other words, all the expansion in value-added share was achieved by majority-owned foreign firms, whereas minority-owned foreign firms (with equity participation within the 10–50 percent range) kept their shares almost constant.[7]

Foreign firms prefer to invest in high-tech industries: their share in value-added is close to 50 percent in medium/high-tech industries, but less that 15 percent in low-tech industries in the late 1990s. The increase in foreign investment in manufacturing since the mid-1980s is mainly due to the attractiveness of medium/high-tech industries.

4. INNOVATIVENESS OF DOMESTIC AND FOREIGN FIRMS

Our main data source is the *Innovation Surveys* conducted by the State Institute of Statistics (SIS). The surveys, the first one conducted in 1998 covering the period 1995–97, and the second one conducted in 2002 covering the period 1998–2000, adopted a questionnaire compatible with the *Community Innovation Survey* of the European Union, and used the concept of 'innovation' as defined in the OECD *Oslo Manual*. The response rates were more than 50 percent in both surveys. The surveys include questions about innovative activities, knowledge sources, interactions, and so on. The SIS performed a non-response analysis and estimated sample weights for each respondent.

Table 7.1 summarizes the data on the innovativeness of domestic and foreign firms in the periods 1995–97 and 1998–2000 for low-tech and medium- and high-tech industries.[8] It is interesting to observe that there is almost no difference in terms of product innovations between domestic and foreign firms in low-tech industries. For example, only 11.2 percent of domestic firms introduced any product innovation in the period 1995–97, whereas the proportion of foreign firms that introduced product innovations in the same period is even lower (9.1 percent). The proportion of innovative firms has increased in the second time period (1998–2000), but the difference between domestic and foreign firms is not significant. Foreign firms in low-tech industries seem to become more successful in process innovations than their domestic counterparts in the second time period.

Firms operating in the high-tech industries are almost twice as innovative as firms operating in low-tech industries, and foreign firms in these

Table 7.1 Innovativeness of domestic and foreign firms,1995–97 and 1998–2000 (proportion of innovative firms)

	1995–97			1998–2000		
	Domestic firms	Foreign firms	Majority-owned foreign firms	Domestic firms	Foreign firms	Majority-owned foreign firms
Product innovations						
Low-tech	0.112	0.091	0.065	0.143	0.162	0.175
Medium- and high-tech	0.278	0.526	0.493	0.325	0.601	0.614
Process innovations						
Low-tech	0.159	0.163	0.126	0.193	0.387	0.435
Medium- and high-tech	0.280	0.453	0.423	0.279	0.483	0.480
Innovative (product and/or process innovations)						
Low-tech	0.191	0.169	0.130	0.250	0.425	0.476
Medium- and high-tech	0.378	0.563	0.541	0.419	0.680	0.685
Product/process innovators ratio						
Low-tech	0.704	0.558	0.516	0.741	0.419	0.402
Medium- and high-tech	0.993	1.161	1.165	1.165	1.244	1.279
n						
Low-tech	1301	68	44	1391	83	66
Medium- and high-tech	646	79	45	770	94	67

Source: SIS, Innovation Surveys, 1998 and 2002.

133

industries are undoubtedly superior to domestic firms in innovativeness. The data provide strong evidence supporting the argument that domestic firms are technologically weaker than foreign firms in high-tech industries.

The relative importance of product and process innovations differs in low-tech and high-tech industries, and the ownership of the firm matters for the type of innovation. Product/process innovators' ratio is much lower in low-tech industries than in high-tech industries. In other words, process innovations are more common than product innovations in low-tech industries. Moreover, MNCs put more emphasis on process innovations than do domestic firms. Since low-tech industries tend to have 'mature' product technologies, process innovations are likely to play a more important role for competitiveness, whereas foreign firms seem to have a competitive advantage over domestic firms.

Product/process innovators' ratio is much higher in high-tech industries than in low-tech industries, and foreign firms have an even higher ratio of product-to-process innovations. This finding supports the perception that high-tech industries play a leading role in developing new products.

The distribution of innovation expenditures over various categories of activities provides additional evidence on the differences in technological activities between domestic and foreign firms (Table 7.2). The major difference is observed in the case of in-house R&D activities: domestic firms in low-tech industries spend relatively more on in-house R&D activities than do foreign firms. In other words, building technological capabilities on the basis of in-house R&D seems to be more important for domestic firms in low-tech industries. Moreover, technology embodied in machinery and equipment and learning-by-doing (production process) have higher shares in domestic firms, whereas marketing-related activities account for almost one-quarter of innovative activities in foreign firms.

As may be expected, in-house R&D has a much higher share in innovation expenditures in high-tech industries, especially in foreign firms: it accounts for exactly half of innovation expenditures in foreign firms, and almost one-third in domestic firms in the period 1998–2000. Domestic firms allocate somewhat higher proportions of expenditures for technology embodied in machinery and equipment and learning-by-doing activities. It is interesting that marketing-related activities have almost the same share in domestic and foreign firms in high-tech industries.

Innovative firms in low- and high-tech industries have a similar pattern of R&D cooperation (Table 7.3). The only noticeable difference is the fact that cooperation with users takes place more frequently in high-tech industries.

More than half of innovative domestic firms are not involved in any type of cooperation in R&D activities. Cooperation with foreign organizations is even less likely for domestic firms (about 10 percent of innovative firms).

Table 7.2 Distribution of innovation expenditures, 1995–97 and 1998–2000

	1995–97			1998–2000		
	Domestic firms	Foreign firms	Majority-owned foreign firms	Domestic firms	Foreign firms	Majority-owned foreign firms
Low-tech industries						
In-house R&D	0.118	0.036	0.032	0.147	0.050	0.048
Contract R&D	0.035	0.077	0.112	0.016	0.006	0.007
Machinery & equipment	0.617	0.587	0.486	0.698	0.606	0.608
Technology transfer	0.026	0.035	0.020	0.020	0.101	0.106
Production process	0.061	0.035	0.029	0.041	0.004	0.004
Training	0.022	0.037	0.056	0.027	0.005	0.006
Marketing	0.121	0.193	0.265	0.051	0.227	0.221
n	301	26	18	223	19	17
Medium-and high-tech industries						
In-house R&D	0.187	0.283	0.227	0.297	0.503	0.502
Contract R&D	0.057	0.038	0.030	0.020	0.010	0.011
Machinery & equipment	0.529	0.477	0.596	0.443	0.352	0.340
Technology transfer	0.018	0.046	0.051	0.034	0.019	0.021
Production process	0.105	0.044	0.017	0.087	0.028	0.033
Training	0.034	0.016	0.018	0.021	0.023	0.027
Marketing	0.070	0.096	0.061	0.098	0.065	0.066
n	264	51	27	228	40	29

Source: SIS, Innovation Surveys, 1998 and 2002.

Table 7.3 *R&D cooperation by ownership, 1998–2000 (proportion of R&D cooperations)*

Partner		1995–97			1998–2000		
		Domestic firms	Foreign firms	Majority-owned foreign firms	Domestic firms	Foreign firms	Majority-owned foreign firms
Low-tech industries							
Domestic	Own group	0.033	0.134	0.075	0.060	0.050	0.044
	Users	0.027	0.178	0.182	0.060	0.074	0.072
	Consultants	0.090	0.112	0.083	0.041	0.213	0.226
	Suppliers	0.035	0.156	0.177	0.087	0.243	0.227
	Universities/non-profit	0.085	0.195	0.183	0.151	0.252	0.247
Foreign	Own group	0.012	0.325	0.413	0.007	0.194	0.194
	Users	0.023	0.000	0.000	0.003	0.089	0.088
	Consultants	0.025	0.140	0.128	0.070	0.031	0.012
	Suppliers	0.037	0.202	0.256	0.037	0.088	0.055
	Universities/non-profit	0.009	0.018	0.028	0.003	0.010	0.011
n		443	37	23	470	49	41

Medium- and high-tech industries

Domestic	Own group	0.081	0.171	0.109	0.051	0.038	0.005
	Users	0.119	0.159	0.096	0.102	0.451	0.552
	Consultants	0.089	0.070	0.033	0.042	0.297	0.353
	Suppliers	0.098	0.106	0.087	0.074	0.176	0.148
	Universities/non-profit	0.183	0.279	0.204	0.094	0.216	0.204
Foreign	Own group	0.028	0.180	0.232	0.002	0.594	0.718
	Users	0.043	0.079	0.054	0.041	0.137	0.129
	Consultants	0.047	0.020	0.000	0.023	0.086	0.027
	Suppliers	0.087	0.177	0.176	0.039	0.132	0.104
	Universities/non-profit	0.010	0.000	0.00	0.008	0.023	0.023
n		321	62	35	402	71	50

Note: The total may exceed one because a firm can cooperate with more than one type of organization.

Source: SIS, Innovation Surveys, 1998 and 2002.

137

On the other hand, irrespective of the sector they operate in, foreign firms have more intensive contacts with other organizations. The most important partner for foreign firms is their sister companies belonging to the same business group. However, it is interesting to observe that foreign firms have closer links with domestic organizations than do domestic firms. In both low- and high-tech industries, foreign firms are more likely than domestic firms to establish R&D cooperation with domestic suppliers and universities/non-profit organizations. Moreover, domestic users are likely to participate in innovation networks of high-tech foreign firms.

5. DETERMINANTS OF INNOVATION AND TECHNOLOGY TRANSFER ACTIVITIES

The descriptive statistics show that there are substantial differences both in terms of innovativeness and in the way innovative activities are performed by domestic and foreign firms. In this section, we will test the impact of foreign ownership and the existence of foreign firms on technological activities.

We assume that technologies acquired through innovative activities improve the productivity of the firm as follows:

$$Q = f(A, K, L, E, M) \tag{7.1}$$

$$A = A_0 e^{\delta \, INNO} \tag{7.2}$$

where Q is (real) output, K, L, E and M are (real) capital, labor, energy and materials inputs. A_0 is the base-line productivity level, and δ is the effects of innovation on productivity. Innovativeness depends on a number of firm- and sector-specific factors as follows:

$$INNO_i = \alpha_0 + \Sigma \alpha_{ij} x_{ij} + \Sigma \alpha_{ij} z_{ij}, \quad i = 1, \ldots, n, \ j = 1, \ldots, k, \ k+1, \ldots, m \tag{7.3}$$

where xs are k firm-specific variables and zs are $m-k$ sector-specific variables. *INNO* is a dummy variable that takes the value 1 if the firm is innovative.[9] Since the innovation variable is endogenous in the output model (equation 7.1), we first estimate equation 7.3, and then estimate the output equation by adding the inverse-Mills ratios (obtained from the estimation of equation 7.3) to have unbiased estimation.[10]

The following variables are included in the innovation equation: *FDI* is a dummy variable that takes the value 1 for joint ventures where foreign ownership is 10 percent or more. *FDIMAJ* is a dummy variable for majority-owned foreign firms. These two dummy variables are used to test if foreign firms are more innovative than domestic firms.

We use three variables to capture the effects of foreign presence on technological activities of manufacturing firms. The first variable, *QFDISH*, measures the share[11] of foreign (*FDI*) firms in the market. If there are sectoral (horizontal) spillovers from foreign firms, other firms in the same market could become more innovative by exploiting these spillovers. The second and third variables, *FDISHSUP* and *FDISHBUY*, measure the weighted average of foreign ownership in supplier and user industries, respectively. These variables are defined as follows:

$$FDISHSUP_i = \Sigma \omega_{ij} s_j$$

$$FDISHBUY_i = \Sigma \acute{\omega}_{ij} s_j$$

where s_j is the market share of foreign firms in market j, ω_{ij} the jth sector's share in inputs used by the ith sector, and $\acute{\omega}_{ij}$ the share of jth sector in the use of ith sector's output. *FDISHSUP* measures the proportion of firm's inputs produced by foreign firms, and *FDISHBUY* measures the proportion of firm's output used by foreign firms. ω and $\acute{\omega}$ variables are calculated from the 1996 Input–Output Table. If vertical relations/networks are used to transfer knowledge from foreign firms, these two variables are expected to have a positive impact on technological activities.

The size of the firm is considered to be one of the main determinants of innovative activities. Thus we include the (log) number of employees (*LL*) to test the impact of firm size on technological activities. Since there could be a non-linear relationship, the square of the size variable (*LL2*) is also included in the models.

The main input for innovation process is investment in R&D activities. The R&D intensity (*RDINT*, R&D expenditures/sales ratio) is used to determine the effect of R&D activities on innovation.

User–producer relations are important elements of a system of innovation, which enables knowledge flows through the exchange of commodities. But *untraded interdependencies* in a system can take the form of 'technological complementarities, synergies, flows of stimuli and constraints' (Dosi, 2000b), not necessarily induced by the flow of commodities, but an informal exchange of knowledge between users and producers. These synergies at the regional and sectoral level are captured by the R&D intensity of firms operating in the same province (*REGRD*) and in the same sector (*SECTRD*), respectively.

The effects of subcontracting relations on technological activities are tested by using two variables, *SINPUT* (the share of subcontracted inputs in total inputs) and *SOUTPUT* (the share of output subcontracted by other firms in total output). These variables are used to check if subcontract-receiving (*SOUTPUT*) and subcontract-offering (*SINPUT*) firms are more innovative.

Finally, there are three additional firm-specific variables: *GROUP* is a dummy variable that takes the value 1 if the firm belongs to a business group. This variable is used to test if membership in a business group yields any benefit for technological activities. The variable *INTERNET* is defined by the proportion of employees who have direct access to the Internet on the job. If technological activities require extensive exchange of information (and, of course, if the Internet provides the basis for information exchange), this variable is expected to have a positive coefficient. The third variable, *LTURN*, is the ratio of the number of employees fired in a year to the average number of employees (average employment plus the number of employees fired). This variable is used to measure labor flexibility, which is likely to have a negative impact on innovative activities (see Kleinknecht, 1998; Michie and Sheehan, 2003).

Table 7.4 presents the descriptive statistics on all variables used in the regression analysis. As mentioned in the previous sections, the shares of innovative and foreign firms are much higher in high-tech industries than in low-tech industries. Firms in high-tech industries are somewhat smaller than firms in low-tech industries, and spend relatively more on R&D activities (however, note that the average R&D intensity is only 0.22 percent for firms in high-tech industries). Regional R&D intensity is almost the same for both groups of firms; that is, high-tech firms do not cluster in specific provinces, but, as expected, the sectoral R&D intensity is much higher in high-tech industries. The average market share of foreign firms is higher in high-tech industries, and foreign firms have a larger market share in their vertically related industries. Most of the firms in low-tech industries operate in textile and food industries, and high-tech firms are observed mainly in engineering and chemicals industries.

The *Innovation Surveys* are available for two time periods, 1995–97 and 1998–2000. The data for these two time periods are pooled together in the regression analysis, and a dummy variable for the second period is used to capture exogenous changes in the dependent variables over time. Moreover, dummy variables for 2-digit industries are added into all models to control for unobserved sector-specific factors.

Regression results summarized in Table 7.5 show that foreign ownership matters for innovativeness neither in low-tech nor in high-tech industries after controlling for all other variables. Both the *FDI* and *FDIMAJ* variables have statistically insignificant coefficients at the 5 percent level.

The market share of foreign firms (*QFDISH*) has a positive impact on innovativeness in low-tech industries whereas it does not have any impact in high-tech industries. This result is somewhat surprising because, as mentioned in the introductory section, technologically advanced domestic firms are expected to take advantage of spillovers. Therefore the positive impact of the presence of foreign firms in low-tech industries can also be taken as an indicator of competitive pressures on domestic firms.

Foreign investment in supplier industries seems to be detrimental to innovative activities in both low-tech and high-tech industries: the higher the share of foreign firms in supplier industries, the lower the innovativeness of firms in user industries. This finding is rather surprising because foreign firms in high-tech industries claim that they cooperate with domestic users in R&D projects (Table 7.3). It is likely that technologically advanced suppliers reduce the incentives to be more innovative because the user firm can benefit from the supplier's technology. On the other hand, foreign investment in user industries induces firms in high-tech industries to be more innovative. This finding may point to the importance of user competence in technological activities.

As expected, R&D intensity is conducive to innovativeness in both low- and high-tech industries. Indeed, R&D intensity is one of the most significant variables, especially for high-tech industries. This evidence provides strong support for the dynamic capability approach. Sectoral knowledge spillovers encourage innovativeness only in low-tech industries.

Firm size has a positive impact on innovative activities in low-tech industries but it is not statistically significant at the 5 percent level. It seems that small firms are as innovative as large firms in high-tech industries where innovativeness is essential for competitiveness (Özçelik and Taymaz, 2004). Business groups fail to improve the innovativeness of their members.

Access to the Internet is another significant variable that has a positive impact on innovativeness in both sectors. Internet access by employees enhances innovativeness of both low- and high-tech firms to a large extent. Labor turnover, that is, labor flexibility, has a negative impact on innovativeness in low-tech industries.

Estimation results of production functions for low-tech and high-tech industries are quite similar. The main difference is observed in the case of labor input. Both the quantity (*LL*) and quality (*SKILLED*) of labor have larger coefficients in high-tech industries.

The *INTERNET* variable, as being one of the most significant variables, picks up much of the variance in the dependent variable. This variable is likely to be influenced by the presence of foreign firms because those domestic firms that are willing to upgrade their technology are likely to adopt the Internet technology. In order to check the robustness of our

Table 7.4 Descriptive statistics (average values for the periods 1995–97 and 1998–2000)

Label	Variable definition	Low-tech industries	Medium- and high-tech industries
Firm-level variables			
INNOVAT	Innovativeness	0.25	0.44
FDI	Foreign-owned firm (foreign ownership 10+)	0.03	0.06
FDIMAJ	Majority-owned foreign firm	0.02	0.05
RDINT	R&D intensity (%)	0.02	0.22
INTERNET	Internet intensity	0.54	0.71
GROUP	Member of a business group	0.07	0.08
SINPUT	Share of subcontracted inputs	0.05	0.03
SOUTPUT	Share of subcontracted outputs	0.07	0.01
LTURN	Labor turnover ratio	0.14	0.15
LL	Employment (log)	3.90	3.75
LQ	Output (log)	10.95	10.90
LK	Depreciation allowances (log)	7.17	7.17
LE	Electricity consumption (log)	12.74	12.39
LM	Inputs (log)	10.50	10.28
SKILLED	Proportion of skilled employees	0.16	0.20
LRW	Real product wage (log)	4.86	5.35

Sector-/region-level variables		
QFDISH	Market share of foreign firms	0.10	0.31
FDISHSUP	Market share of foreign firms in supplier ind	0.07	0.12
FDISHBUY	Market share of foreign firms in user ind	0.03	0.07
REGRD	Regional R&D intensity (%)	0.10	0.12
SECTRD	Sectoral R&D intensity (%)	0.02	0.17
Sectoral distribution of firms			
ISIC 31	Food industries	0.23	0.00
ISIC 32	Textile industries	0.48	0.00
ISIC 33	Wood industries	0.04	0.00
ISIC 34	Paper industries	0.04	0.00
ISIC 35	Chemical industries	0.00	0.30
ISIC 36	Non-metallic minerals industries	0.08	0.00
ISIC 37	Basic metal industries	0.03	0.05
ISIC 38	Engineering industries	0.09	0.65
n	Number of observations	1978	1042

Table 7.5 *Determinants of innovativeness and productivity*

| | Low-tech industries | | | | Medium- and high-tech industries | | | |
| | Innovativeness | | Production | | Innovativeness | | Production | |
	Coeff.	Std dev.	Coeff.	Std dev.	Coeff.	Std dev.	Coeff.	Std dev.
FDI	−0.26	0.14			0.06	0.41		
FDIMAJ	0.46	0.46			0.46	0.44		
QFDISH	0.97	0.27**			0.02	0.18		
FDISHSUP	−2.17	0.95*			−2.28	0.66**		
FDISHBUY	0.79	0.83			2.39	0.87**		
LL	0.31	0.19	0.12	0.01**	−0.19	0.26	0.22	0.02**
LL2	−0.02	0.02			0.03	0.03		
GROUP	0.14	0.12			−0.04	0.19		
INTERNET	0.80	0.08**			1.05	0.12**		
RDINT	0.27	0.13*			0.25	0.07**		
REGRD	0.17	0.27			0.25	0.38		
SECTRD	6.13	1.35**			−0.06	0.24		
SINPUT	−0.68	0.36			−0.16	0.71		
SOUTPUT	0.16	0.18			−0.52	0.62		
LTURN	−0.58	0.26*			−0.62	0.37		

	(1) n = 1978	(2) n = 1978	(3) n = 1042	(4) n = 1042
LM		0.69 (0.01**)		0.68 (0.01**)
LE		0.06 (0.01**)		0.03 (0.01**)
LK		0.08 (0.01**)		0.07 (0.01**)
SKILLED		0.05 (0.05)		0.33 (0.09**)
LRW		0.11 (0.01**)		0.04 (0.01**)
INNOVAT		0.34 (0.07**)		0.32 (0.07**)
λ_{INNO}		-0.17 (0.04**)		-0.17 (0.05**)
ρ		-0.45		-0.44
n	1978	1978	1042	1042
Log-likelihood	-966.6	-807.5	-621.5	-434.6
χ^2/F-test	655.0**	2236.0**	186.2**	1582.5**
Predictions/Adj.R^2	0.685	0.944	0.641	0.948

Note: All models include sector dummies for ISIC 2-digit industries, a dummy for year 2000, and a constant term. **(*) means statistically significant at the 1% (5%) level, two-tailed test.

findings, we estimated the model without the *INTERNET* variable. Estimation results for innovation models remained almost unchanged when the *INTERNET* variable is omitted.[12] The coefficient of the innovation variable (*INNOVATE*) in the production function remained statistically significant but its point estimate was somewhat smaller (0.27 for low-tech and 0.21 for high-tech industries). In other words, our findings do not change qualitatively when the *INTERNET* variable is omitted from the innovation model.

6. CONCLUSIONS

Recent efforts to analyze the complex process of technical change with a systems view contributed to our understanding of the experience of developing countries. This approach is an appropriate framework for explaining the dynamics of lagging behind, catching up and forging ahead observed especially after World War II in which the world economy has extensively and increasingly become knowledge-intensive.

Our analysis of Turkish manufacturing industries shows that foreign firms are more innovative in high-tech industries than their domestic counterparts, transfer technology from (their sister companies) abroad, and tend to establish more cooperative relations with domestic organizations. The superior innovative performance of foreign firms is explained by various firm-specific factors (R&D intensity, Internet access, labor flexibility, etc.). After controlling for all these variables, we found that foreign ownership does not matter for innovativeness. The effects of foreign firms on technological activities of other firms in horizontally and vertically related industries are ambiguous. Foreign presence in user industries induces innovation in high-tech industries, but foreign presence in supplier industries is harmful for innovation in both types of industries.

The poor performance of domestic firms in high-tech industries is worth mentioning. Our descriptive statistics show that domestic firms in high-tech are more innovative than their counterparts in low-tech industries. This can be attributed to the fact that the pace of technological change in high-tech industries is faster than in low-tech ones. However, innovativeness of domestic high-tech firms versus MNCs in the same industry is considerably low. The innovative performance of domestic low-tech firms, on the other hand, is not very different from that of MNCs, especially in the case of product technologies. This implies that there is a technological gap in Turkey in high-tech firms, whereas low-tech domestic firms are close to the frontier. When there is a 'discontinuity in technologies', or a difference in paradigms, as defined by Dosi (2000a), backwardness may not be an advantage for a successful catch-up. On the other hand, when no such differences in para-digms exist, backward countries may be in an advantageous position, as observed in the relatively innovative performance of domestic firms in low-tech industries. Therefore, the catch-up approach based on developmental-ist/modernist understanding is inadequate to explain the technological performance of developing country firms.

NOTES

* The earlier versions of this chapter were presented at the conference in honor of Keith Pavitt, 13–15 November 2003, University of Sussex, Brighton, UK; and in the International Workshop 'Public Research Institutions, International Business, and Technological and Economic Catch-Up in Developing Regions', 19–20 March 2004, University of Catania, Catania, Italy. We are grateful to the participants of both events, in particular John Cantwell and Richard R. Nelson, and the anonymous referee for this volume for their valuable comments and critiques. This chapter partly derives from a background study prepared for the Technology Capability Project that was carried out by the Scientific and Technical Research Council of Turkey.

1. The systems of innovation are called sectoral (Malerba, 2002) and regional (Cooke, 2001), depending on the focus and accepted unit of analysis.
2. However, empirical studies show that host-country characteristics, such as the industry and policy environment (Blomström and Kokko, 1998), the level of human capital stock (Borensztein et al., 1995; Noorbaksh et al., 2001), and absorptive capacity of domestic firms (Kinoshita, 2001) are important determinants of the net benefits the host country can enjoy from MNCs.
3. For the data on inward FDI and a list of all firms with foreign equity participation, see the web site of the Undersecretariat of Treasury (http://www.hazine.gov.tr).
4. The share of manufacturing industry in total FDI was about 88 percent in 1977 (Öniş, 1994, p. 9).
5. Following the usual convention, 'foreign firms' are defined as those joint ventures where foreign ownership is 10 percent or more. If the foreign share is less than 10 percent, it is considered to be portfolio investment. Joint ventures with more than 50 percent foreign ownership are 'majority-owned foreign firms'.
6. The data refer to all *private* establishments employing ten or more people, and all public establishments. The data source is the State Institute of Statistics (SIS) Longitudinal Database. The statistical unit is the 'establishment', which is the main decision-making unit.
7. Cieslik and Ryan (2002) also found a similar shift from minority-owned joint ventures in Central and Eastern Europe in favor of wholly owned foreign firms.
8. We use OECD's definition of low-, medium- and high-tech industries. Since the number of firms operating in high-tech industries is small, medium- and high-tech industries are grouped together, and defined as 'high-tech'.
9. Since product and process innovations are highly correlated, we use a single innovative-ness variable. The *INNO* variable takes the value 1 if the firm introduced a product and/or process innovation in the periods under consideration (1995–97 and 1998–2000).
10. We use the Cobb–Douglas functional form for the production function. Two variables, the proportion of skilled employees and real product wages, are used to control for labor quality.
11. The 'market' is defined at the ISIC 4-digit level (Rev. 2).
12. The only noteworthy change is observed in the coefficient of the size (LL) variable in low-tech industries. Although its sign did not change, it became statistically significant.

REFERENCES

Bell, Clive (1989), 'Development economics', in John Eatwell, Murray Milgate and Peter Newman (eds), *The New Palgrave: Economic Development*, New York: Macmillan, pp. 1–17.

Blomström, Magnus and Ari Kokko (1998), 'The impact of foreign investment on host countries: A review of the empirical evidence', *Journal of Economic Surveys*, **12**, 247–77.

Borensztein, E., J. De Gregorio and J.W. Lee (1995), 'How does foreign direct investment affect economic growth?', NBER Working Papers, No. W5057.

Braga, Helson and Larry Willmore (1991), 'Technological imports and technological effort: An analysis of their determinants in Brazilian firms', *Journal of Industrial Economics*, **39** (4), 421–32.

Cantwell, John (1994), 'Introduction: Transnational corporations and innovatory activities', in John Cantwell (ed.), *Transnational Corporations and Innovatory Activities*, UN Library on Transnational Corporations, vol. 17, London and New York: Routledge.

Chen, Jin and W.G. Qu (2003), 'A new technological learning in China', *Technovation*, **23**, 861–67.

Cieslik, Andrej and Michael Ryan (2002), 'Characterising Japanese direct investment in Central and Eastern Europe: A firm level investigation of the stylized facts and investment characteristics', *Post-Communist Economies*, **14** (4), 509–28.

Cooke, Philip (2001), 'Regional innovation systems, clusters, and the knowledge economy', *Industrial and Corporate Change*, **10** (4), 945–74.

Dahlman, C.J., B. Ross-Larson and Larry Westphal (1987), 'Managing technological development: Lessons from newly industrializing countries', *World Development*, **15** (6), 759–75.

Dosi, Giovanni (1999), 'Some notes on national systems of innovation and production, and their implications for economic analysis', in Daniele Archibugi, Jeremy Howells and Jonathan Michie (eds), *Innovation Policy in a Global Economy*, Cambridge: Cambridge University Press.

Dosi, Giovanni (2000a), 'Technological paradigms and technological trajectories', in *Innovation, Organization and Economic Dynamics: Selected Essays*, Cheltenham, UK and Northampton, MA, USA: Edward Elgar, pp. 47–62 [1982].

Dosi, Giovanni (2000b), 'Sources, procedures and microeconomic effects of innovation', in *Innovation, Organization and Economic Dynamics: Selected Essays*, Cheltenham, UK and Northampton, MA, USA: Edward Elgar, pp. 63–114 [1988].

Dosi, Giovanni (2000c), 'Institutions and markets in a dynamic world', in *Innovation, Organization and Economic Dynamics: Selected Essays*, Cheltenham, UK and Northampton, MA, USA: Edward Elgar, pp. 593–620 [1988].

Dosi, Giovanni and Luigi Marengo (2000), 'Some elements of evolutionary theory of organizational competences', in Giovanni Dosi (ed.), *Innovation, Organization and Economic Dynamics: Selected Essays*, Cheltenham, UK and Northampton, MA, USA: Edward Elgar, pp. 211–35 [1994].

Erdilek, Asim (1982), *Direct Foreign Investment in Turkish Manufacturing*, Tübingen: J.C.B. Mohr.

Erdilek, Asim (1986), 'Turkey's new open-door policy of direct foreign investment: A critical analysis of problems and prospects', *METU Studies in Development*, **13**, 171–91.

Freeman, Chris (1987), *Technology Policy and Economic Performance: Lessons from Japan*, London: Pinter.

Freeman, Chris (1988), 'Japan: a new institutional system of innovation?', in Giovanni Dosi, Christopher Freeman, Richard Nelson, Gerald Silverberg and Luc Soete (eds), *Technical Change and Economic Theory*, London and New York: Pinter.

Freeman, Chris (2002), 'Continental, national and sub-national innovation systems – complementarity and economic growth', *Research Policy*, **31**, 191–211.

Katrak, Homi (1997), 'Developing countries imports of technology, in-house technological capabilities and efforts: An analysis of the Indian experience', *Journal of Development Economics*, **53**, 67–83.

Kepenek, Yakup and Nurhan Yentürk (2000), *Türkiye Ekonomisi*, 10th ed, Istanbul: Remzi Kitapevi.

Kinoshita, Y. (2001), 'R&D and Technology Spillovers via FDI: Innovation and Absorptive Capacity', University of Michigan Business School Working Papers, No. 349a, William Davidson Institute.

Kim, Linsu (2000), 'Korea's national innovation system in transition', in Linsu Kim and Richard R Nelson (eds), *Technology, Learning and Innovation*, Cambridge: Cambridge University Press, pp. 335–60.

Kleinknecht, A. (1998), 'Is labour market flexibility harmful to innovation?', *Cambridge Journal of Economics*, **22**, 387–96.

Lall, Sanjaya (1980), 'Promoting technology development: The role of technology transfer and indigenous effort', *Third World Quarterly*, **14** (1), 95–109.

Lall, Sanjaya (1992), 'Technological capabilities and industrialization', *World Development*, **20** (2), 165–86.

Lundvall, Bengt-Åke (1988), 'Innovation as an interactive process: From user–producer interaction to national systems of innovation', in Giovanni Dosi, Christopher Freeman, Richard Nelson, Gerald Silverberg and Luc Soete (eds), *Technological Change and Economic Theory*, London and New York: Pinter.

Lundvall, Bengt-Åke (1992), 'Introduction', *National Systems of Innovation: Towards a Theory of Innovation and Interactive Learning*, London: Pinter.

Malerba, Franco (2002), 'Sectoral systems of innovation and production', *Research Policy*, **31**, 247–64.

Mansfield, Edwin (1994), 'Technology and technological change', in John Cantwell (ed.), *Transnational Corporations and Innovatory Activities*, UN Library on Transnational Corporations, vol. 17, London and New York: Routledge.

Metcalfe, J.S. (1994), 'Evolutionary economics and technology policy', *The Economic Journal*, **104** (July), 931–44.

Michie, J. and M. Sheehan (2003), 'Labour market deregulation, "flexibility", and innovation', *Cambridge Journal of Economics*, **27**, 123–43.

Nelson, Richard R. (1988), 'Institutions supporting technical change in the United States' in Giovanni Dosi, Christopher Freeman, Richard Nelson, Gerald Silverberg and Luc Soete (eds), *Technological Change and Economic Theory*, London and New York: Pinter.

Nelson, Richard R. (1993), *National Innovation Systems: A Comparative Analysis*, New York: Oxford University Press.

Nelson, Richard R. and Nathan Rosenberg (1993), 'Technical innovation and national systems', in R.R. Nelson (ed.), *National Innovation Systems: A Comparative Analysis*, New York: Oxford University Press.

Nelson, Richard R. and Sydney Winter (1982), *Evolutionary Theory of Economic Change*, Boston, MA: Harvard University Press.

Noorbaksh, F., A. Paloni and A. Youssef (2001), 'Human capital and FDI flows into developing countries: New empirical evidence', *World Development*, **29**, 1593–610.

OECD (1999), *Boosting Innovation: The Cluster Approach*, OECD Proceedings, Paris: OECD.

OECD (2000), *Innovation and Economic Performance*, Paris: OECD.

Öniş, Ziya. (1994), 'Liberalization, transnational corporations and foreign direct investment in Turkey: The experience of the 1980s', in Ş. Fikret (ed.), *Recent Industrialization Experience of Turkey in a Global Context*, Westport, CT and London: Greenwood Press, pp. 91–109.

Özçelik, Emre and Erol Taymaz (2004), 'Does technology matter for international competitiveness in developing countries? The case of Turkish manufacturing industries', *Research Policy*, **33**, 409–24.

Pavitt, Keith and Parimal Patel (1999), 'Global corporations and national systems of innovation: Who dominates whom?', in D. Archibugi, J. Howells and J. Michie (eds), *Innovation Policy in a Global Economy*, Cambridge: Cambridge University Press, pp. 94–119.

Radosevic, Slavo (1999), *International Technology Transfer and Catch-up in Economic Development*, Cheltenham, UK and Northampton, MA, USA: Edward Edgar.

Rosenberg, Nathan (1982), *Inside the Black Box: Technology and Economics*, Cambridge: Cambridge University Press.

Smith, Keith (1995), 'Interactions in knowledge systems: Foundations, policy implications and empirical methods', *Science, Technology, Industry*, **16**, 69–102.

Teece, David J. (1994), 'Profiting from technological innovation: Implications for integration, collaboration and public policy', in John Cantwell (ed.), *Transnational Corporations and Innovatory Activities*, UN Library on Transnational Corporations, vol. 17, London and New York: Routledge, pp. 73–106 [1986].

Teece, David J. (2000), 'Firm capabilities and economic development: Implications for newly industrializing economies', in Linsu Kim and Richard R Nelson (eds), *Technology, Learning and Innovation*, Cambridge: Cambridge University Press, pp. 105–28.

Teece, David J., Gary Pisano and Amy Shuen (2000), 'Dynamic capabilities and strategic management', in *Nature and Dynamics of Organizational Capabilities*, Oxford: Oxford University Press, pp. 334–63.

Veugelers, Reinhilde (1997), 'Internal R&D expenditures and external technology sourcing', *Research Policy*, **26**, 303–15.

Veugelers, Reinhilde and Bruno Cassiman (1999), 'Make and buy in innovation strategies: Evidence from Belgian manufacturing firms', *Research Policy*, **28** (1), 63–80.

8. Multinationality and innovative behaviour in Italian manufacturing firms

Davide Castellani and Antonello Zanfei

1. INTRODUCTION

Over the past decade there has been a remarkable increase in the foreign ownership of assets in Europe. This has attracted the interest of both scholars and practitioners in the effects of inward investments, and *inter alia* in technological opportunities provided by foreign firms in advanced economies. From this perspective, a key issue is whether and to what extent foreign-owned companies possess superior technology as compared to domestic firms. Several empirical studies have attempted to address this issue by analysing differences in productivity of foreign and domestic companies, controlling for a number of attributes of firms. There is substantial evidence that foreign-owned firms outperform domestic firms in host countries, but more recent works have shown that multinationality is more relevant than foreign ownership as a determinant of performance gaps (see Bellak, 2002 for a review). In particular, foreign-owned firms, which are by definition *multinational companies*, exhibit a higher productivity as compared to domestic *uni-national* firms, while non-significant (or even negative) differences emerge with reference to domestic multinationals (Doms and Jensen, 1998; Pfaffermayer and Bellak, 2002; Bellman and Jungnickel, 2002; Criscuolo and Martin, 2003; De Backer and Sleuwaegen, 2003).

This is consistent with the theory that firms, whether foreign or domestic owned, need to have some form of *ex ante* advantage in order to be able to compete in international markets (Dunning, 1970; Caves, 1974; Markusen, 1995). And it is also consistent with the increasing perception that multinationality can generate further (*ex post*) advantages, as it allows access to multiple, geographically dispersed sources of knowledge (Dunning, 1993; Fosfuri and Motta, 1999; Siotis, 1999; Zanfei, 2000; Cantwell and Narula, 2001).

151

This chapter builds on this growing literature, and provides evidence on differences in technological performances of foreign and domestic manufacturing firms active in Italy over the second half of the 1990s, focusing on the role of multinationality as a source of heterogeneity. We improve on existing literature from two points of view. First, we use data on innovative behaviour for 1994–96, based on the Second Community Innovation Survey (CIS II), and we compare them with data on productivity of foreign and domestic (multinational and uni-national) firms. This has never been done for Italy; nor do we have knowledge of other works systematically comparing innovative activities across the same categories of firms for the whole of manufacturing industry in any country.[1] Considering productivity alone would provide only a spurious and indirect measure of technology. Although recent studies have attempted to disentangle technical efficiency from scale and monopoly power effects underlying differences in productivity (Girma and Gorg, 2002), it is still the case that not all technical change will translate into a higher output-to-input ratio. For example, Parisi et al. (2002) find that while an increase in process innovation is normally associated with higher total factor productivity, product innovation does not have any effect. It thus appears to be useful to consider other, more direct measures of innovative activity and behaviour, indicating for instance whether firms have actually introduced process and product innovation, whether they were engaged in R&D and patenting activities, and whether they were involved in different forms of technological collaborations with third parties.

Second, we also attempt to improve the analysis of technological diversity across firms by introducing a more useful categorization of multinationals. Not only do we distinguish between foreign-owned multinationals, domestic multinationals and domestic uni-national firms, as is more and more frequently done in the empirical literature; we also break down the subset of domestic multinationals according to the nature of activities carried out by their affiliates abroad, and according to the position of firms within the multinational group they belong to. More precisely, we first separate 'domestic manufacturing MNCs' (owned by domestic companies and having at least one manufacturing subsidiary abroad) from 'domestic non-manufacturing MNCs' (owned by domestic companies and having foreign affiliates carrying out *only* non-manufacturing activities, mainly sales).[2] Domestic firms belonging to the two types of multinationals may have different productivity and innovative behaviour, reflecting their distinct structural characteristics and motivations. In fact, the creation of manufacturing subsidiaries appears to correspond to a greater commitment to foreign markets, as compared with the mere setting up of sales affiliates abroad. Higher sunk costs associated with the former strategy can be more easily dealt with by more productive firms. A similar line of argument has been recently formalized by Helpman et al. (2004) with reference to the export versus FDI alternative. Furthermore, other streams of literature have emphasized that the higher the engagement in international production, the wider the access to foreign knowledge sources (see Narula and Zanfei, 2005 for a review). This view would also help explain why firms creating manufacturing affiliates abroad would perform better than those with foreign commercialization facilities only.

The second distinction we make is between firms that are affiliates of a domestic multinational group, and those that are parent companies. Given this distinction, one can highlight how foreign affiliates in Italy differ from affiliates of domestic multinationals active in the same country, but also from the headquarters of domestic multinationals. While the former comparison may make more sense from an organizational point of view, as firms would occupy a similar position in each other's multinational group, the latter comparison may be more relevant from an industrial policy point of view. It might be suggested that it is particularly worth favouring the presence of foreign-owned investors when these have significantly higher technological levels than parent companies of domestic multinationals. If this were not the case, the costs of promoting inward direct investments would most likely exceed the benefits, and stimulating the birth and growth of dynamic domestic-owned multinationals would be preferable. In fact, parent companies of domestic multinationals can have access to foreign sources of knowledge much like foreign multinationals, but have closer access to national sources of innovation (including their own central R&D facilities at home, if they exist), and may have higher incentives to interact, and exchange technology, with other domestic firms.

The rest of this chapter is structured as follows. Section 2 illustrates our data sets, the firm categories we use, and the econometric specification we adopt to analyse differences in productivity and innovation. Section 3 discusses the main results of comparisons between affiliates of foreign firms, domestic multinationals, and domestic uni-national firms. Section 4 concludes.

2.   DATA AND SPECIFICATION

The empirical analysis presented in this chapter is based on a data set resulting from the intersection of two different sources: the Second Community Innovation Survey (CIS II) and ELIOS (European Linkages and Ownership Structure). The former is a survey based on a common questionnaire administered by Eurostat to firms from all European countries which aims to assess various aspects of firms' innovative behaviour and performances. Subject to a confidentiality agreement, we were allowed to access micro-data for Italy from the survey carried out in 1996 and covering innovation occurring in 1994–96.[3] Innovation data were complemented by ownership, multinationality and economic performance data from the ELIOS data set developed by the University of Urbino, Italy, which combines information from Dun & Bradstreet's Who Owns Whom and Bureau Van Dijck's Amadeus. The sample resulting from this matching is 1114 manufacturing firms. Balcet and Evangelista (2003) utilize part of the same data set to characterize innovative patterns of foreign-owned firms in Italy. In contrast to that work, we not only draw information on foreign-owned firms (i.e. affiliates of foreign multinationals located in Italy), but also on domestic-owned firms. As mentioned in the introduction, we break down the subset of domestic firms, distinguishing between uni-national firms and different categories of domestic multinational firms, namely those that are part of a multinational group with manufacturing subsidiaries abroad, and those which are part of a multinational group with non-manufacturing (mainly sales) subsidiaries in foreign markets. For each of these categories of domestic multinational firms we also distinguish headquarters and subsidiaries active in Italy. Figure 8.1 provides a graphical representation of the sample and of its various subsets of firms. To summarize, the 1114 sample firms are all active in manufacturing sectors in Italy, of which 325 are foreign-owned firms (i.e. Italian affiliates of foreign MNCs) denoted as *FOR*, 467 are firms part of an Italian multinational (*MNCGRP*), while 322 are domestic uni-national firms (DOM). Out of the 467 firms part of a multinational group, only 275 belong to groups controlling at least one foreign manufacturing firm; that is, they are part of 'domestic manufacturing multinationals'.[4]

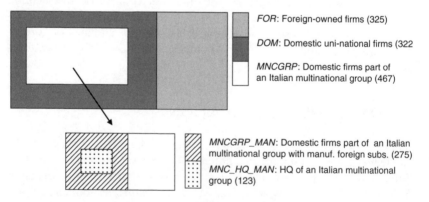

Figure 8.1   Definition of groups of firms in the sample

We denote this subset *MNCGRP_MAN*. Some 123 of these firms are head-quarter companies of domestic manufacturing multinationals.[5] Firms that are not headquarters but do belong to a domestic manufacturing multina-tional, and hence are national subsidiaries of such an MNC, will then add up to 152. This subsample is the most closely 'comparable' to the subsam-ple of Italian subsidiaries of foreign firms (FOR), at least from an organi-zational point of view.

Table 8.1 provides some further details on the sectoral composition of firms, including their size, together with the main indicators of their tech-nological activities, as expressed in terms of total factor productivity, the share of innovative firms and product-to-process-innovation ratio in each of the examined subsamples. It suffices here to note three important features of the examined sample. First, the average size of sampled firms is relatively high, certainly higher relative to the universe of manufacturing firms in Italy, but the distribution of firms by Pavitt sectors and by low–medium–high technology classes substantially corresponds to the specialization of Italy's industry: a high overall weight of traditional, supplier-dominated and scale-intensive industries, and a very small share of firms active in science-based industries (an even smaller share in the case of high-technology industries, as classified by OECD).[6] Second, the share of science-based (and high-tech) activities is slightly higher in the case of affiliates of foreign-owned multi-nationals (FOR) than is the case of domestic firms. This largely corresponds to the sectoral distribution of foreign affiliates as recorded by available sta-tistics produced by Reprint Dataset and ultimately published in OECD's *Measuring globalisation* for Italy (CNEL, 2002; OECD, 2002). Third and finally, foreign-owned manufacturing affiliates (FOR) appear to be system-atically more productive and more innovative by all indicators in Table 8.1, as compared to domestic uni-national firms (DOM), and the former also have a higher product-to-process-innovation ratio than the latter. However, the scenario is much more blurred once we compare foreign affiliates to the other categories of domestic-owned multinational firms.

Of course, the figures in Table 8.1 only allow for rough comparisons without any controls. A more precise analysis requires the use of multi-variate techniques. We shall first estimate the following expression:

$$y_t = \alpha + \beta\ FOR_t + \delta_1 MNCGRP_t + Z'_t\gamma + \varepsilon_t,$$

where *y* denotes a measure of firm performance or a characteristic of its innovative behaviour (see Table 8.2), **Z** is a vector of controls such as firm age, sector, region and size dummies, and *FOR* and *MNCGRP* are defined as above. Within this context, β and δ_1 represent the difference in

Table 8.1 *Descriptive statistics*

	DOM	FOR	MNCGRP	MNCGRP MAN	MNC_HQ MAN	Total
No. of firms	322	325	467	275	123	1114
%	28.9	29.2	41.9	24.7	11.0	100
No. of firms						
By Pavitt sectors						
Science-based	8.3	15.6	9.8	10.1	8.1	10.5
Scale-intensive	39.9	46.7	38.9	46.5	39.8	41.9
Specialized suppliers	19.2	22.1	20.7	21	26.8	20.1
Supplier-dominated	32.4	15.3	30.4	22.1	25.2	27.4
	100	100	100	100	100	100
By tech.class						
Low-tech	32.8	17.1	29.0	26.8	26.0	28.2
Medium–low-tech	27.2	24.6	27.3	24.6	25.2	26.4
Medium–high-tech	34.3	46.7	37	40.1	43.0	38.0
High-tech	5.5	11.5	6.6	8.3	5.6	7.3
	100	100	100	100	100	100
No. of employees	90 199	209 136	512 208	345 649	202 395	811 543
%	11.1	25.8	63.1	42.6	24.9	100
Avg. no. employees	338	706	1208	1382	1732	822
Avg. TFP	1.02	1.05	1.05	1.08	1.10	1.04
No. product innov.	169	225	306	184	98	700
Share in total firms (%)	52	69	66	67	80	63
No. process innov.	179	206	304	188	95	689
Share in total firms (%)	56	63	65	68	77	62
Product/process innov.	0.94	1.09	1.01	0.98	1.03	1.02

Table 8.2   Indicators of firm performance and innovative behaviour

Variable	Description	Source
Performance		
TFP	Log of the *TFP* of firm *i*	ELIOS
WAGE	Log of the (gross) cost of labour per employee	ELIOS
Innovation		
INPDT	= 1 if firm *i* introduced product innovation in 1994–96	CIS2
INPCS	= 1 if firm *i* introduced process innovation in 1994–96	CIS2
RTOT	= 1 if firm *i* spent any money in R&D activities (both intra and extra muros)	CIS2
PAT	= 1 if firm *i* applied for at least one patent in 1994–96	CIS2
CO_NAZ	= 1 if firm *i* had some technological cooperation with Italian counterparts in 1994–96	CIS2
CO_INT	= 1 if firm *i* had some technological cooperation with foreign counterparts in 1994–96	CIS2
CO1	= 1 if firm *i* had some technological cooperation with firms within the same group	CIS2
CO3	= 1 if firm *i* had some technological cooperation with clients	CIS2
CO5	= 1 if firm *i* had some technological cooperation with suppliers	CIS2
CO6	= 1 if firm *i* had some technological cooperation with universities	CIS2

performance or innovative behaviour of foreign-owned firms and of firms belonging to a domestic multinational group relative to domestic uni-national firms (the baseline category).

We then extend this specification in order to test whether it makes any difference to be part of a domestic manufacturing multinational or the headquarters of such a group. In other words, we estimate:

$$y_t = \alpha + \beta\, FOR_t + \delta_1 MNCGRP_t + \delta_2 MNCGRP\_MAN_t$$
$$+ \delta_3 MNCGRP\_HQ\_MAN_t + Z_t'\gamma + \varepsilon_t$$

In this case, β can be interpreted as before, δ_1 captures differences in performance or innovation between firms belonging to domestic non-manufacturing multinationals and domestic uni-national firms, while δ_2

measures any gap between firms belonging to domestic manufacturing MNCs and firms belonging to other domestic multinational companies, and δ_3 denotes the additional differential at the headquarter level relative to other manufacturing firms belonging to the same multinational group. The difference between parent companies and domestic uni-national firms is the sum of δ_1, δ_2 and δ_3.

3.   RESULTS: COMPARING PRODUCTIVITY AND INNOVATIVE BEHAVIOUR

Results in Table 8.3a are consistent with our prior analysis, derived from the theoretical and empirical literature, that firms belonging to multinational groups (either foreign or domestic owned) outperform domestic uni-national firms and exhibit different innovative patterns. In particular, OLS regression coefficients on *FOR* and *MNCGRP* in TFP and wage equations suggest that foreign-owned firms (and firms belonging to domestic multinationals respectively) are 2.4 per cent (3.8 per cent) more productive and pay 8.7 per cent (4.5 per cent) higher wages than uni-national firms.[7] As regards the probit regressions of the different innovation indicators, the marginal effects reported in Tables 8.3a–c and 8.4 indicate that foreign-owned firms (and firms belonging to domestic multinationals respectively) have a 6.8 per cent (7.4 per cent) higher probability of introducing a product innovation. However, interesting results emerge when we distinguish within domestic multinationals (see Table 8.3b). First, only manufacturing MNCs have higher productivity and pay higher wages *relative to domestic uni-nationals*. In fact, once controlled for *MNCGRP_MAN*, the dummy *MNCGRP* turns non-significantly different from zero, suggesting that TFP and wages in firms belonging to non-manufacturing multinationals are not statistically different from those in uni-national firms. Second, while productivity and wages are not different in headquarters than in other firms belonging to a multinational controlling manufacturing subsidiaries abroad, the probability of carrying out the most crucial innovative activities, including product innovation, R&D, patenting and technological cooperation with foreign parties, appears to be significantly higher at the headquarter level than in the domestic subsidiaries.

It thus appears that productivity premiums are more diffuse across firms belonging to domestic multinationals than is the case with innovative activities. This might have to do with the different nature of indicators used to capture technology gaps across firms. Even setting aside the problem of disentangling efficiency effects from scale and monopoly power effects, productivity indicators are rather limited measures of technology. Changes in

Table 8.3a Differences in performance and innovation, by multinationality and foreign ownership

Dep. var. Estimation method Sample	TFP OLS All firms 1996–2000	WAGE OLS All firms 1996–2000	INPDT Probit All firms 1996	INPCS Probit All firms 1996	PAT* Probit Innov. firms 1996	RTOT* Probit Innov. firms 1996	CO_NAZ* Probit Innov. firms 1996	CO_INT* Probit Innov. firms 1996
FOR	0.024**	0.083**	0.068*	-0.019	-0.095*	0.029	0.011	0.763*
	(0.011)	(0.011)	(0.042)	(0.043)	(0.054)	(0.020)	(0.047)	(0.048)
MNCGRP	0.037**	0.044**	0.074*	0.014	-0.030	0.052**	0.054	0.026
	(0.010)	(0.009)	(0.039)	(0.038)	(0.052)	(0.022)	(0.044)	(0.044)
Test 1	-0.013	0.039**	-0.006	-0.033	-0.065	-0.023	-0.043	0.737
(p-value)	(0.150)	(0.000)	(0.891)	(0.389)	(0.170)	(0.383)	(0.271)	(0.199)
No. obs.	4407	4417	1075	1109	769	634	778	769

Notes: * CIS2 provides detailed information on innovative behaviour only for innovative firms.
Estimated equation: $y_i = \alpha + \beta\,FOR_i + \delta_i MNCGRP_i + Z'_i\gamma + \varepsilon_i$
All regressions are estimated with a constant and controlling for age of the firm, sector, region and size dummies. Standard errors in parentheses below estimates. Asterisks denote confidence levels (**: p<0.05; *: p<0.10).

Test 1: Difference between β and δ_1. Asterisks denote whether it is statistically different from zero.

Table 8.3b Differences in performance and innovative behaviour, by multinationality and foreign ownership

Dep. var. Est. method Sample	TFP OLS All firms 1996–2000	WAGE OLS All firms 1996–2000	INPDT Probit All firms 1996	INPCS Probit All firms 1996	PAT* Probit Innov. firms 1996	RTOT* Probit Innov. firms 1996	CO_NAZ* Probit Innov. firms 1996	CO_INT* Probit Innov. firms 1996
FOR	0.026**	0.086**	0.073*	−0.015	−0.096*	0.028	0.017	0.080*
	(0.011)	(0.011)	(0.042)	(0.043)	(0.054)	(0.018)	(0.047)	(0.048)
MNCGRP	0.010	0.002	0.058	−0.008	−0.003	0.038	−0.033	−0.067
	(0.012)	(0.011)	(0.047)	(0.047)	(0.064)	(0.024)	(0.055)	(0.054)
MNCGRP_MAN	0.042**	0.071**	−0.037	0.001	−0.110	0.015	0.110*	0.083
	(0.144)	(0.013)	(0.060)	(0.057)	(0.072)	(0.034)	(0.067)	(0.066)
MNCGRP_ HQ_MAN	0.014	0.003	0.154**	0.098	0.129*	0.062**	0.071	0.136**
	(0.016)	(0.015)	(0.055)	(0.060)	(0.079)	(0.016)	(0.065)	(0.069)
Test 2	−0.026**	0.013	0.052	−0.008	0.017	−0.025	−0.06**	0.064
(p-value)	(0.048)	(0.318)	(0.330)	(0.876)	(0.786)	(0.792)	(0.030)	(0.188)
Test 3	−0.04**	0.01	−0.102**	−0.106*	−0.112*	−0.087**	−0.131**	−0.072
(p-value)	(0.003)	(0.499)	(0.05)	(0.057)	(0.089)	(0.032)	(0.016)	(0.238)
No. obs.	4407	4417	1075	1109	769	634	778	769

Notes: * CIS2 provides detailed information on innovative behaviour only for innovative firms.
Estimated equation: $y_t = \alpha + \beta\, FOR_t + \delta_1 MNCGRP_t + \delta_2 MNCGRP\_MAN_t$
$\qquad + \delta_3 MNCGRP\_HQ\_MAN_t + Z_t \gamma + \varepsilon_t$

All regressions are estimated with a constant and controlling for age of the firm, sector, region and size dummies. Standard errors in parentheses below estimates. Asterisks denote confidence levels (**: p<0.05; *: p<0.10)

Test 2: Difference between β and ($\delta_1 + \delta_2$). Asterisks denote whether it is statistically different from zero.
Test 3: Difference between β and ($\delta_1 + \delta_2 + \delta_3$). Asterisks denote whether it is statistically different from zero.

Table 8.3c *Differences in technological cooperation, by multinationality and foreign ownership in innovative firms**

Dep. var.	CO1_NAZ	CO1_INT	CO3_NAZ	CO5_NAZ	CO6_NAZ	CO6_INT
Estimation method	Probit	Probit	Probit	Probit	Probit	Probit
Sample	Innovative firms 1996	Innovative firms 1996	Innovative firms 1996	Innovative firms 1996	Innovative firms 1996	Innovative firms 1996
FOR	0.012	0.184**	0.011	0.001	−0.025	−0.007
	(0.029)	(0.047)	(0.028)	(0.022)	(0.028)	(0.018)
MNCGRP	−0.005	−0.041	−0.033	−0.032	−0.036	0.028
	(0.035)	(0.043)	(0.034)	(0.026)	(0.036)	(0.028)
MNCGRP_MAN	0.064	0.096*	0.040	0.090**	0.080*	−0.040**
	(0.048)	(0.067)	(0.048)	(0.051)	(0.053)	(0.019)
MNCGRP_HQ_MAN	0.070*	0.096**	0.022	0.017	0.044	0.164**
	(0.047)	(0.057)	(0.042)	(0.029)	(0.044)	(0.096)
Test 2	−0.047	0.129**	0.004	−0.057	−0.069*	0.005
(p-value)	(0.196)	(0.000)	(0.756)	(0.195)	(0.069)	(0.391)
Test 3	−0.117**	0.033	−0.018	−0.074**	−0.113*	−0.159**
(p-value)	(0.007)	(0.249)	(0.704)	(0.027)	(0.001)	(0.002)
No. obs.	743	760	654	676	723	498

Notes: * CIS2 provides detailed information on innovative behaviour only for innovative firms.

Estimated equation: $y_t = \alpha + \beta\ FOR_t + \delta_1 MNCGRP_t + \delta_2 MNCGRP\_MAN_t$
$+ \delta_3 MNCGRP\_HQ\_MAN_t + Z_t\gamma + \varepsilon_t$

All regressions are estimated with a constant and controlling for age of the firm, sector, region and size dummies. Standard errors in parentheses below estimates. Asterisks denote confidence levels (**: p<0.05; *: p<0.10).

Test 2: Difference between β and $(\delta_1 + \delta_2)$. Asterisks denote whether it is statistically different from zero.
Test 3: Difference between β and $(\delta_1 + \delta_2 + \delta_3)$. Asterisks denote whether it is statistically different from zero.

productivity may well reflect modifications in managerial practices, in the organization of labour and improvements in manufacturing procedures. However, they can hardly account for other innovative activities, such as the introduction of new products or the setting up of technical alliances, which will possibly, but not immediately or necessarily, translate into changes of output per unit inputs. It is not surprising that these innovative activities, which tend to require significant R&D efforts and strategic decision making, are relatively concentrated at both the geographical and organizational level. Conversely, one might venture to say that these results support the hypothesis that managerial practices, organization of labour and improvements in manufacturing procedures can be more easily transferred to all firms belonging to the multinational group than the ability to introduce new products.

Having highlighted some important diversities across domestic multinationals relative to domestic uni-national firms, some remarkable differences also emerge between foreign-owned firms and domestic firms belonging to Italian multinationals (see tests 1, 2 and 3 in Tables 8.3a through 8.3c). Relative to foreign multinationals, headquarters of domestic multinationals have much the same propensity to set up international technological cooperation, but they have 10.2 per cent higher probability of introducing a product innovation, 8.7 per cent higher probability of carrying out R&D, 11.2 per cent higher probability of patenting new technologies and 13.1 per cent higher propensity to engage in cooperation with national partners than affiliates of foreign-owned companies. This is consistent with Balcet and Evangelista (2003), who find that foreign affiliates in Italy are often less innovative than domestic firms (including Italian MNEs) and are characterized by relatively low technological profiles (especially in science-based industries). The point to be made, however, is that the potential for spillovers for the Italian economy is even higher from headquarters of domestic multinationals than in the case of affiliates of foreign firms. This seems to apply in terms of both technological opportunities provided to other domestic firms and in terms of linkage creation with local counterparts. In particular, as shown in Table 8.3c, domestic multinationals have a higher propensity to cooperate with other Italian firms (11.7 per cent) within the same group but also, and most importantly, with domestic suppliers and universities (7.4 per cent and 15.9 per cent respectively). Linkage creation has long been considered perhaps the most important channel through which investment can create technology and productivity spillovers. This view, originally put forward by Hirschman (1958) with reference to all categories of investment creating new demands for inputs and/or new opportunities for downstream activities, has usually been applied to the case of foreign direct investment (see, *inter alia*, Rodriguez-Clare, 1996), although empirical evidence is scarce and most often based on indirect measures of linkage creation. In the case of Italy, we find direct evidence of higher linkage creation for investment by domestic multinationals than is the case for foreign investors.

By contrast, the other (non-headquarter) domestic firms belonging to manufacturing MNCs pay much the same salaries as Italian affiliates of foreign-owned firms and have even higher productivity, but have a lower propensity to innovate products, or to set up technological alliances with foreign partners. There are at least four reasons for such differences. First, foreign subsidiaries need to overcome the cost of operating in a foreign market; hence the parent company may decide to transfer a higher share of strategic activities to affiliates active abroad than to domestic affiliates. Second, foreign affiliates may learn through the interaction with firms and institutions in the host country, thus increasing their innovative ability. Third, a home-country effect may play a role, causing multinationals from relatively more advanced economies and systems of innovation to exhibit better innovation performance. Fourth, foreign multinationals may acquire better firms (the 'cherries') in the host country. In a companion paper we address the 'Cherry-picking' issue (Castellani and Zanfei, 2004), while in Table 8.4 we shed some light on the home-country effect, estimating performance and innovative differentials for foreign-owned firms originating from European countries, from the USA and from other countries (mainly Japan). Results suggest that EU-owned multinationals have a higher probability of carrying out R&D and innovative activities in their Italian affiliates than US multinationals. Furthermore, the latter, consistently with a general characteristic of US firms, tend to pay higher wages and show a very high propensity to engage in international technological cooperation.[8]

4.   CONCLUDING REMARKS

We have shown that significant differences exist in productivity and innovation behaviour of manufacturing firms active in Italy and that multinationality accounts for a large part of this heterogeneity. Foreign and domestic multinationals both pay higher wages, exhibit a higher productivity and a greater propensity to get involved in R&D, product innovation and technological collaboration than domestic uni-national firms. On closer examination, it appears that among domestic multinationals, those with at least some manufacturing activity abroad (and not those with non-manufacturing activity only) exhibit higher productivity. Furthermore, while higher productivity is diffuse throughout all firms belonging to manufacturing multinational groups, crucial innovative activities, including R&D, product innovation and international technological cooperation, are

Table 8.4 Differences in performance and innovative behaviour, by area of origin

Dep. var. Est. method Sample	TFP OLS All firms 1996–2000	WAGE OLS All firms 1996–2000	INPDT Probit All firms 1996	INPCS Probit All firms 1996	PAT* Probit Innov. firms 1996	RDTOT* Probit Innov. firms 1996	CO_NAZ* Probit Innov. firms 1996	CO_INT* Probit Innov. firms 1996
US	0.055**	0.121**	0.042	0.024	−0.088	−0.005	0.003	0.125*
	(0.015)	(0.016)	(0.062)	(0.063)	(0.074)	(0.031)	(0.064)	(0.075)
EU	0.012	0.069**	0.088*	−0.015	−0.090	0.037*	0.031	0.077
	(0.011)	(0.011)	(0.045)	(0.047)	(0.058)	(0.016)	(0.052)	(0.053)
OTH	0.096**	0.150**	−0.019	−0.348	−0.293	0.037	–	–
	(0.048)	(0.039)	(0.186)	(0.176)	(0.164)	(0.024)		
MNCGRP	0.010	0.002	0.058	−0.008	−0.003	−0.015	−0.035	−0.070
	(0.012)	(0.011)	(0.047)	(0.047)	(0.064)	(0.033)	(0.055)	(0.054)
MNCGRP_MAN	0.043**	0.072**	−0.038	0.002	−0.109	−0.015	0.111*	0.086
	(0.014)	(0.013)	(0.060)	(0.057)	(0.072)	(0.033)	(0.067)	(0.067)
MNCGRP_HQ_MAN	0.013	0.002	0.155**	0.098	0.129*	0.061**	0.072	0.137**
	(0.016)	(0.015)	(0.055)	(0.060)	(0.079)	(0.016)	(0.066)	(0.069)
Test 4	0.043**	0.052**	−0.046	0.039	−0.002	−0.042*	−0.028	0.048
(p-value)	(0.003)	(0.001)	(0.467)	(0.531)	(0.985)	(0.097)	(0.657)	(0.500)
No. obs.	4407	4417	1075	1109	769	631	774	769

Notes: * CIS2 provides detailed information on innovative behaviour only for innovative firms.
Estimated equation: $y_i = \alpha + \beta_{US}US_i + \beta_{EU}EU_i + \beta_{OTH}OTH_i + \delta_1 MNCGRP_i + \delta_2 MNCGRP\_MAN_i + \delta_3 MNCGRP\_HQ\_MAN_i + Z_i\gamma + \varepsilon_i.$

All regressions are estimated with a constant and controlling for age of the firm, sector, region and size dummies. Standard errors in parentheses below estimates. Asterisks denote confidence levels (**: p<0.05; *: p<0.10).
Test 4: Difference between β_{US} and β_{EU}. Asterisks denote whether it is statistically different from zero.

more concentrated at the headquarter level. Finally, headquarters of domestic multinationals are even more innovative, and set up more linkages with local firms and institutions, than affiliates of foreign firms in Italy.

It is thus highly desirable that the share of dynamic domestic multinationals grows in the Italian manufacturing industry. However, this does not necessarily mean that a lower inflow of foreign capital is also desirable. First, the inflow is already very low, and foreign-owned assets represent a much lower share of fixed capital formation in Italy than in other EU countries. Second, evidence from previous studies suggests that incoming foreign firms are not gaining control of the most innovative and productive Italian firms (i.e. there is no 'Cherry-picking' effect) (Castellani and Zanfei, 2004) and that there have been positive spillovers from foreign to domestic firms in Italy over the 1990s, at least in terms of productivity (Castellani and Zanfei, 2003). In other words, we may conclude that foreign multinationals are more likely to add to, rather than substitute for, the capacity of domestic firms to innovate and improve their economic performance. Therefore, a case could probably be made for a better promotion and selection of inward investments so as to favour foreign multinationals into higher value-added activities.

NOTES

1. Frenz and Ietto-Gillies (2003) have analysed patterns of innovative activities of multinational and uni-national firms in the UK, but they did not compare innovation with productivity performances in this sector.
2. It might be worth noting that firms included in our sample are only manufacturing firms *active in Italy*, including those belonging to these two types of domestic MNCs. What thus distinguishes Italian manufacturing from non-manufacturing MNCs is the composition of their affiliates *active abroad*.
3. We thank Giulio Perani from the Italian National Statistical Office for allowing us access to these data.
4. However, 192 firms belong to multinational groups controlling only non-manufacturing subsidiaries. We define this kind of multinational group as 'non-manufacturing MNCs'.
5. This suggests that a large proportion of Italian multinationals control only non-manufacturing subsidiaries abroad. In particular, 158 firms can be classified as headquarters of multinationals without any foreign manufacturing subsidiary.
6. In a more detailed analysis, the NACE two-digit sectoral distribution of sample firms turns out to be not significantly different from the Eurostat universe of firms over 50 employees.
7. The implied percentage differences across groups can be obtained directly from the estimated coefficients applying the following formula: percentage difference = exp (coefficient) − 1.
8. Similar patterns of involvement in international technological cooperation by US multinationals have been found by Hagedoorn (2002) with reference to most high-technology industries monitored by the Merit–Cati database. The propensity to pay higher salaries of US multinational companies in Europe has been highlighted *inter alia* by Basile et al. (2003).

REFERENCES

Balcet, G. and Evangelista, R. (2003), 'Global technology: innovative strategies of multinational affiliates in Italy', mimeo.

Basile, R., Castellani, D. and Zanfei, A. (2003), 'Location choices of multinational firms in Europe: the role of national boundaries and EU policy', *Quaderni di Economia, Matematica e Statistica*, no. 78, Università di Urbino.

Bellak, C. (2002), 'How performance gaps between domestic and foreign firms matter for policy', European International Business Academy Conference, Athens, December.

Bellman, L. and Jungnickel, R. (2002), '(Why) do foreign-owned firms in Germany achieve above-average productivity?', in R. Jungnickel (ed.), *Foreign-owned firms: are they different?*, Basingstoke, UK: Palgrave Macmillan.

Cantwell, J. and Narula, R. (2001), 'The eclectic paradigm in the global economy', *International Journal of the Economics of Business*, **8** (2), 155–72.

Castellani, D. and Zanfei, A. (2003), 'Technology gaps, absorptive capacity and the impact of inward investments on productivity of European firms', *Economics of Innovation and New Technology*, **12** (6), 555–76.

Castellani, D. and Zanfei, A. (2004), '"Cherry-picking" and self-selection. Empirical evidence on ex-ante advantages of multinational firms in Italy', *Applied Economics Quarterly*, **50** (1), 5–20.

Caves, R. (1974), 'Multinational firms, competition and productivity in host economies', *Economica*, **41**, 176–93.

CNEL (2002), *Italia Multinazionale 2000*, Consiglio Nazionale per l'Economia e il Lavoro, Roma.

Criscuolo, C. and Martin, R. (2003), 'Multinationals, foreign ownership and US productivity leadership: evidence from the UK', mimeo.

De Backer, K. and Sleuwaegen, L. (2003), 'Why are foreign firms more productive than domestic firms?', mimeo.

Doms, M. and Jensen, B. (1998), 'Comparing wages, skills, and productivity between domestically and foreign-owned manufacturing establishments in the United States', in R. Baldwin, R. Lipsey and J.D. Richardson (eds), *Geography and Ownership as Basis for Economic Accounting*, Chicago, IL: University of Chicago Press.

Dunning, J. (1970), *Studies in International Investment*, London: Allen & Unwin.

Dunning, J. (1993), *Multinational Enterprises and the Global Economy*, Wokingham, UK: Addison Wesley.

Fosfuri, A. and Motta, M. (1999), 'Multinationals without advantages', *Scandinavian Journal of Economics*, **101** (4), 617–30.

Frenz, M. and Ietto-Gillies, G. (2003), 'The impact of multinationality on the propensity to innovate: an analysis of the UK Community Innovation Survey 3', presented at the Workshop on 'Empirical studies on innovation in Europe', Urbino, 1–2 December.

Girma, S. and Gorg, H. (2002), 'Multinationals' productivity advantage: scale or technology?', CEPR Discussion Paper.

Hagedoorn, J. (2002), 'Inter-firm R&D partnerships: an overview of patterns and trends since 1960', *Research Policy*, **31**, 477–92.

Helpman, E., Meliz, M. and Yeaple, S. (2004), 'Export versus FDI with heterogenous firms', *American Economic Review*, **94** (1), 300–316.

Hirschman, A.O. (1958), *The Strategy of Economic Development*, New Haven, CT: Yale University Press.

Markusen, J. (1995), 'The boundaries of multinational firms and the theory of international trade', *Journal of Economic Perspectives*, **92**, 169–89.

Narula, R. and Zanfei, A. (2005), 'The globalization of innovation: the role of multinational enterprises', in J. Fagerberg, D. Mowery and R. Nelson (eds), *Handbook of Innovation*, Oxford: Oxford University Press.

OECD (2002), *Measuring Globalisation. The Role of Multinationals in OECD Economies*, Paris: OECD, CD-ROM edition.

Parisi, M.L., Schiantarelli, F. and Sembenelli, A. (2002), 'Productivity, innovation creation and absorption, and R&D: micro evidence for Italy', mimeo.

Pfaffermayer, M. and Bellak, C. (2002), 'Why foreign-owned firms are different: a conceptual framework and empirical evidence for Austria', in R. Jungnickel (ed.), *Foreign-owned Firms: Are They Different?*, Basingstoke, UK: Palgrave Macmillan.

Rodriguez-Clare, A. (1996), 'Multinationals, linkages and economic development', *American Economic Review*, **86** (4), 852–73.

Siotis, G. (1999), 'Foreign direct investment strategies and firms' capabilities', *Journal of Economics and Management Strategy*, **8** (2), 251–70.

Zanfei, A. (2000), 'Transnational firms and changing organization of innovative activities', *Cambridge Journal of Economics*, **24**, 515–42.

PART III

Catch-up and Innovative Activity in
Backward Areas

9. Catching up or standing still? National innovative productivity among 'follower' countries, 1978–1999*

Jeffrey L. Furman and Richard Hayes*

1. INTRODUCTION

Examining the state of British industrial performance in 1980, Keith Pavitt cautioned that unless the nation made substantial improvements in its innovative capacity, both through additional industrial R&D and improved linkages between R&D and product development, its prospects for long-run economic growth would dim (Pavitt, 1980a, 1980b). This sentiment resonates with those of economists and policymakers, who have focused increasing attention in the years since World War II on the centrality of scientific and technological advance in driving economic progress and who have argued that increasing national investments to innovation are essential to ensure countries' economic growth (Schumpeter, 1942; Bush, 1945; Solow, 1956; Abramovitz, 1956; Romer, 1990; Jones, 1995).

In the near quarter-century since Pavitt's initial appeal, Great Britain has made investments in its innovative capacity; its level of R&D expenditures and its realized level of USPTO (US Patent & Trademark Office) patenting have increased by approximately 30 percent each. At the same time, neighboring Ireland, whose standard of living in the early 1980s was substantially lower than Britain's, has vastly increased its economic and policy commitments to innovation, boosting its count of R&D personnel nearly tenfold and achieving a 350 percent increase in USPTO patents, thus achieving a rate of per capita patenting comparable with that of a number of the more innovative countries in the world. The experience of these countries is illustrative of two striking facts about country-level innovative output over the last few decades.

* Reprinted from a draft version of the paper that ultimately appeared as *Research Policy*, **33**(9), J.L. Furman and R. Hayes, 'Catching up or standing still? National innovative productivity in 'follower' countries, 1978–1999', 1329–54, Copyright 2004, with permission from Elsevier.

First, among the set of countries that have historically generated significant numbers of innovations at the world's technological frontier, the difference in the relative innovative productivity of the most innovative countries and other innovative countries has decreased. While the world's leading innovator economies, including the USA, Switzerland and Japan, have continued to increase investments in innovative capacity, other members of the group of innovator countries have increased their commitments to innovation at an even greater rate. Thus, although the absolute gap in innovative productivity between the world's most innovative economies and other innovator countries remains, this gap is relatively smaller at the end of the twentieth century than it was 20 years before.

Second, the set of countries that generate numerous new-to-the-world innovations has expanded over the past quarter-century, as a number of formerly industrializing countries have sufficiently increased their levels of innovative productivity to begin introducing new-to-the-world innovations with regularity. These countries include a number of late industrializing countries that had been primarily imitators (and consumers) of innovations at the world's technological frontier. Ireland, Israel, Singapore, South Korea and Taiwan are among the nations that have achieved remarkable increases in innovative output per capita, suggesting that their innovative capacities have overtaken those of some countries whose economic conditions were more favorable as recently as the 1980s.

The fact that some countries have increased their innovative capacities so substantially while others have not presents a puzzle for the study of national systems of innovation (Freeman, 1987; Dosi et al., 1988; Lundvall, 1992; Nelson, 1993), a literature that does not issue strong predictions about the emergence of innovative leaders among former follower countries. In this chapter, we investigate developments in national innovative capacities, focusing on the country-level investments, institutional configurations and national policy decisions that shape the success of follower nations in catching up to the world's leading innovator countries in terms of per capita innovative output. By studying the emergence of innovative capacity in former industrializing and imitator countries and examining the relative leveling of investments in innovation in some historical innovator countries, we build directly on a set of issues central to Keith Pavitt's work (Pavitt, 1979, 1980a, 1980b; Patel and Pavitt, 1987, 1989; Bell and Pavitt, 1992, 1993). Further, in adopting an approach that focuses on statistical analysis, we contribute to research that addresses Patel and Pavitt's (1994) appeal for quantitative analysis clarifying the properties of national innovation systems.

We base our analysis on the conceptual framework for understanding national innovative capacity outlined in Furman et al. (2002), which builds in particular on literature in macroeconomic growth (Romer, 1990), national industrial competitive advantage (Porter, 1990) and national innovation systems (Nelson, 1993).[1] The core of our empirical analysis involves the estimation of a production function for economically significant technological innovations. The framework on which we based our estimation suggests that an economy's innovative productivity depends on (a) investments in broadly available resources for innovation, which we refer to as the common innovation infrastructure, (b) the environment for innovation in its industrial clusters, and (c) linkages between these components.

To evaluate this empirically, we employ a panel dataset of 23 countries between 1978 and 1999. Consistent with prior research, these regressions show a tight fit between predictors of national innovative capacity and economically significant innovations. These models also bear out the striking result that a number of former follower countries are becoming increasingly productive in their innovative productivity. To explore more fully the factors driving this phenomenon, we categorize countries into four groups based on historical patterns in their levels of innovative capacity: (1) leading innovator countries; (2) middle-tier innovator countries; (3) third-tier innovator countries; and (4) emerging innovator countries. Over the course of the sample, the leading innovator countries have the highest levels of innovative capacity, followed by the middle-tier countries, and the third-tier countries. Average innovative capacity in emerging innovator countries grows substantially over the course of the sample, from levels slightly higher than those of third-tier innovators to levels that exceed those of the average middle-tier economies. Although not quite catching up to the world's most innovative countries, emerging innovator countries as a group surpass economies whose historical levels of wealth and innovation had vastly exceeded their own.

The improvements in national innovative capacity in emerging innovator countries do not arise from any single factor alone but rather from increased investment and commitment across a number of the drivers of national innovative capacity. Moreover, emerging innovator countries differ from each other with respect to their geographic region of origin and their national systems of innovation. Just as alternative institutional arrangements can support continuous innovation, there appears to be no single dictate prescribing the ideal institutional configuration necessary for catch-up in innovative productivity and output.

Commonality does, however, exist across emerging innovator countries: they exhibit ever-deepening investments in the drivers of national innovative capacity, both by committing to innovation-enhancing policies and investing in R&D and human capital. We examine the drivers of catch-up more precisely by creating indices that decompose a country's commitments to innovative capacity into components associated with (a) its policies and infrastructure and (b) its investments in innovation. This descriptive

counterfactual exercise exposes critical differences between groups of innovator countries. It demonstrates that leading innovator countries, middle-tier
innovator countries and emerging innovator countries have committed in relatively similar ways to innovation-enhancing policies. Middle-tier innovator
countries and emerging innovators are, however, distinguished by the extent
to which each has increased investments in R&D and human capital. By contrast, third-tier innovator countries have neither substantially increased their
investments in R&D expenditures and human capital nor their commitments
to innovation-enhancing policies. We explore both the public policy and theoretical implications of these results in greater detail in our discussion.

The remainder of the chapter is structured as follows: Section 2 reviews the
historical background for this study and discusses prior research on catch-up
and the determinants of national innovative productivity. Section 3 introduces the conceptual framework that drives our analysis. Section 4 outlines
our empirical approach. Our empirical results appear in Section 5. Section 6
concludes, discussing the findings of the chapter in greater generality.

2. LEADERSHIP AND CATCH-UP IN NATIONAL INNOVATIVE PRODUCTIVITY

2.1   Historical Background

In the years since World War II, the set of countries contributing regularly
to innovation at the world's technological frontier has expanded, raising a
number of questions for conceptual and empirical study. The 'economic
miracles' of postwar Germany and Japan involved vast improvements in
physical and human capital and culminated in the 1970s and 1980s with
remarkable increases in innovative productivity. It is curious that, despite
the destruction of their economies in the wake of World War II, Germany
and Japan accomplished such leaps in national innovative productivity
while countries such as England and France did not. Although the USA
played a critical role in rebuilding innovative capabilities in Germany and
Japan in the years after World War II, their most significant gains in innovative capacity occurred in the 1970s and 1980s, when national choices
rather than US edicts drove commitments to innovation.

This experience recurs in a different form in the final two decades of the
twentieth century, as a set of countries nearly joins the group of elite innovator countries, although their economic and political circumstances at the
start of the 1980s are similar to or less favorable than a set of countries whose
innovative productivity does not increase substantially over this period.
These emerging innovators do not appear to have the same historical

advantages that benefited Germany and Japan. For example, emerging innovator countries such as South Korea, Singapore, Ireland and Finland were not rebuilding shattered economies that had historical legacies of innovative leadership. Instead, these countries developed imitator economies and transformed them into innovative leaders by systematically and continuously increasing their commitments to innovation over time.

We focus our empirical analysis in this chapter on this most recent time period, from 1978 to 1999, for which international data availability enables statistical analysis on the country-level determinants of innovative output. This proves to be an empirically interesting time frame: during this period, the set of countries listed above, as well as some other Scandinavian and Asian countries, vastly increased their innovative productivity. At the same time, a number of other countries with similar initial economic conditions and similarly low initial levels of new-to-the-world innovation, including, for example, numerous Latin American and southern European countries, did not improve their capacities for innovation as substantially (Porter et al., 2000; Furman and Stern, 2000). For example, between 1976 and 1980 a sample of emerging Latin American and Asian countries received a similar number of USPTO patents; by the second half of the 1990s, however, patenting in the Asian economies dwarfs Latin American countries' output (Appendix Table 9A.1). (For more detailed studies of country-specific innovative development, see Amsden 1989; Kim, 1997; O'Sullivan, 2000; and Trajtenberg, 2001.) In some cases, innovative productivity increases concomitant with economic development. However, the example of Great Britain and Ireland presented in the introduction demonstrates that initial economic wealth alone does not fully explain levels of or increases in innovative productivity.

2.2 Perspectives on Innovation in Economic Growth and Catch-up

The factors that affect economic progress across countries have been of primary interest to political scientists, economic historians, economists and policymakers – and the role of technology has been principal in the debates. Veblen (1915) was pioneering in comparing countries' relative economic standing and identifying penalties associated with initial industrial advantages. Gerschenkron's (1962) view of catch-up expands on Veblen, suggesting that later-industrializing countries may be able to accelerate their growth rates by adopting technology developed by leader countries and, although considerable obstacles exist, may be able to leapfrog leader countries by developing institutions that deal with contemporaneous challenges more effectively than those developed in previous periods. These authors identify a fundamental question regarding whether laggard countries' wealth and technological progress increase at a higher rate than those of leader countries.

Debate about the factors affecting catch-up and the extent of convergence in economic conditions across countries has intensified since World War II. Since Solow (1956) and Abramovitz (1956) identified the importance of technological progress in economic growth, questions about the role of innovation have been a central feature of this debate.[2] A number of distinct research traditions has emerged around these issues, each of which conceives of and incorporates technology in a different way. On one hand, most formal models of economic growth conceive of technology as a key input (along with labor and capital) in determining economic output and long-run growth. Such modeling efforts often require simplifying assumptions about the nature of technology and do not incorporate its more nuanced characteristics. By contrast, research in more historical, descriptive, or evolutionary (e.g. Nelson and Winter, 1982) traditions rejects strict simplifying assumptions about technology and focuses on more fine-grained factors that affect the rate and direction of technical change. For example, while some formal models make the simplifying assumption that technology flows freely across place and time, economic historians and evolutionary theorists document the limitations of such assumptions.[3]

Within the tradition of formal economic models, this distinction is quite important. In early neoclassical growth models, technology is viewed as spilling over freely across countries, leading to certain convergence in levels of economic progress, leaving only 'transitional dynamics' (Fagerberg, 1994, p. 1149) to explain differences across countries, subject to constraints associated with capital mobility.[4] Follow-on efforts in the 1960s incorporate learning-by-doing into formal models, but these ideas do not have an immediate impact on mainstream economics. The importance of a country's stock of knowledge and the parameters affecting the mobility of knowledge across borders is more fully incorporated in the early 1990s, in models of ideas-driven, endogenous growth (Romer, 1990; Grossman and Helpman, 1991). In these models, the ability to apply existing technology and generate new innovations differs systematically across economies and convergence in economic wealth is not inevitable.

Empirical literature assessing drivers of economic growth and the extent of convergence across countries is deep and varied (Barro and Sala-i-Martin, 1992, 1995; Islam, 1995; Sala-i-Martin, 1996; Quah, 1997). Several authors in a primary strand of this literature conclude that conditional convergence has occurred among industrialized economies (Baumol, 1986), but that this result does not hold if one selects countries based on economic leadership in the late 1800s rather than selecting from among the economic leaders in more recent periods (DeLong, 1988; Baumol et al.,

1989). Convergence appears to apply to a greater set of countries in the 1990s, as formerly industrializing economies in Asia experience total factor productivity and economic growth. Young (1995) documents this experience in Hong Kong, Singapore, South Korea and Taiwan, concluding that vast improvements in these countries' levels of per capita income result from substantial growth in labor and capital over the period.

Complementing formal models and large-scale empirical analysis, economic historians and technology scholars have developed a perspective on the role of technology in economic advance in which a more nuanced understanding of innovation is central.[5] Fagerberg (1994) describes this perspective as the 'technology gap' approach, and identifies a number of its central tenets. Specifically, he notes that authors in this view (including Ames and Rosenberg, 1963; Nelson, 1981; Nelson and Winter, 1982; and Nelson and Wright; 1992) emphasize that technological innovation does not flow freely across economic actors or distances because its creation and use are so closely tied to specific firms, networks and economic institutions. In this view, the ability of economically lagging countries to catch up to leader countries depends on the investments in technology, as incorporating advances made elsewhere is essential to the process of catch-up. Ohkawa and Rosovsky (1973) note this explicitly, and characterize the ability to assimilate external technologies as 'social capability'. Consistent with the argument that specific investments in innovative capabilities are essential for assimilating new-to-the-country innovation, Abramovitz (1986) proposes that countries whose economic environments more closely match that of the leader country will have better 'technological congruence' and will, thus, be more successful in incorporating advances made elsewhere. For related reasons, Bell and Pavitt (1992, 1993) argue that investments in innovative capacity are essential for catch-up in developing countries, as investments in production equipment alone are insufficient for incorporating technical advances made elsewhere.

The natural progeny of the technology gap perspective, the literature on national innovation systems (Freeman, 1987; Dosi et al., 1988; Lundvall, 1992; Nelson, 1993; Edquist, 1997),[6] focuses on the particular configurations of firms, networks and institutions that affect innovative outcomes in different countries.[7] Unlike the technology gap or economic growth literatures, research in the national innovation systems tradition has not focused explicitly on relative levels of economic or technological development. Instead, this research has emphasized rich, descriptive accounts of the constellations of organizations and policies that contribute to patterns of innovative behavior in particular countries, highlighting the institutions and actors whose roles in important industries are particularly decisive and emphasizing the diversity in national approaches to innovation. Such actors include private firms, universities, public and quasi-public research organizations, governmental departments and ministries (e.g. military, aeronautics and health), as well as the institutions, legal authorities, budget-setting agencies and norms that influence the nature and extent of innovative efforts in an economy.[8] Consistent with evolutionary theorizing (Nelson and Winter, 1982), this perspective also emphasizes that processes leading to technical advance involve detailed search efforts, iterative learning and complex interactions among the actors described above (Lundvall, 1992). Understanding the processes operating in a country's (or region's) innovative system requires far-reaching examinations of the relationships among its actors and technological infrastructure. As a consequence, research in this tradition has been predominantly qualitative, prompting Patel and Pavitt's (1994) call for follow-on research quantifying the characteristics, inputs and outputs of national innovation systems.

Although the national innovation systems tradition has not yet generated a great deal of large-scale empirical analysis, the nuanced national innovation systems and technology gap literatures have helped focus research efforts on exploring the determinants of national innovative output as well as overall economic output. This development occurred parallel and complementary to advances in the literature on macroeconomic growth that model the ideas-generating sector (innovation-generating sector) of the economy as an endogenous determinant of economic growth (Romer, 1990; Jones, 1995; Porter and Stern, 2000). In investigating the drivers of innovative outputs in the OECD, Furman et al. (2002) is among a number of recent papers that build on both of these research streams to evaluate the determinants of innovation and innovative productivity at the country level. For example, Hu and Mathews (2004) investigate developments in innovative capacity in a sample of five East Asian countries, concluding that public financing played a key role in fostering the growth of their innovative capacities. We design this chapter to contribute to that emerging line of research, focusing on the factors that have allowed a number of former follower countries to achieve substantial improvements in their ability to generate new-to-the-world innovations. The next section introduces the conceptual lens we employ in order to understand these developments.

3. CONCEPTUAL APPROACH

3.1 Overview and Introduction

Informed by the research traditions described in the previous section, we pursue a conceptual and empirical approach with the aim of acknowledging the subtleties of the national innovation systems and technology gap litera-tures and incorporating its lessons in a way that also allows us to assess the drivers of national innovative output. In order to measure key constructs in a way that is comparable across a broad range of countries, we sacrifice some of the rich detail of the national innovation systems literature; at the same time, we are able to incorporate a greater degree of sensitivity to institutional variation than is characteristic of more formal economic approaches. We interpret our approach as complementary to, rather than a substitute for, both case-based research in innovation studies and more formal modeling efforts.

Accordingly, the framework we employ for understanding the drivers of national innovative productivity is fairly eclectic. It builds on recent models of ideas-driven economic growth (Romer, 1990; Jones, 1998), in which eco-nomic growth depends in great measure on the production of the ideas-generating sector of the economy. The rate at which new ideas are produced depends, in turn, on the stock of knowledge (previously generated ideas) and the extent of efforts (human and financial capital) devoted to the ideas-generating portion of the economy. The notion of an ideas production function forms the core of our empirical approach to understanding catch-up in innovative productivity.

We build, as well, on ideas developed by Rosenberg (1963) and Porter (1990) regarding the manner in which microeconomic processes interact with the macroenvironment and national institutions to affect the overall level of innovative activity in an economy. We incorporate this under-standing of the importance of the microstructure of competition in our view of national innovative productivity and catch-up.

The final pillar of our approach to understanding the drivers of innova-tive output comes from the national innovation systems literature, which emphasizes the array of national policies, institutions and relationships that drive the nature and extent of country-specific innovative output.

3.2 Determinants of National Innovative Capacity

To explain the sources of differences among countries in the production of innovations at the world's technical frontier, we employ the framework introduced by Furman et al. (2002). According to this framework, national innovative capacity is understood as an economy's potential for producing a stream of commercially relevant innovations. In part, this capacity depends on the technical sophistication and labor force in a given economy; however, it also reflects the investments, policies and behaviors of the private sector and the government that affect the incentives to engage in R&D and the productivity of the country's R&D enterprise. The framework organizes the determinants of national innovative capacity into three main elements (see Figure 9.1): (1) a common pool of institutions, resource commitments and policies that support innovation, referred to as the common innovation infrastructure; (2) the particular innovation orientation of groups of inter-connected national industrial clusters; and (3) the quality of linkages between the two.

The innovative performance of a country's economy ultimately depends upon the activities of individual firms and industrial clusters. Some of the most critical investments that support innovative activity operate across all innovation-oriented sectors in an economy. These cross-cutting factors comprise the *common innovation infrastructure* (represented by the left-hand portion of Figure 9.1). Consistent with models of ideas-based growth (Romer, 1990), the framework suggests that a country's R&D productivity depends upon its historical stock of knowledge (denoted A_t) as well as the amount of scientific and technical talent dedicated to the production of new technologies (denoted $H_{A,t}$). Innovative productivity also depends on national investments and policy choices (denoted as X^{INF}), including factors such as expenditures on higher education, intellectual property protection, and openness to international competition, which will exert an over-arching impact on innovativeness across the range of a country's economic sectors (Nelson, 1993).

While the common innovation infrastructure provides resources for innovation throughout an economy, it is the firms in specific industrial clusters that introduce and commercialize those innovations. The innovative capacity of an economy, then, depends upon the extent to which a country's

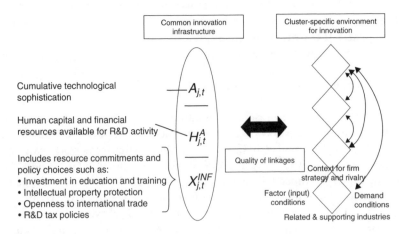

Figure 9.1   National innovative capacity

industrial clusters support and compete on the basis of technological innovation. Drawing on the 'diamond' framework developed in Porter (1990), we emphasize four key elements of the microeconomic environment – the presence of high-quality and specialized inputs; a context that encourages investment and intense local rivalry; pressure and insight gleaned from sophisticated local demand; and the presence of a cluster of related and supporting industries – that have a central influence on the rate of innovation in a given national industrial cluster (these are the diamonds on the right-hand side of Figure 9.1). The potential also exists for productivity-enhancing knowledge to spill over across industrial clusters (this is represented by the lines connecting the diamonds on the right-hand side of Figure 9.1).

Finally, the extent to which the potential for innovation supported by the common innovation infrastructure is translated into specific innovative outputs in a nation's industrial clusters will be determined by the quality of linkages between these two areas. In the absence of strong linking mechanisms, upstream scientific and technical activity may spill over to other countries more quickly than opportunities can be exploited by domestic industries. For example, while the underlying technology for creating the chemical dye industry was the result of the discoveries of the British chemist Perkin, the sector quickly developed and became a major exporting industry for Germany, not Britain. At least in part, this migration of the fruits of scientific discovery to Germany was due to that country's stronger university–industry relationships and the greater availability of capital for technology-intensive ventures (Arora et al., 1998; Murmann, 2003).

4. EMPIRICAL APPROACH AND DATA

4.1 Empirical Approach – Estimating National Innovative Productivity

We base our approach to assessing national innovative productivity on the ideas production function articulated by Romer (1990), Jones (1995) and Porter and Stern (2000). We use the national innovative capacity framework described above as a guide to direct our model and analysis. Specifically, we describe a production function for economically significant technological innovations, choosing a specification in which innovations are produced as a function of the factors underlying national innovative productivity:

$$\dot{A}_{j,t} = \delta(X_{j,t}^{INF}, Y_{j,t}^{CLUST}, Z_{j,t}^{LINK}) H_{j,t}^{A\lambda} A_{j,t}^{\phi} \tag{9.1}$$

where, for each country j in year t, $\dot{A}_{j,t}$ represents the flow of new-to-the-world innovations, $H^A_{j,t}$ reflects the total level of capital and labor resources devoted to the ideas sector of the economy, and $A_{j,t}$ symbolizes the stock of useful knowledge available to drive future ideas production. In addition, X^{INF} refers to the level of cross-cutting resource commitments and policy choices which constitute the common innovation infrastructure, Y^{CLUS} refers to the particular environments for innovation in a country's industrial clusters, and Z^{LINK} captures the strength of linkages between the common infrastructure and the nation's industrial clusters.

The reasoning we apply to arrive at an empirical model to estimate (9.1) follows the logic of Furman et al. (2002) and reflects our principal aim of allowing the data to illustrate the phenomenon to the greatest possible extent. As the source of statistical identification, we employ a panel dataset over a time period of more than 20 years. We can therefore take advantage of both cross-sectional and time-series variation in estimating the parameters associated with (9.1). Recognizing the benefits (and pitfalls) associated with each identification strategy, our analysis explicitly compares how estimates vary depending on the source of identification.[9] We are careful in our analysis to include year dummies to account for the evolving differences across time in the overall level of innovative output. We also include either country dummies or other measures to control for aggregate differences in technological sophistication (e.g. as reflected in GDP per capita). By controlling for year and country effects in most of our analysis, we address some of the principal endogeneity and autocorrelation concerns.[10]

We base our specification of the innovation production function on the assumption that each of the terms of (9.1) is complementary with each other, in the sense that the marginal productivity associated with increasing one factor is increasing in the levels of each of the other factors. (More precisely, this simplification is based on the assumption that the factors X^{INF}, Y^{CLUS} and Z^{LINK} enter (9.1) exponentially. Thus, (9.1) becomes $\dot{A}_{j,t} = \delta X^{\delta_{INF}}_{j,t} Y^{\delta_{CLUS}}_{j,t} Z^{\delta_{LINK}}_{j,t} H^{A\lambda}_{j,t} A^{\phi}_{j,t}$ and simplifies to (9.2) after logarithmic transformation.) Denoting the natural logarithm of X as $L\,X$, our main specification reduces to the following form:

$$L\dot{A}_{j,t} = \delta + \delta_{INF} LX^{INF}_{j,t} + \delta_{CLUS} L Y^{CLUS}_{j,t}$$
$$+ \delta_{LINK} LZ^{LINK}_{j,t} + \lambda LH^A_{j,t} + \phi LA_{j,t} + \varepsilon_{j,t} \qquad (9.2)$$

The log-log form of this specification allows many of the variables to be interpreted in a straightforward way in terms of elasticities, is less sensitive to outliers, and is consistent with prior research in this area (Jones, 1998).

4.2   Measuring Innovative Output across Countries and Time

To perform our proposed analysis, we must identify observable measures that characterize new-to-the-world innovation and the concepts underlying national innovative capacity and develop a dataset that tracks these measures across countries and over time. Constructing a measure of commercializable innovations that is comparable and available across countries over the course of our dataset and is indicative of national innovative output is an extraordinarily difficult task. Consistent with Furman et al. (2002), we focus our analysis of visible commercializable innovations on 'international patents' (*PATENTS*), which we define as the number of patents granted by the USPTO to inventors from foreign countries.[11]

We recognize that no measure is perfect in characterizing the precise extent of innovation in an economy and readily acknowledge the well-understood hazards of using patenting as an indicator of innovative activity (Schmookler, 1966; Pavitt, 1982, 1985, 1988; Griliches, 1984, 1990; Trajtenberg, 1990). As Griliches notes succinctly, 'not all inventions are patentable, not all inventions are patented, and the inventions that are patented differ greatly in "quality," in the magnitude of inventive output associated with them' (1990, p. 1669). Such difficulties are exacerbated when comparing innovation across countries because the propensity to patent also differs across country (Eaton and Kortum, 1996, 1999; Kortum and Lerner, 1999).

At the same time, we focus on international patenting rates as 'the only observable manifestation of inventive activity with a well-grounded claim for universality' (Trajtenberg, 1990, p. 183) and, thus, the most useful measure available for comparing innovative output across countries and over time. Though we believe that the advantages of international patent data suggest it as the best measure for our purposes, we exercise caution in our use and interpretation of the data. For example, we construct *PATENTS* to include only commercially significant innovations at the world's technical frontier.[12] Moreover, in using realized international patents as an indicator of national innovative activity, we draw on a wide range of research in economics and innovation studies, including Soete and Wyatt (1983); Evenson (1984); Patel and Pavitt (1987, 1989); Dosi et al. (1990); Eaton and Kortum (1996, 1999); Kortum (1997); Vertova (1999); and Furman et al. (2002).[13]

While we acknowledge that the 'true' rate of technological innovation is unobservable and that *PATENTS* is an imperfect proxy, our decision to use this variable rests on the belief that *PATENTS* is positively correlated with the true level of new-to-the-world innovative output in our panel dataset and that it represents the best available indicator that allow us to compare national innovative output across a broad set of countries over time. We remain aware of the limitations of this measure, test it carefully for robustness, and bear these in mind when interpreting our results.[14]

A list of our variables, definitions, and sources appears in Table 9.1; the set of countries included in our analysis is listed in Table 9.2; and summary statistics appear in Table 9.3. For all countries except the USA, we define *PATENTS* as the number of patents granted in year $t+2$ in the USA. This accounts for the average lag between patent application and approval. For the USA, we use the number of patents granted to government and corporations (non-individuals), in the USA in year $t+2$.[15]

Across all years, the average country in our sample obtains approximately 3550 *PATENTS*. Reflecting the skewness in the data, the standard deviation in international patenting is substantially higher than the mean (nearly 9200). At the country level, these data evidence an increase in *PATENTS* in countries such as Japan, Finland and South Korea, a solid increase in *PATENTS* in many Western European countries, and only modest increases in *PATENTS* in countries such as Italy, Spain and New Zealand.

4.3   Measuring the Drivers of Innovative Output

Limitations in the quality and extent of available data constitute the principal challenge in developing a dataset that allows us to measure the drivers of innovative productivity in emerging innovator countries. We obtain the majority of our data from series published by the OECD Science and Technology Indicators, the World Bank, the USPTO and the Penn World Tables. Before the 1990s, few countries outside of the OECD kept regular, reliable records on science and engineering or R&D-related activities. Thus our ability to compile a comprehensive historical dataset for a large sample of countries remains limited.[16] As economists and policymakers have focused increasing attention on innovation as a source of economic growth, national statistical agencies and international bodies have undertaken more concerted efforts at gathering these data. As a consequence, we are able to expand on previous data collection efforts to develop a dataset that reflects investments in the drivers of national innovative productivity for 29 countries between 1978 and 1999. Our core dataset, on which we run our regressions, includes 23 countries for which consistent data series are available over the course of the sample period.[17] In additional analyses, we are able to include six additional countries for which consistent data are available for a subset of years.[18]

We measure the strength of the common innovation infrastructure using variables that reflect the extent of a country's accumulated knowledge stock (A), country-level investments in R&D and human capital (H^A), and

Table 9.1   Variables and Definitions

	Variable	Full variable name	Definition	Source
Innovative output				
$PATENTS_{j\,t+2}$		International patents granted in year $t+2$	For non-US countries, patents granted by the USPTO. For the USA, patents granted by the USPTO to corporations or governments. To ensure this asymmetry does not affect the results we include a US dummy variable in the regressions	USPTO patent database
Quality of the common innovation infrastructure				
A	$GDP\ PER\ CAPITA_{j,t}$	GDP per capita	Gross domestic product per capita, constant price, chain series, US$	Penn World Tables, OECD Science & Technology Indicators
A	$GDP78_{j,t}$	GDP 1978	1978 gross domestic product constant price, chain series, billions of year 2000 US$	Penn World Tables
H^A	$FTE\ R\&D\ PERS_{j,t}$	Aggregate personnel employed in R&D	Full-time equivalent R&D personnel in all sectors	OECD Science & Technology Indicators
H^A	$R\&D\ \$_{j,t}$	Aggregate expenditure on R&D	Total R&D expenditures in year millions of year 2000 US$	OECD Science & Technology Indicators

Table 9.1 (continued)

	Variable	Full variable name	Definition	Source
X^{INF}	$OPENNESS_{j,t}$	Openness to international trade and investment	Exports plus imports, in constant dollar prices, divided by GDP, expressed as a %	Penn World Tables
X^{INF}	$IP_{j,t}$	Strength of protection for intellectual property	Average survey response by executives on a 1–10 scale regarding relative strength of *IP* (available from 1989)	IMD World Competitiveness Report
X^{INF}	$ED\ SHARE_{j,t}$	Share of GDP spent on secondary and tertiary education	Public spending on secondary and tertiary education divided by GDP	World Bank, OECD Education at a Glance

Quality of the cluster-specific innovation environment

	Variable	Full variable name	Definition	Source
Y^{CLUS}	$PRIVATE\ R\&D\ FUNDING_{j,t}$	Percentage of R&D funded by private industry	R&D expenditures funded by industry divided by total R&D expenditures	OECD Science & Technology Indicators

Quality of linkages

	Variable	Full variable name	Definition	Source
Z^{LINK}	$UNIV\ R\&D\ PERF_{j,t}$	Percentage of R&D performed by universities	R&D expenditures performed by universities divided by total R&D expenditures	OECD Science & Technology Indicators

Table 9.2   Sample countries

Australia	Finland	Ireland	Norway	Sweden
Austria	France	Italy	Poland*	Switzerland
Belgium	Germany†	Japan	Portugal*	Turkey*
Canada	Greece*	Mexico	Slovak	UK
Czech	Hungary	Netherlands	Republic*	USA
Republic*	Iceland	New Zealand	South Korea	
Denmark			Spain	

Notes:
* These countries are included in supplemental analyses, but are omitted from the regression analyses because of data limitations.
† Before 1990, data are for West Germany only; after 1990, results include all federal states.

Table 9.3   Means and standard deviations

Variable		N	Mean	Standard deviation
Innovation output				
PATENTS		473	3550.20	9193.53
Quality of the common innovation infrastructure				
A	GDP PER CAPITA	473	18324.53	4582.88
A	GDP78	473	578.57	1000.85
H^A	FTE R&D PERS	473	199797.80	383363.60
H^A	R&D $	473	15941.54	35650.40
X^{INF}	OPENNESS	473	63.57	28.63
X^{INF}	IP	245	6.72	1.09
X^{INF}	ED SHARE	473	3.23	1.01
Cluster-specific innovation environment				
Y^{CLUS}	PRIVATE R&D FUNDING	473	50.64	14.31
Quality of linkages				
Z^{LINK}	UNIV R&D PERF	473	22.25	6.55

national policies (X^{INF}). *GDP78* and *GDP PER CAPITA* measure the knowledge stock indirectly, reflecting the extent to which ideas are embodied in goods and services. *GDP78* equals the gross domestic product in 1978, the initial year of our sample. *GDP78* is a fixed measure, which reflects the initial stock of knowledge in the economy, while *GDP PER CAPITA* constitutes a variable measure. Measured in year 2000 US$, *GDP78*

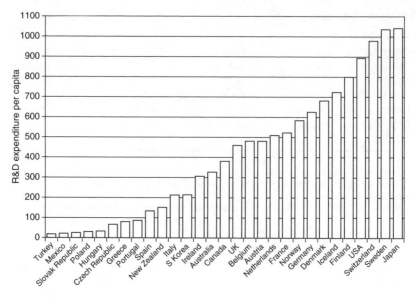

*Note:** In year 2000 US$.

Figure 9.2   R&D Expenditure per capita, selected countries (1999)*

averages nearly US$580 billion across countries. *GDP PER CAPITA* aver-
ages US$18 324 over the sample.

Measures of R&D human capital and country-level investments in R&D
(*FTE R&D PERS and R&D $*) reflect the extent of R&D effort in the
economy. Countries in the dataset employ an average of nearly 200 000
full-time equivalent R&D workers and invest nearly US$16 billion annu-
ally on R&D over the sample period. Figure 9.2 depicts the substantial dispersion in per capita R&D investment in 1999 and Figure 9.3 the growth of
R&D expenditures over the sample period. While leading innovator countries like Japan, Sweden and Switzerland invest more than US$900 in R&D
per capita, countries with lower levels of innovative capacity, such as
Mexico, Poland and Portugal, report less than US$100 in per capita R&D
expenditures in 1999. Consistent with the observation that countries' levels
of visible innovative output become more similar over time, many of the
countries with the lowest levels of R&D investment are among those with
the greatest relative increases in R&D investment over the period. For
example, although South Korea invests less than the median amount of
R&D per capita in 1999, its level of investment represents a staggering
increase of 5570 percent relative to its expenditures in 1978. Likewise,

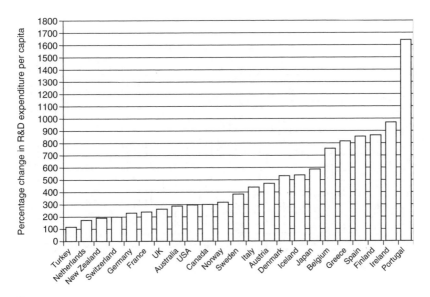

Figure 9.3   Percentage increase in R&D expenditure per capita, * *1978–99*[†]

Portugal, whose per capita R&D expenditures are among the lowest in the
sample, had increased its R&D investment by more than 1600 percent
between 1978 and 1999.

We measure the final component of the common innovation infrastructure X^{INF}, using indicators of national policies regarding openness to international trade (*OPENNESS*), the strength of intellectual property
protection (*IP*), and the share of GDP allocated to expenditures for secondary and tertiary education (*ED SHARE*). In this chapter, we employ a
direct measure of the *OPENNESS*.[19] Specifically, we use data from the
Penn World Tables to compute total trade (equal to exports plus imports)
as a proportion of GDP. This measure correlates with the ability of firms
in an economy to target larger international markets and with the ability of
foreign firms to exploit their innovations in the local economy. Across the
sample, the mean level of trade openness is 63.6 percent; not surprisingly,
this figure is higher in EU countries. *IP* is measured using executives'
responses in the World Competitiveness Report. On a Likert scale between
1 and 10 (where 10 represents the strongest degree of protection), sample

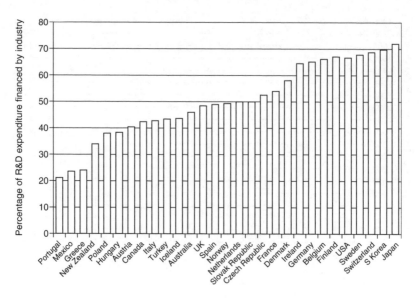

Figure 9.4   Percentage of R&D expenditure financed by industry, 1999

countries earn an IP average of 6.7. The average country in the sample devotes 3.2 percent of GDP to secondary and tertiary education.

To gauge the innovation orientation of industrial clusters and the strength of linkages, we employ compositional variables that reflect the relative sources of R&D funding between the public and private sector (*PRIVATE R&D FUNDING*) and the degree to which R&D performance takes place in the university sector (*UNIV R&D PERFORMANCE*).[20] For our sample countries, industry sources fund slightly more than 50 percent of all R&D expenditures. As demonstrated in Figure 9.4, this measure varies substantially across countries. In 1999, private sources contribute less than 30 percent of R&D funds in countries such as Portugal, Mexico, and Greece, although they account for approximately 70 percent of funding in South Korea and Japan. There is also substantial variation in changes in *PRIVATE R&D FUNDING* over the sample period (Figure 9.5). While private sources in Iceland and Ireland increased their fraction of R&D funding by more than 30 percent, *PRIVATE R&D FUNDING* declined in Austria, Portugal and Switzerland. Note that declines in *PRIVATE R&D FUNDING* in Austria and Portugal are, in a sense, more meaningful than those in Switzerland, as private sources fund a substantially higher fraction of its national R&D in Switzerland. *UNIV R&D PERF* averages 22.2 percent across the sample and evidences similar variation across countries.

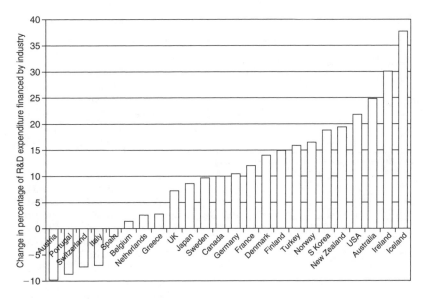

Figure 9.5   Percent change in fraction of R&D expenditure financed by industry, 1978–1999

5.   EMPIRICAL RESULTS

5.1   Econometric Analysis

Our econometric analysis applies the specification in (9.2) to the core dataset of 473 observations. The results appear in Tables 9.4 and 9.5. This specification yields a number of advantages from the perspective of interpretation. First, most of the variables in the specification enter in log form; consequently, their coefficients have a natural interpretation as elasticities. Variables expressed as ratios are included as levels, allowing us to also use an elasticity interpretation for their coefficients. Second, the log–log specification minimizes the leverage of outliers on the results. In all models, R-squared is greater than 0.94; for models including year dummy variables, it is greater than 0.997.

Table 9.4 reports the primary national innovative capacity results. Equation (4–1) estimates a specification that reproduces the Romer–Jones ideas production function model. The results show that *GDP PER CAPITA* and *FTE R&D PERS* have a significant and economically important impact on *PATENTS*. The coefficient on *FTE R&D PERS* implies that a 10 percent increase in science and engineering employment is associated with an 11.6 percent increase in *PATENTS*. Equations (4–2) and (4–3) incorporate the

Table 9.4 Determinants of the production of new-to-the-world technologies

		Dependent variable $= \ln(PATENTS)_{j,t+2}$			
		(4–1) Baseline ideas production function	(4–2) Common innovation infrastructure	(4–3) National innovative capacity: including all variables	(4–4) National innovative capacity: preferred model
Quality of the common innovation infrastructure					
A	L GDP PER CAPITA	**1.584** (0.069)	**0.697** (0.130)	**0.870** (0.138)	**0.836** (0.134)
H_A	L FT R&D PERS	**1.161** (0.013)	**0.737** (0.101)	**0.865** (0.097)	**0.850** (0.099)
A	L GDP78		**−0.355** (0.055)	**−0.299** (0.062)	**−0.289** 0.063
H^A	L R&D $		**0.757** (0.076)	**0.556** (0.077)	**0.556** (0.078)
X^{INF}	ED SHARE		**0.069** (0.018)	**0.091** (0.018)	**0.089** (0.018)
X^{INF}	IP		0.027 (0.042)	0.018 (0.040)	
X^{INF}	OPENNESS		**0.004** (0.001)	**0.0023** (0.0008)	**0.0018** (0.0008)
X^{INF}	ANTI-TRUST		−0.044 (0.033)	0.002 (0.031)	
Cluster-specific innovation environment					
Y^{CLUS}	PRIVATE R&D FUNDING			**0.011** (0.002)	**0.012** (0.002)
Quality of the linkages					
Z^{LINK}	UNIV R&D PERFORMANCE			**0.011** (0.004)	**0.011** (0.004)
Z^{LINK}	VENTURE CAPITAL			**−0.047** (0.018)	
Controls					
Year fixed effects			**Significant**	**Significant**	**Significant**
US dummy			0.136 (0.086)	**0.246** (0.085)	**0.185** (0.076)
Constant		**−21.931** (0.687)			
R-squared		0.9470	0.9971	0.9974	0.9973
Observations		473	473	473	473

Table 9.5   Exploring robustness

		Dependent Variable = ln($PATENTS$)$_{j,t+2}$		
		(5–1) (4–4), with country fixed effects	(5–2) Baseline ideas production function (w/ *PAT STOCK*)	(5–3) National innovative capacity model (w/ *PAT STOCK*)
Quality of the common innovation infrastructure				
A	L *GDP PER CAPITA*	**2.121** **(0.307)**		
A	L *PATENT STOCK*		**0.807** **(0.049)**	**0.557** **(0.034)**
H^A	L *FT R&D PERS*	**0.954** **(0.129)**	**0.616** **(0.118)**	**0.422** **(0.040)**
H^A	L *R&D $*	**0.218** **(0.093)**		**0.289** **(0.057)**
X^{INF}	*ED SHARE*	0.024 (0.023)		**0.047** **(0.018)**
X^{INF}	*OPENNESS*	**−0.006** **(0.002)**		0.0003 (0.0007)
Cluster-specific innovation environment				
Y^{CLUS}	*PRIVATE R&D FUNDING*	**0.006** **(0.003)**		**0.006** **(0.002)**
Quality of the linkages				
Z^{LINK}	*UNIV R&D PERFORMANCE*	0.002 (0.003)		0.001 (0.003)
Controls				
Country fixed effects		**Significant**	**Significant**	
Year fixed effects		**Significant**	**Significant**	
YEAR				**−0.045** **(0.003)**
L *GDP 1978*				**−0.255** **(0.045)**
US dummy				**0.213** **(0.071)**
R-squared		0.9991	0.9994	0.9979
Observations		473	473	473

elements of the common innovation infrastructure and the complete national innovative capacity model, respectively. Consistent with prior work, the key measures of the common innovation infrastructure, the environment for innovation in national clusters, and the extent of linkages between the two, enter in a statistically and economically significant manner.

Coefficients on the variable expressed as a share (including as *ED SHARE* and *OPENNESS*) can be interpreted as the percentage increase in *PATENTS* resulting from a one percentage point increase in those variables. Equation (4–4) presents the preferred national innovative capacity regression. In this model, elements of the common innovation infrastructure, the environment for innovation in industrial clusters, and the linkages between the two enter in a statistically and economically significant manner.

Table 9.5 explores the robustness of the model to a number of modifications. In order to isolate the extent to which the results are driven by time-series rather than cross-sectional variation, we add country fixed effects to the model in (5–1), with all country fixed effects entering significantly. (We omit *GDP78* from this model; since its value is fixed over time, it is effectively incorporated into the country fixed effect.) Key measures of the extent of ideas in the economy and the commitment to R&D financial and human capital remain significant and of the expected valence in this equation; many of the more nuanced measures of national innovative capacity become insignificant, however. The positive and significant coefficient on *PRIVATE R&D FUNDING* is robust to this modification, although *ED SHARE* and *UNIV R&D PERFORMANCE* lose their significance, suggesting that cross-sectional variation is what drives significance in these variables. *OPENNESS* becomes negative and significant in this formulation, suggesting that countries that have, over time, increased their openness to international trade have generated fewer *PATENTS*. The magnitude of the coefficient on *GDP PER CAPITA* changes substantially when country fixed effects are added, suggesting that the impact of within-country changes in *GDP PER CAPITA* over time is different from their impact across the cross-section.

Equations (5–2) and (5–3) reproduce key results from Table 9.4, substituting *PATENT STOCK* for *GDP PER CAPITA* as a measure of the stock of knowledge in the economy. The results of these equations echo those of the core national innovative capacity equations presented in Table 9.4.

In addition to the robustness of the results, stationarity is a potential concern given the way we model international patenting. To test for stationarity in our ln(*PATENTS*) data series, we followed the panel data unit root tests of Levin et al. (2002) and Im et al. (2003), which rely on pooled Augmented Dickey–Fuller testing for unit roots. In the case of ln(*PATENTS*), each test rejected the null hypothesis of nonstationarity, demonstrating that the series is not I(1).

5.2   Categorizing Innovator Countries

To understand more thoroughly differences and changes in the level of innovative productivity across differences across countries, we undertake a counterfactual analysis in which we predict per capita international patenting as a function of countries' realized levels of investments in innovation and their policies towards innovation. Essentially, this exercise consists of predicting a country's expected international patenting rate by applying its observed levels of the drivers of national innovative capacity to the regression coefficients obtained in (4–4) and then normalizing by national population. In Figure 9.6, we plot the results of this exercise for all of the countries in our core and expanded samples.

Several notable results emerge from this counterfactual analysis. The first is consistent with a catch-up phenomenon. While the USA and Switzerland have the highest levels of predicted per capita international patenting across the period, the relative difference in predicted per capita international patenting between these countries and others has declined over time as other countries have begun to invest more substantially in the drivers of national innovative capacity. For example, Japan dramatically improved its predicted international patenting between the early 1970s and the present, and a number of Scandinavian economies, including Denmark and Finland, have made investments that led to increased expected international patenting since the mid-1980s. This catch-up phenomenon has not, however, occurred uniformly across all countries. For example, the estimates associated with several Western European economies, including the UK, France and Italy, do not evidence marked increases in relative levels of innovative capacity.

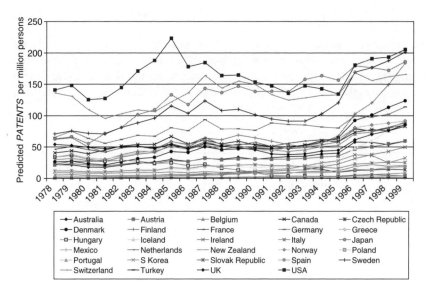

Figure 9.6   Predicted patents per million persons, by country

While initial levels of innovative productivity are, at least in part, the legacies of historical conditions, differential rates of catch-up constitute a separate empirical puzzle. As a descriptive exercise that enables us to understand the factors driving differential rates of catch-up in innovative productivity, we classify the countries in our dataset into categories based on the historical evolution of their innovative capacity (Table 9.6). We designate four categories: leading innovators, middle-tier innovators, third-tier innovator, and emerging innovator countries.

Leading innovator countries, including the USA, Switzerland, Germany, Japan and Sweden, maintain high levels of innovative capacity throughout the sample period, with Germany, Japan and Sweden experiencing particular growth in their innovative capacities in the early 1980s. Average expected per capita patenting rates for this group range from a minimum of 80 *PATENTS* per million persons to a maximum of over 170 over the sample period.

Middle-tier innovator countries, which include a number of the Western European countries, as well as Australia, Canada and Norway, maintain relatively stable levels or slowly increasing level of innovative capacity for much of the sample period. From 1978 to 1995, middle-tier innovator countries average patenting rates increase from approximately 38 to slightly more than 50 *PATENTS* per million persons. Predicted patenting rates rose somewhat more rapidly starting in 1995, and reached nearly 80 *PATENTS* per million by 1999. Even by 1999, however, middle-tier countries have not reached an average level of innovative capacity equal to that of the leading innovators in 1978.

Third-tier innovator countries, which include Italy, New Zealand and Spain, experience relatively low levels of innovative capacity throughout the sample period, although their investments in innovation drivers also increase in the final few years of the 1990s. Expected international patenting

Table 9.6 Categorizing innovator countries

Leading innovator	Middle-tier	Third-tier	Emerging innovator
Germany	Australia	Hungary	Denmark
Japan	Austria	Italy	Finland
Sweden	Belgium	Mexico	Iceland
Switzerland	Canada	New Zealand	Ireland
USA	France	Spain	South Korea
	Netherlands		
	Norway		
	UK		

rates in these countries are generally fewer than 30 *PATENTS* per million persons throughout the sample period.

Emerging innovator countries, Denmark, Finland, Iceland, Ireland and South Korea, evidence a dramatically different pattern. Beginning with relatively low expected patenting rates, these countries have increased their commitments to innovation by a relatively greater fraction than other countries in the sample. As a consequence, by 1999, their average expected patenting rates have exceeded those of the middle-tier countries. Finland and South Korea constitute striking examples. In 1978, the predicted international patenting rate was approximately 26 for Denmark and less than 1 for South Korea. Over the subsequent two decades, these countries invested substantially their financial and human capital in innovation and raised their commitments to innovation-supporting policies. By the end of the 1990s, Denmark and South Korea had surpassed many countries whose historical levels of innovative capacity had exceeded their own.

Figure 9.7 traces the historical average innovative capacity levels of these groups.[21] The figure also reports averages for countries in the *expanded dataset*.[22] Data for these countries are not sufficiently complete to allow us to include these countries in our historical regressions, but do enable us to compute predicted patenting rates in the late 1990s. Levels of innovative capacity in these countries are less than half those of third-tier

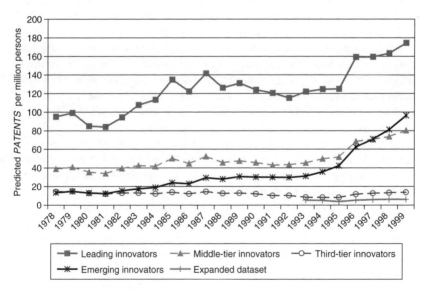

Figure 9.7   Predicted PATENTS *per million persons, grouped by innovator country category*

innovators over the course of the few years for which reliable data are available.

5.3 Examining the Drivers of Catch-up

The unpredictable pattern according to which some countries increased their innovative productivity dramatically over the past quarter-century while others lagged behind constitutes an empirical puzzle. Our counterfactual exercise in the previous section demonstrates that part of the resolution to this puzzle lies in the extent to which these countries increased their commitments to the drivers of innovative capacity. In this section we decompose the factors that drive innovative capacity, in order to shed more light on the extent to which investments and policy commitments have contributed to the rapid and substantial increases in innovative capacity in emerging innovator countries and the more modest increases achieved by middle- and third-tier countries. In order to do this, we develop two indices, which incorporate realized levels of the drivers of innovative capacity along with the weights derived in model (4–4 in the econometric analysis).

The first index, which we call the investment index, reflects the contribution of country-level investments in R&D and human capital, and growth in the stock of ideas. Essentially, it is a population-adjusted measure of A and H^A. Specifically, it is calculated as the linear combination of the realized levels of *FTE R&D PERS*, *R&D EXPENDITURES*, and *GDP PER CAPITA*, multiplied by their matching coefficient estimates from (4–4), exponentiated and normalized by population. The second index, which we call the policy index for the purposes of discussion, is based on values of X^{INF}, Y^{CLUS}, and Z^{LINK}. It is constructed in the same manner as the investment index, using *ED SHARE*, *OPENNESS*, *PRIVATE R&D FUNDING* and *UNIV R&D PERFORMANCE*. As these measures are not subject to scaling, we do not adjust this index for population.

We plot the historical Investment and Policy indices for each group of innovator countries in Figures 9.8 and 9.9. A number of interesting observations emerge. First, important differences in investment index levels are apparent across the categories. The initial investment index for leading innovator countries is more than twice that of the middle-tier innovators and approximately ten times that of third-tier innovator countries, and substantial differences among these groups remain at the end of the sample period. By contrast, the percentage difference among innovator country categories in the policy index is substantially smaller, and even third-tier innovator countries have policy index values that are comparable to (though nonetheless below) those of the leading innovator and middle-tier countries over the sample period.

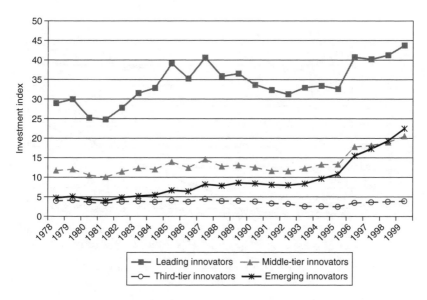

Figure 9.8 Investment index

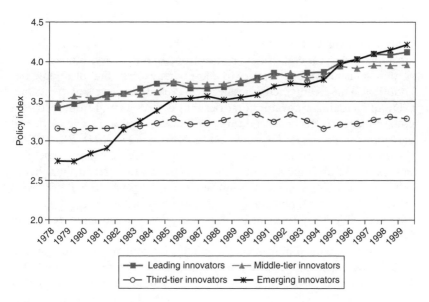

Figure 9.9 Policy index

Catch-up in backward areas

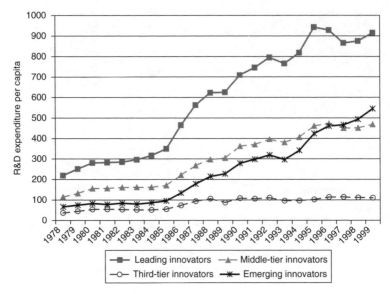

Note: *In year 2000 US$.

Figure 9.10   R&D expenditures per capita* by innovator category,
1978–99

Over the course of the 1980s and 1990s, the average investment index for
emerging innovator countries increases from an initial level similar to that
of third-tier innovator countries to a level that exceeds that of middle-tier
countries. This steady increase reflects, in part, rising levels of per capita
GDP in emerging innovator countries, but derives as well from increased
commitments to R&D expenditure and human capital. Figures 9.10 and
9.11 plot levels of *R&D$ PER CAPITA* and *FTE R&D PERS PER*
CAPITA by innovator category over time. In each category, emerging
innovator countries increase their investments at a rate greater than that of
other categories of innovator countries. The increase in *FTE R&D PERS*
PER CAPITA among emerging innovator countries is so significant that
per capita R&D employment in these countries is nearly equal to that of
leading innovator countries by the end of the 1990s.

Differences in the timing of catch-up in the investment and policy indices
constitute a second observation of interest in Figures 9.8 and 9.9.
Beginning in the 1980s, leading innovator and middle-tier innovator countries have nearly equal policy index values and the differences between these
countries' index values and those of the third-tier innovators is less than
25 percent. Again the emerging innovator countries have made startling

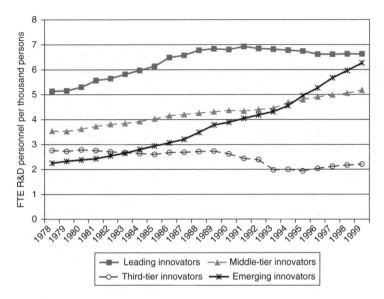

Figure 9.11   Full-time equivalent R&D personnel per thousand persons, by innovator category, 1978–99

progress, with policy progress taking them to a comparable level to the leading innovator countries. It is also interesting to note that, with the exception of a few years in the late 1980s and early 1990s, the policy index does not increase significantly in third-tier innovator countries over the sample period.

The coefficient of variation decreases over time for both the investment index and policy index across the sample of countries. Although both coefficients of variation decrease over time, the investment index exhibits greater variation across countries than the policy index. Similarly, the coefficients of variation decrease over time for both the predicted and actual international patenting rates. These results provide preliminary evidence of a 'narrowing of the gap' in national innovation rates, driven by decreases in the variation of both investment levels and policy effects.

Taken together, the elements of this descriptive exercise suggest that both changes in the policy environment (i.e. changes in X^{INF}, Y^{CLUS} and Z^{LINK}) and changes in investment levels (H^A) have affected catch-up dynamics in innovative productivity. The larger source of variation and catch-up across countries and innovator categories appears to derive from the investment index, suggesting that its elements have had the most impact in affecting relative levels of innovative capacity.

6. DISCUSSION

In this chapter we contribute to a line of research that investigates the factors affecting national innovative output. We pursue an approach at an intermediate level of abstraction that combines elements from formal economic modeling and the more qualitative and appreciative traditions of research in innovation studies. In this effort, we aim to build on one of the core areas of Keith Pavitt's research, and to do so in a manner consistent with his principled, eclectic approach to understanding the phenomena associated with innovation. Specifically, we examine the factors that drive levels of innovative output in a sample of 29 countries, including the majority of the world's most innovative economies during the years 1978–99. A number of key observations emerge. Consistent with prior research, we find that a parsimonious model based on the national innovative capacity performs in a statistically precise way in predicting our measure of national innovative output, international patents. Although our econometric models are based on a particular measure that does not capture the universe of innovation in a country, we believe that this measure correlates well with our underlying concept of interest and that our results provide useful evidence that the factors that drive national innovative capacity are important in affecting country-level innovation.

This econometric analysis serves as the underpinning for our efforts to understand the factors that explain recent developments in innovative productivity. Specifically, we investigate why some countries were able to dramatically increase their ability to generate a stream of leading-edge innovations while other countries – including a number of countries with historically higher levels of innovation – did not. The results suggest that there is no 'magic bullet' that explains these changes. Rather, innovative leadership arises from a range of sustained investments and policy commitments. Our analysis suggests that innovation-oriented policies and an appropriate composition of innovation-oriented investments are prerequites for innovative leadership, in the sense that these characterize each of the world's leading innovator countries. Further, our results provide evidence that, though necessary, these choices alone are not sufficient to ensure innovative leadership. In fact, countries that we classify as middle-tier innovators – countries whose levels of innovative capacity have been fairly stable, and consistently less than those of leading innovators – evidence policy commitments quite similar to the leading countries throughout the sample period, although their levels of innovative capacity remain substantially lower than those of the leading innovators. While no country achieves a relatively high level of innovative capacity without such innovation-oriented policy commitments, policy commitments appear to be insufficient in the absence of vastly increased investments in the drivers of innovative capacity.

The data do suggest that continuously increasing investment in innovation is, ultimately, essential for achieving innovative leadership. Japan, consistently among the world's most innovative countries during the sample period, experienced an increase in R&D personnel of approximately 85 percent; by contrast, France, which begins the period with a lower fraction of R&D workers in its labor force and is consistently a middle-tier innovator country, only experiences a 32 percent increase in R&D personnel. The results of our counterfactual index suggest that substantial increases in investments characterize the emerging innovator countries whose innovative capacity develops most over the period. For example, Finland's real R&D expenditures increase fourteen-fold over the period and South Korea's real R&D expenditures were more than 450 times greater in 1999 than they were in 1978. These increases are significant in both relative and absolute terms, and constitute some of the factors that enable their substantial increases in overall innovative capacity.

In some sense, a straightforward implication of our results is that greater inputs into innovation at the country level are associated with greater outputs; however, a simplistic interpretation of this result would be incomplete. Whereas all countries that achieve substantial increases in innovative capacity increased investments in key drivers of innovation over the period, each of these countries also maintained innovation-enhancing policies. A number of countries achieved policies supportive of innovation, but did not invest in R&D to the same degree. By contrast, no country appears to achieve high levels of investment in innovation without innovation-oriented policies. Together, these findings suggest to us that a well-functioning innovation infrastructure is necessary but not sufficient to create the environment required to achieve sustained innovation at the world's technological frontier.

Moreover, the finding that a number of wealthy economies with well-functioning science and innovation systems do not increase their investments in innovation sufficiently to enter the 'club' of leading innovator countries suggests either that national innovative leadership is a strategy that countries choose not to pursue or that continuously deepening commitments to innovation are difficult to achieve, even for middle-tier innovator economies. Although it is important to exercise caution in interpreting the results for policy, the results suggest that, for such middle-tier countries, the greatest challenge in enhancing innovative productivity lies in increasing their levels of investment in innovation rather than in adjusting their national policies or innovation systems. For third-tier innovators, it appears as if there is room for improvement on both dimensions. While the success of a number of emerging innovator economies allows for hope, the results also quantify the magnitude of the challenges faced by historically less innovative economies in increasing their innovative capacity substantially enough to achieve innovative productivity commensurate with the world's innovator countries.

Researchers in innovation studies, including authors in the national innovation systems approach, have often asked about the country-specific factors that affect the composition of inputs into innovation – and often report on the levels of inputs into the innovation process.[23] The results of this study suggest deepening this research agenda to focus as well on the determinants of the *level* of innovative inputs achieved by an economy. In the tradition of Keith Pavitt's research, both qualitative and quantitative approaches could bear fruit. Large-scale empirical analyses that jointly estimate the determinants of innovative inputs and outputs could tackle endogeneity issues not addressed by a reduced-form approach; detailed, cased-based research would, however, be a necessary complement that elucidates the underlying mechanisms by which these processes occur.

The complementarity between detailed qualitative work and large-scale empirical analysis is also important for understanding the phenomenon associated with emerging innovator countries. While emerging innovator countries share the fact that they have managed to increase their commitments to innovative capacity in a way not matched by middle-tier or third-tier innovator countries, these countries – e.g. Iceland, Ireland and South Korea – vary substantially in the institutional configurations that characterize their national innovation systems. That they are all able to achieve relatively high levels of innovative capacity underscores the point that there is no universal recipe that enables follower countries to catch up to leading innovator economies. Understanding both the unique circumstances that have led these countries to make substantial commitments to innovative capacity and the common relationships that allow these countries' investments to bear fruit requires the interplay between qualitative and quantitative research methods.

NOTES

*   This paper builds on research conducted jointly with Michael E. Porter and Scott Stern and additional research conducted by Joshua Gans in conjunction with Scott Stern. We thank each of these researchers for thoughtful discussion, four anonymous reviewers for their insightful suggestions, and Virginia Acha, Richard Nelson and Orietta Marsili for stewarding this paper through the editorial process at *Research Policy,* and Grazia Santangelo for organizing this conference volume. We are grateful to Mercedes Delgado for excellent research assistance. All errors are our own. We acknowledge the gracious support of the Boston University Junior Faculty Research Fund, the Victorian Department of Treasury & Finance and the Intellectual Property Research Institute of Australia. We are grateful for the comments of participants in the conferences at the Sussex Policy Research Unit and the University of Catania Faculty of Political Science.

1. We employ the term 'innovative capacity' to describe a country's potential – as both an economic and political entity – to produce a stream of commercially relevant innovations. The term 'innovative capacity' has been used by a broad range of researchers in literature in economics, geography and innovation policy. For example, Keith Pavitt (1980b) employed the term in a manner similar to that in this chapter (and Pavitt, 1980a, applied a variant of the term) in his broad-based research in innovation policy and economics. Suarez-Villa (1990, 1993) applies the concept within the geography literature, emphasizing the linkage between invention and innovation. Neely and Hii (1998) provide a detailed discussion of the origins and definition of innovative capacity in the academic literature. The framework presented here builds directly on research reported in Porter and Stern (1999) and Furman et al. (2000, 2002) and the references cited therein.

2. Similarly, Vannevar Bush's report, *Science: The Endless Frontier* (1945) identified scientific and technological progress as a key element of national policy debates, particularly in the USA.

3. It is important to note that these literatures are not necessarily at odds, and that some authors have made important contributions to both streams. For example, Romer's (1990) model of endogenous technical change employs a concept of technology that is less nuanced than that of his historical essay examining the causes of the USA's technical leadership in manufacturing (1996). Likewise, Abramovitz's early growth accounting research (1956) was a keystone for early formal models, though his later research on catch-up (1986) adopts a more phenomenon-driven approach, e.g. proposing 'technical congruence' as a notion to explain why knowledge flows imperfectly across countries.

4. For additional elaboration, see also Fagerberg (1987, 1988) and Fagerberg and Verspagen (2002).

5. Keller and Gong (2003) also provide a recent review of the evolution of economic growth and the role of technology.

6. This perspective is first articulated fully in the papers by Nelson, Lundvall and Freeman in Part V of Dosi et al. (1988).

7. These authors echo Gerschenkron (1962) and North (1990), who are among the numerous economic historians to point to importance of national institutions in affecting the structure and nature of competition across countries and describe how these institutions have a long-run impact on national economic fortunes.

8. It is important to note that important though subtle differences exist among authors within the national innovation systems literature. McKelvey (1991) reviews some of these perspectives.

9. Cross-sectional variation allows inter-country comparisons that can reveal the importance of specific determinants of national innovative capacity, yet it may be subject to unobserved heterogeneity. On the other hand, time-series variation yields insight into how national choices manifest themselves in terms of observed innovative output, but may be subject to its own sources of endogeneity (e.g. changes in a country's fundamental characteristics may reflect idiosyncratic changes in its environment).

10. Porter and Stern (2000) have investigated potential problems with endogeneity in an innovation production function specification similar to the one used here.

11. Furman et al. (2002) discuss the use of international patenting as a proxy for national innovative output in greater detail.

12. Focusing on international patents helps satisfy this criterion. First, obtaining a patent in a foreign country is a costly undertaking that is only worthwhile for organizations anticipating a return in excess of these substantial costs. Second, USPTO-granted 'international' patenting (*PATENTS*) constitutes a measure of technologically and economically significant innovations at the world's commercial technology frontier that should be consistent across countries. Third, we are careful to accommodate the potential

for differences in the propensity to apply for patent protection across countries and over time (as highlighted by Scherer, 1983) by evaluating robustness of our results to year- and country-specific fixed effects.

13. For example, Patel and Pavitt (1987, 1989) compare the relative innovativeness of European countries using USPTO-approved patents as a benchmark.

14. In previous work (Furman et al., 2002), we explored several alternative measures to *PATENTS*, including the rate of publication in scientific journals (*JOURNALS*), the realized market share of a country in 'high-technology' industries (*MARKET SHARE*), and total factor productivity (*TFP*) and discuss the relative advantages and disadvantages of using these measures.

15. To ensure that this asymmetry between US and non-US patents does not affect our results we include a US dummy variable in all regressions that include US data. Note that the key results are also robust to the use of *PATENTS* based on date of application, and are also robust to the use of alternative lag structures.

16. Some additional data are available from country-specific publications and offices. These are often available only in local languages and for recent years, and questions exist about their comparability across countries and over time. Hu and Mathews (2004) address these issues in compiling innovation statistics for their sample of East Asian economics. The ability to analyze a complete set of data for a wider array of countries – including both those that have achieved apparent innovative success, (e.g. Israel, Singapore, Taiwan) as well as currently industrializing countries – would greatly enhance research in this area.

17. Our dataset is similar to that compiled by Gans and Stern (2003), and used in their investigation of Australia's innovative capacity.

18. For the countries in the core dataset, we interpolated data from existing years to obtain occasional missing values. For example, several countries only report educational expenditure data every second year. For these we used an average of the immediately preceding and following years.

19. Note that this differs from Furman et al. (2002), in which *OPENNESS* is based on data from the World Competitiveness Report, an annual survey in which leading executives ranked their perceptions of their country's openness to trade. Although the measure we use here differs, the results are qualitatively similar.

20. We have also examined alternative drivers in our background analysis, including policy variables such as *ANTITRUST* and measures of the extent to which venture funding is available (*VC*). These variables do not enter our models in a consistently statistically significant manner, and thus do not appear in the preferred model (4–4). In prior work, we have also modeled *SPECIALIZATION* as a factor reflecting the cluster-specific environment for innovation. The core results in this chapter are also robust to the inclusion of *SPECIALIZATION*.

21. Preliminary analysis applying the techniques elaborated by Islam (1995, 2003) to the data underlying Figure 9.7 provides suggestive evidence of statistical convergence in innovative capacity. Further research on statistical convergence in innovative outputs may be a promising avenue for future work.

22. *Expanded dataset* countries include the Czech Republic, Greece, Poland, Portugal, the Slovak Republic and Turkey.

23. Romer (2000), for example, investigates whether US government subsidies for scientist and engineering are essential or excessive.

REFERENCES

Abramovitz, M. (1956), 'Resource and Output Trends in the United States since 1870', *American Economic Review*, **46** (2), 5–23.

Abramovitz, M. (1986), 'Catching Up, Forging Ahead and Falling Behind', *Journal of Economic History*, **46**, 385–406.

Ames, E. and N. Rosenberg (1963), 'Changing Technological Leadership and Industrial Growth', *Economic* Journal, **74**, 13–31.

Amsden, Alice H. (1989), *Asia's Next Giant*, New York: Oxford University Press.

Arora, A., R. Landau and N. Rosenberg (1998), *Chemicals and Long-Term Economic Growth: Insights from the Chemical Industry*, New York: Wiley.

Barro, R. and X. Sala-i-Martin (1992), 'Convergence', *Journal of Political Economy*, **100** (2), 223–51.

Barro, R. and X. Sala-i-Martin (1995), *Economic Growth*, New York: McGraw-Hill.

Baumol, W.J. (1986), 'Productivity Growth, Convergence, and Welfare: What the Long-Run Data Show', *American Economic Review*, **76** (5), 1072–85.

Baumol, W.J., S.A. Batey and E.N. Wolff (1989), *Productivity and American Leadership: The Long View*, Cambridge, MA: MIT Press.

Bell, M. and K. Pavitt (1992), 'Accumulating Technological Capability in Developing Countries', *The World Bank Research Observer*, 257–72.

Bell, M. and K. Pavitt (1993), 'Technological Accumulation and Industrial Growth: Contrasts Between Developed and Developing Countries', *Industrial and Corporate Change*, **2**, 157–210.

Bush, V. (1945), *Science: The Endless Frontier. A Report to the President on a Program for Postwar Scientific Research*, Washington, DC: National Science Foundation.

DeLong, J.B. (1988) 'Productivity Growth, Convergence, and Welfare: Comment', *American Economic Review*, **78** (5), 1138–54.

Dosi, G., C. Freeman, G. Silverberg and L. Soete (eds) (1988), *Technical Change and Economic Theory*, London: Pinter Publishers.

Dosi, G., K. Pavitt and L. Soete (1990), *The Economics of Technical Change and International Trade*, New York: Columbia University Press.

Eaton, J. and S. Kortum (1996), 'Trade in Ideas: Patenting & Productivity in the OECD,' *Journal of International Economics*, **40** (3–4), 251–78.

Eaton, J. and S. Kortum (1999), 'International Technology Diffusion: Theory and Measurement', *International Economic Review*, **40** (3), 537–70.

Edquist, C. (ed.) (1997), *Systems of Innovation: Technologies, Institutions, and Organizations*, London: Pinter Publishers.

Evenson, R. (1984), 'International Invention: Implications for Technology Market Analysis', in Zvi Griliches (ed.), *R&D, Patents, and Productivity*, Chicago, IL: University of Chicago Press, pp. 89–126.

Fagerberg, J. (1987), 'A Technology Gap Approach to Why Growth Rates Differ', *Research Policy*, **16** (2–4), 87–99.

Fagerberg, J. (1988), 'Innovation, Catching Up, and Growth', in *Technology and Productivity: The Challenge for Economic Policy*, Paris: OECD, pp. 37–46.

Fagerberg, J. (1994), 'Technology and International Differences in Growth Rates', *Journal of Economic Literature*, **32** (3), 1147–75.

Fagerberg, J. and B. Verspagen (2002), 'Technology-Gaps, Innovation-Diffusion, and Transformation: An Evolutionary Interpretation', *Research Policy*, **31**, 1291–304.

Freeman, C. (1987), *Technology Policy and Economic Performance: Lessons from Japan*, London: Pinter Publishers.

Freeman, C. (1988), 'Japan: A New System of Innovation', in G. Dosi, C. Freeman, G. Silverberg and L. Soete (eds), *Technical Change and Economic Theory*, London: Pinter Publishers, pp. 330–48.

Furman, J.L., M.E. Porter and S. Stern (2002), 'The Determinants of National Innovative Capacity', *Research Policy*, **31**, 899–933.
Furman, J.L., M.E. Porter and S. Stern (2000), 'Understanding the Drivers of National Innovative Capacity', *Academy of Management Best Papers in Proceedings*.
Furman, J.L. and S. Stern (2000), 'Understanding the Drivers of National Innovative Capacity – Implications for Central European Economies', *Wirtschaftspolitische Blätter*, **47**(2).
Gans, J.S. and S. Stern (2003), 'Assessing Australia's Innovative Capacity in the 21st Century', Intellectual Property Research Institute of Australia Working Paper.
Gerschenkron, A. (1962), *Economic Backwardness in Historical Perspective*, Cambridge, MA: Belknap Press of Harvard University Press.
Griliches, Z. (ed.) (1984), *R&D, Patents and Productivity*, Chicago, IL: Chicago University Press.
Griliches, Z. (1990), 'Patent Statistics as Economic Indicators: A Survey', *Journal of Economic Literature*, **28**(4), 1661–707.
Grossman, G. and Helpman, E. (1991), *Innovation and Growth in the Global Economy*, Cambridge, MA: MIT Press.
Hu, M.-C. and J.A. Mathews (2004), 'National Innovative Capacity in East Asia', Macquarie University Working Paper.
Im, K., M. Pesaran and Y. Shin (2003), 'Testing for Unit Roots in Heterogeneous Panels', *Journal of Econometrics*, **115**, 53–74.
Islam, N., (1995), 'Growth Empirics: A Panel Data Approach', *Quarterly Journal of Economics*, **110**, 1127–70.
Islam, N. (2003), 'What Have We Learnt from the Convergence Debate?' *Journal of Economic Surveys*, **17**(3), 309–62.
Jones, C. (1995), 'R&D Based Models of Economic Growth', *Journal of Political Economy*, **103**, 739–84.
Jones, C. (1998) *Introduction to Economic Growth*, New York: W.W. Norton & Company.
Keller, W. and G. Gong (2003), 'Convergence and Polarization in Global Income Levels: A Review of Recent Results on the Role of International Technology Diffusion', *Research Policy* **32**(6), 1055–79.
Kim, L. (1997), *Imitation to Innovation: The Dynamics of Korea's Technological Learning*, Cambridge, MA: Harvard Business School Press.
Kortum, S. (1997), 'Research, Patenting, and Technological Change', *Econometrica*, **65**(6), 1389–419.
Kortum, S. and Lerner, J. (1999), 'What is Behind the Recent Surge in Patenting?', *Research Policy*, **28**(1), 1–22.
Levin, A., C. Lin and C. Chu (2002), 'Unit Root Tests in Panel Data: Asymptotic and Finite-sample Properties', *Journal of Econometrics*, **108**, 1–24.
Lundvall, B.-A. (1988), 'Innovation as an Interactive Process: From User–Producer Interaction to the National System of Innovation', in G. Dosi, C. Freeman, G. Silverberg and L. Soete (eds), *Technical Change and Economic Theory*, London: Pinter Publishers, pp. 349–69.
Lundvall, B.-A. (1992), *National Systems of Innovation: Towards a Theory of Innovation and Interactive Learning*, London: Pinter.
McKelvey, M. (1991), 'How do National Systems of Innovation Differ? A Critical Analysis of Porter, Freeman, Lundvall, and Nelson', in G.M. Hodgson and

E. Screpanti (eds), *Rethinking Economics – Markets, Technology, and Economic Evolution,* Aldershot, UK: Edward Elgar.

Murmann, J.P. (2003), *Knowledge and Competitive Advantage: The Coevolution of Firms, Technology, and National Institutions,* Cambridge, UK: Cambridge University Press.

Neely, A. and J. Hii (1998), 'Innovation and Business Performance: A Literature Review', mimeo, Judge Institute of Management Studies, University of Cambridge.

Nelson, R.R. (1981), 'Research on Productivity Growth and Productivity Differences: Dead Ends and New Directions', *Journal of Economic Literature,* **19** (3), 1029–64.

Nelson, R.R. (ed.) (1993), *National Innovation Systems: A Comparative Analysis,* New York: Oxford University Press.

Nelson, R.R. and S. Winter (1982), *An Evolutionary Theory of Economic Change,* Cambridge, MA: Harvard University Press.

Nelson R.R. and G. Wright (1992), 'The Rise and Fall of American Technological Leadership: The Postwar Era in Historical Perspective', *Journal of Economic Literature,* **30** (4), 1931–64.

North, D.C. (1990), *Institutions, Institutional Change, and Economic Performance,* Cambridge, UK: Cambridge University Press.

Ohkawa, K. and H. Rosovsky (1973), *Japanese Economic Growth,* Palo Alto, CA: Stanford University Press.

O'Sullivan, M. (2000), 'The Sustainability of Industrial Development in Ireland', *Regional Studies,* **34** (3), 277–90.

Patel, P. and K. Pavitt (1987), 'Is Western Europe Losing the Technological Race?', *Research Policy,* **16** (2–4), 59–86.

Patel, P. and K. Pavitt (1989), 'A Comparison of Technological Activities in West Germany and the United Kingdom', *National Westminster Bank Quarterly Review,* 27–42.

Patel, P. and K. Pavitt (1994), 'National Innovation Systems: Why They Are Important, and How They Might Be Measured and Compared', *Economics of Innovation and New Technology,* **3** (1), 77–95.

Pavitt, K. (1979), 'Technical Innovation and Industrial Development', *Futures,* **11** (6), 458–70.

Pavitt, K. (1980a), 'Industrial R&D and the British Economic Problem', *R&D Management,* **10,** 149.

Pavitt, K. (ed.) (1980b), *Technical Innovation and British Economic Performance,* Sussex, UK: SPRU.

Pavitt, K. (1982), 'R&D, Patenting, and Innovative Activities: A Statistical Exploration', *Research Policy,* **11** (1), 33–51.

Pavitt, K. (1985), 'Patent Statistics as Indicators of Innovative Activities: Possibilities and Problems', *Scientometrics,* **7,** 77–99.

Pavitt, K. (1988), 'Uses and Abuses of Patent Statistics', in A. van Raan (ed.), *Handbook of Quantitative Studies of Science Policy,* Amsterdam: North-Holland.

Porter, M.E. (1990), *The Competitive Advantage of Nations,* New York: The Free Press.

Porter, M.E. and S. Stern (1999), *The New Challenge to America's Prosperity: Findings from the Innovation Index,* Washington, DC: Council on Competitiveness.

Porter, M.E. and S. Stern, (2000), 'Measuring the "Ideas" Production Function: Evidence from International Patent Output', NBER Working Paper 7891.

Porter, M.E., J.L. Furman and S. Stern (2000), 'Los Factores Impulsores de la Capacidad Innovadora Nacional: Implicaciones para Espana y America Latina', (English title: The Drivers of National Innovative Capacity: Implications for Spain and Latin America), in *Claves de la Economia Mundial,* Madrid, Spain: ICEX, pp. 78–88.

Quah, D.T. (1997), 'Empirics for Growth and Distribution: Stratification, Polarization, and Convergence Clubs', *Journal of Economic Growth,* **2**, 27–59.

Romer, P. (1990), 'Endogenous Technological Change', *Journal of Political Economy,* **98**, S71-S102.

Romer, P. (1996), 'Why, Indeed, in America?', *American Economic Review,* **86** (2), 202–6.

Romer, P. (2000), 'Should the Government Subsidize Supply or Demand in the Market for Scientists and Engineers?', NBER Working Paper No. w7723.

Rosenberg, N. (1963), 'Technological Change in the Machine Tool Industry, 1840–1910', *Journal of Economic History*, **23**, 414–43.

Scherer, F.M. (1983), 'The Propensity to Patent', *International Journal of Industrial Organization*, **1**, 107–28.

Sala-i-Martin, X. (1996), 'The Classical Approach to Convergence Analysis', *The Economic Journal*, **106**, 1019–36.

Schumpeter, Joseph (1942), *Capitalism, Socialism and Democracy*, 2nd ed, London: George Allen & Unwin.

Schmookler, J. (1966), *Invention and Economic Growth,* Cambridge, MA: Harvard University Press.

Soete, L.G. and S. Wyatt. (1983), 'The Use of Foreign Patenting as an Internationally Comparable Science and Technology Output Indicator', *Scientometrics*, **5**(1): 31–4.

Solow, R.M. (1956), 'A Contribution to the Theory of Economic Growth', *Quarterly Journal of Economics,* **70**, 65–94.

Suarez-Villa, Luis (1990), 'Invention, Inventive Learning, and Innovative Capacity', *Behavioral Science*, **35**: 290–310.

Suarez-Villa, Luis (1993), 'The Dynamics of Regional Invention and Innovation: Innovative Capacity and Regional Change in the Twentieth Century', *Geographical Analysis*, **25** (2), 147–64.

Trajtenberg, M. (1990), 'Patents as Indicators of Innovation', *Economic Analysis of Product Innovation,* Cambridge, MA: Harvard University Press.

Trajtenberg, M. (2001), 'Innovation in Israel 1968–1997: A Comparative Analysis Using Patent Data', *Research Policy*, **30** (3), 363.

Veblen, T. (1915), *Imperial Germany and the Industrial Revolution,* New York: Macmillan.

Vertova, G. (1999), 'Stability in National Patterns of Technological Specialisation: Some Historical Evidence from Patent Data', *Economics of Innovation and New Technology*, **8** (4), 331–54.

Young, A. (1995), 'The Tyranny of Numbers: Confronting the Statistical Realities of the East Asian Growth Experience', *Quarterly Journal of Economics*, **110**, 641–80.

APPENDIX

Table 9A.1   *Patents in a sample of emerging Latin American and Asian economies*

Country	1976–80	1995–99	Growth rate
Emerging Latin American economies			
Argentina	115	228	0.98
Brazil	136	492	2.62
Chile	12	60	4.00
Colombia	28	42	0.50
Costa Rica	22	48	1.18
Mexico	124	431	2.48
Venezuela	50	182	2.64
Emerging Asian economies			
China	3	577	191.33
Hong Kong	176	1 694	8.63
India	89	485	4.45
Malaysia	13	175	12.46
Singapore	17	725	41.65
South Korea	23	12 062	523.43
Taiwan	135	15 871	116.56

Source: Porter et al. (2000).

10. Positive forces and vicious mechanisms behind innovative activity in a lagging region

Rosalia Epifanio

INTRODUCTION

Innovation is today generally considered a fundamental component of the engine of growth. This is true for various economic scenarios. Therefore it is crucial to take account of the particular features that different scenarios present.

Literature on the economic growth of lagging regions is traditionally concerned with problems related to gaps. What is at issue are the ways in which such regions may 'run after' or even catch up with the more advanced economies. This is very often debated through the application of growth models built on successful experiences of development.

On the other hand, approaches based on development theories refer mainly to third world realities and deal essentially with issues peculiar to the economic and social development of low-income countries.

Finally, traditional literature on technological change generally analyses growth processes of advanced industrialized countries and aims at identifying general patterns and models that reflect the successful cases on which they are built.

Even if these three research streams contribute to address some crucial issues, they do not seem to be fully suitable for analysing cases of lagging industrialized regions and their growth processes and potentials.

To grasp the various aspects of innovation processes taking place in lagging regions, theoretical frameworks which examine the role of 'context' variables and of systemic processes have provided useful interpretative guidelines.

In this chapter, therefore, the role of 'context' variables for innovative activity in a lagging self-contained region will be analysed. In particular the innovative behaviour of a sample of Sicilian firms will be considered.

'CONTEXT' VARIABLES AND GROWTH THROUGH INNOVATION

Industrial districts literature is a cornerstone when studying the means to economic success of areas characterized by small, low-technology firms.

Such literature, in the light of the 1970s 'Third Italy' experience, has emphasized the importance of the 'Marshallian atmosphere' determined by proximity, small size and sense of community. In the case of industrial districts, this special 'atmosphere' provided an incentive for cooperative and competitive behaviours; this resulted in a process of innovative bottom–up stimulus that enhanced growth of industrial districts and inspired the creation of new institutions devoted to the promotion of local growth. Existing local public actors have thus been forced to improve their efficiency (Becattini, 1987; Brusco, 1983).

However, the subsequent crisis of Italian districts implied a revision of the approach (Pyke and Sengenberger, 1992). In particular the collapse of bottom–up mechanisms had shown the need for an institutional top–down intervention directed to coordinate resources, especially with regard to collective goods provision and real services markets.

On the wave of the industrial districts case, notwithstanding the relevance of structural and productive variables (Breschi and Malerba, 1997), the role of 'context' has attracted economists and geographers interested in technological change of delimited areas.

The general hypothesis that innovative performance is influenced by a set of synergetic factors characterizing the context has found a full formulation in the system of innovation approach (Freeman, 1987; Nelson, 1993). In its initial version, it particularly emphasized the relevance for technological growth of interactions among economic, political and cultural spheres at national level.

Innovations, intended as new combinations of existing knowledge (Lundvall, 1992), are strongly dependent on learning processes. In this perspective, interactions between economic and extra-economic subjects are fundamental for the diffusion of innovation and, hence, the interactions within the industrial context and those between this and the institutions turn out to be extremely relevant. In particular, formal and informal user–producer relationships within the economic–productive sphere are crucial: they involve flows of information and knowledge and stimulate learning processes (Lundvall, 1992).[1]

The emphasis placed on synergies and interactions leads to the relevance attributed to meso-economic structures. In particular, considering the system of innovation as a dynamic cycle of knowledge and innovation, the determinants of its functioning can be found in Carlsson (1997):

1. the initial conditions of the system, which are influenced by the economic, technical and social history;
2. receiver competencies, which determine the learning capacity of firms;
3. connectivity, corresponding to the firms' attitude to interaction with other subjects;
4. mechanisms of reactions to changing situations, which explain the system capacity to find different solutions to continuous selection mechanisms.

The success of an innovation system depends strongly on the existence of internal spillover mechanisms, linked to labour mobility and internal mechanisms of knowledge diffusion, together with openness to external relationships. This has proved to be significant also for areas smaller than nations, as in the cases analysed by regional systems of innovation (Cooke and Morgan, 1998) and 'milieux innovateurs' (Camagni, 1991) studies.

The same interpretative scheme of change through innovation outlined above might, in my view, be used to analyse the cases of lagging industrialized regions. The same sort of factors and mechanisms, in fact, strongly influence the economic performance of such regions. The economies of lagging regions usually rely on industry and, thus, the analysis of technological change is crucial for their growth. Moreover, an approach based on a system of innovation interpretative framework allows us to take into account incremental innovations, small firms, collaborations, institutions and other factors that characterize such areas.

In detail, however, lagging regions might present some anomalies in the functioning of the system or might even lack some of the key factors and mechanisms.

It can generally be hypothesized that difficulties could arise relating to various stages of the process (Epifanio et al., 2002) and particularly:

- in the generation of innovation;
- in the functioning of those mechanisms which drive firms to interact with other subjects (that affect 'connectivity');
- in the learning processes. This could happen both at single firm level, due to the absence or bad coordination of internal firm competencies, and at the 'context' level, where various obstacles could hamper flows of knowledge;
- in the access of individuals to collective learning and, therefore, in its application to innovative activity;

- in the absence of exogenous factors which can trigger the virtuous process;
- in the dynamic capacity of the system.

SICILY: RESOURCES AND PERFORMANCE OF A LAGGING REGION

Among Southern Italian regions, Sicily is rather distinct because of its institutional as well as geographical characteristics. In this sense, Sicily can be considered a self-contained system and could be looked at as a prototype of the regional system of innovation.[2] The case of Sicily is, therefore, of great interest in an analysis of the role of the 'context' as an influence on the innovative performance of a region.

From an economic point of view, Sicily can be considered a lagging region. Such a lag is self-evident if some of the most significant indicators of efficiency are taken into consideration (Table 10.1).

Looking at human resources, the data point to a situation typical of late development; the Sicilian regional system is characterized by a dramatic gap between human resources and the labour market. Table 10.2 synthesizes some indicators of human capital, components which usually play a significant role in economic growth through technological change.

The productive system is characterized by a sector distribution where

Table 10.1   Sicilian economic performance: principal efficiency indicators

Main Italian geographical areas	Export/GDP (%)		Net imports[a] GDP (%)		Investments/ GDP (%)		R&D/GDP[b] (%)	
	1995	2000	1995	2000	1995	2000	1995	2000
Sicily	5.2	8.1	20.9	22.0	19.2	20.1	0.04	0.21
Italy	21.3	22.3	−2.8	0.1	18.3	19.8	0.53	0.54
North-west	29.8	28.5	−13.6	−9.1	17.4	19.4	1.00	0.96
North-east	28.4	30.9	−6.8	−3.4	19.7	21.5	0.35	0.38
Centre	15.7	17.8	−4.4	−2.5	17.5	17.9	0.43	0.42
Mezzogiorno	8.2	10.1	17.0	18.0	19.0	20.6	0.16	0.21
Regions Ob. 1	7.2	9.0	18.2	18.9	19.1	20.5	0.13	0.19

Notes:
[a] Net imports represent the import–export balance and include goods and services flows with foreign countries and other regions. A positive value indicates an excess of imports over exports.
[b] R&D is measured in terms of intra-moenia expenses for R&D both of private and public firms.

Source: *Indicatori di contesto chiave regionali QCS 2000–06.* ISTAT, novembre 2002.

Table 10.2   Human resources: principal indicators

Main Italian geographical areas	Graduated with technical–scientific degree [a]/ total graduated (%)		Youth unemployment rate [b] (%)		Workers participating in training activities (%)	
	1995	2001	1995	2001	1995	2001
Sicily	33.9	35.3	58.4	54.7	1.4	2.5
Italy	32.0	33.0	33.8	28.2	2.9	4.0
North-west	36.6	35.3	22.6	12.6	3.3	4.1
North-east	31.6	34.1	15.3	9.3	4.2	6.2
Centre	29.1	30.3	34.1	24.2	2.9	3.9
Mezzogiorno	30.2	31.5	54.7	50.8	1.6	2.4
Regions Ob. 1	31.1	31.6	56.0	52.3	1.6	2.5

Notes:
[a] Graduated in the following Faculties: Engineering, Medicine, Veterinary Sciences, Agriculture, Mathematics, Physics and Natural Sciences, Pharmacy, Industrial Chemistry.
[b] Number of people unemployed – aged 15–24 – as a percentage of the labour force aged 15–24.

Source: As for Table 10.1.

industry accounts for 19 per cent (in terms of local units and employees), commerce 39 per cent (20 per cent of employees) and other services 34 per cent (26.5 per cent employees) (Figures 10.1 and 10.2). The presence of the public sector in economic activity, with particular reference to the proportion of employees working for public institutions, is impressive. The prominent role of the state in the Sicilian economy is especially relevant when considering the high unemployment rate of the region, which heavily influences market efficiency.[3]

The relatively low incidence of industry[4] confirms the profile of a lagging industrialized region in which the public productive sector is highly relevant, especially in the labour market.

More specifically, in the Sicilian manufacturing sector, as in total regional industry, small – or even micro-sized – firms prevail. About 97 per cent of Sicily's manufacturing firms have fewer than 20 employees[5] and this characterizes all the productive compartments of the sector.

Furthermore, the level and trend of investments are lower than in the rest of Italy, and firm internationalization is limited.

Another characteristic of Sicilian industry, shown also by the manufacturing sector, is firms' spatial agglomeration: about half of the Sicilian manufacturing firms are located in the two principal provinces of Palermo and Catania.

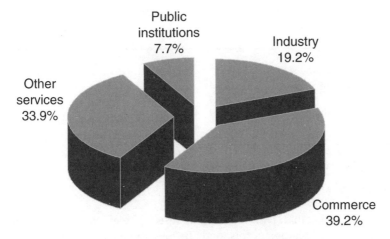

Source: *Based on 8° Censimento dell'Industria e dei Servizi*, ISTAT 2001.

Figure 10.1   Distribution of local units

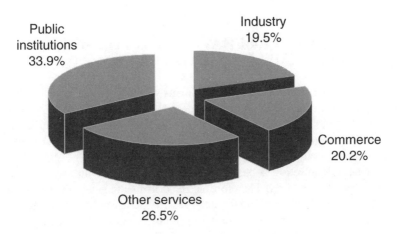

Source: As for Figure 10.1.

Figure 10.2   Distribution of employees

As in most lagging industrialized economies, traditional manufacturing industries prevail. In particular the food-processing industry – due to Sicily's historical and natural agricultural background – and the mechanical industry are the main actors. The textile and clothing industry is prominent in the low-technology sector (Table 10.3).

Sicilian industry shows a limited innovative activity compared to the

Table 10.3   Food-processing, mechanical and textile industries in Sicily (1996)*

	Palermo	Catania	Sicily
Food processing	24.1	24.9	26.8
Mechanical	14.4	14.4	15.3
Textiles & clothing	6.3	6.0	5.4
Total	44.8	45.3	47.5

Note: * Percentages of manufacturing sector measured in terms of number of firms.

Source: As for Figure 10.1.

national average that, besides being the result of regional specialization in low-technology sectors, corresponds to lower innovative performance of each specific sector. Most of the innovations are incremental or organizational, as is also the case of firms located in Sicilian para-district systems (Mazzola and Asmundo, 1999).

THE INNOVATIVE BEHAVIOUR IN THE SICILIAN CASE: THE SAMPLE AND THE DATA

A sample of 72 small manufacturing firms was selected to answer the key research questions.

The chosen firms belong to the food-processing, mechanical and textiles & clothing sectors which, as outlined above, constitute the most relevant industries in Sicily.[6]

The sample selection is based on indications given by industrial associations, experts and so on. Therefore, selected firms are generally well known for their external presence and for activities not exclusively linked to their own business. Even if from a strict statistical point of view such selection criteria could appear biased, they guarantee good-quality responses, and avoid the inclusion of firms pursuing a simple survival strategy. Moreover, response quality is particularly crucial in the case of such a limited size sample.[7]

The sample firms, despite the selection method, represent the universe of Sicilian manufacturing firms in terms of distribution by industry, size and age. The location and industrial sector of sample firms is shown in Table 10.4.

As evidenced in Table 10.4, according to the actual distribution of economic activity in the region, the firms considered in the research are located mainly in Palermo and Catania (the two principal Sicilian provinces).

Table 10.4   Sample firms distribution (number of firms)

	Palermo	Catania	Other provinces	Total	%
Food processing	11	3	14	28	38.9
Mechanical	8	15	2	25	34.7
Textiles & clothing	7	1	11	19	26.4
Total	26	19	27	72	100.0

Data have been collected over two periods through structured questionnaires and direct interviews with entrepreneurs or their delegates. The data in particular refer to innovative activity carried out over three five-year periods from 1981 to 2000. In particular, for a group of 30 firms, the data regarding the two periods 1981–90 and 1991–95 have been collected, while for the remaining 42 firms the collected data refer to the period 1996–2000.

The collected data relate to the firms' innovative activity. Innovations have been classified according to the Oslo Manual guidelines as:

- innovations new to the firm,
- innovations new to the region,
- innovations new to the nation,
- innovations new to the world.

Such a classification allows us, in my opinion, to deepen the analysis of the mechanisms driving innovative behaviours. This is rather significant, since the object of the analysis is not the firms on the technological frontier. The understanding of the role played by the different variables in the different phases and levels of technological change is crucial for development policy.

Firms from the sample have then been classified in three principal groups, in order to stress the differences among their innovative behaviours.

1. more innovative firms, that is, firms introducing innovations which were new at least to the region (this group includes firms introducing innovations to the region, the country, or to the world);
2. less innovative firms, that is, firms introducing innovations new merely at the firm level;
3. non-innovative firms.

This has allowed us to overcome the risk of a quantitative misrepresentation of innovative activity, given the difficulty of objectively identifying single innovations.

Catch-up in backward areas

The characteristics of sample firms

Table 10.5 synthetically shows the distributions of firms, grouped by innovative levels, according to their dimension and productive sector.

Looking at the structural characteristics of the firms within the sample (Table 10.6) among the three groups, we can observe a remarkable difference in the average age (of the firms), the number of the employees and the sales. In particular, the more innovative firms are, on average, younger and show higher levels of sales and employees. On the other hand, it is not surprising to find, within the less innovative firms group, an average level of sales far lower than in the previous group examined.

Finally, the sales/employee index is higher for the more innovative firms, whereas it is almost the same within the other groups.

Considering the type of innovations introduced, a certain prevalence of process innovations in less innovative firms (about 57 per cent of the whole innovations in this group) emerges. This reflects the main characteristics of the innovations introduced by this category of firms (i.e. innovations which are new only to the firm, mostly through the acquisition of instrumental goods).

Table 10.5   Distribution of sample firms by degree of innovation

Industry/firm size (no. of employees)		More innovative	Less innovative	Non-innovative	Total
Food processing	Number	8	13	7	28
	%	28.6	46.4	25.0	100.0
Mechanical	Number	8	12	5	25
	%	32.0	48.0	20.0	100.0
Textiles & clothing	Number	10	5	4	19
	%	52.6	26.3	21.1	100.0
1–19	Number	13	15	9	37
	%	35.1	40.5	24.3	100.0
20–49	Number	4	11	2	17
	%	23.5	64.7	11.8	100.0
50–99	Number	5	3	3	11
	%	45.5	27.3	27.3	100.0
100 +	Number	4	0	0	4
	%	100.0	0	0	100.0
n.a.	Number		1	2	3
	%		33.3	66.7	100.0

Note: n.a.   Reported results from firms that did not declare their size.

The average number of innovations per firm[8] does not seem to be an effective indicator of the innovation behaviour of companies and it is non-sensitive to the technological content of the introduced innovations. This therefore confirms the appropriateness of the choice made: to impute the introduction of innovation on a binary base.

In the light of the above-mentioned relevance of public intervention in the Sicilian economy, the access to public funds by the firms of the sample is a significant piece of information. In fact, it is very interesting to examine the distribution by localization and size of the firms given these incentives (Table 10.7).

Table 10.6   Structural and innovative characteristics of sample firms

	More innovative	Less innovative	Non-innovative	Total
Number of firms	26	30	16	72
Age	19	31	26	27
Sales	16862	6755	5603	10706
Employees	44	25	26	32
Sales/employees	383	270	216	335
Process innovations	17	25		42
Product innovations	13	15		28
Product + process innovations	7	4		11

Table 10.7   Firms receiving public funding (classified according to the awarding institutions)

Provinces – firm size	Total[a] %	Regional[b] %	National[b] %	European[b] %
Palermo	53.8	50.0	57.1	35.7
Catania	73.7	35.7	64.3	7.1
Other	84.6	40.9	59.1	22.7
0–19	64.9	50.0	45.8	16.7
20–49	70.6	50.0	75.0	41.7
50–99	81.8	33.3	66.7	22.2
100 +	75.0	0.0	100.0	0.0

Notes:
[a] Percentage is calculated on the total number of firms for each category.
[b] Percentage is calculated on the number of firms which have been awarded public funds.

Table 10.8   Firms and public funding (%)[a]

	More innovative	Less innovative	Non-innovative
Obtained funding	70.8	76.7	62.5
No public funding	29.2	23.3	37.5
Regional funding	43.7	57.1	20.0
National funding	75.0	42.9	90.0
European funding	18.7	19.0	40.0

Note: [a] Percentage values have been calculated on the number of firms which have received public funding. Columns sum to more than 100 because, on average, each firm has used more than one typology of incentive.

It is worth mentioning, first of all, the fact that 50 per cent of the firms located in Palermo have been awarded regional public funding. This is particularly significant in the light of the lower incidence of firms benefiting from regional resources located in other provinces.

The distribution of public funding as a function of firm size demonstrates that bigger firms show a higher propensity (or ability) to get public incentives in general, whereas regional incentives appear to be prevalent among small firms.

The analysis of the access to public incentives according to the innovatory level is even more interesting for the object of the present research (Table 10.8). The largest recipient of public incentives is constituted by firms which are laggards in the innovative arena. On the other hand, all the more innovative firms, which accessed public funds, received them through more than one public agency.[9]

To evaluate the relevance of interactions with other firms, information has been gathered on the formal and informal collaboration between firms. Data reported in Table 10.9 point to a general uniformity in the propensity to collaboration among firms which are located in different areas.

The distinction among classes ranged by number of employees is more articulated: collaborative relationships increase according to the increase in size. This general trend reflects, however, different patterns within groups classified by the location of partner firms.

Collaboration relationships established by firms located in the province of Palermo are mostly at a national level (69 per cent), whereas firms located in the other provinces tend to cooperate with regional partners.

In this case also, the data analysis is quite interesting if one looks at the grouping by innovative attitude (Table 10.10). First of all, more innovative firms show a very high propensity to collaborate (62.5 per cent of the

Table 10.9   *Firms collaborating with other firms: distribution by location and by firm size (%)*

Provinces and Firm size	Total collaborations[a]	Firms with regional partners[b]	Firms with national partners[b]	Firms with international partners[b]
Palermo	57.7	46.7	60.0	46.7
Catania	52.6	60.0	50.0	10.0
Others	50.0	69.2	46.2	7.7
0–19	40.5	53.3	53.3	26.7
20–49	58.8	60.0	50.0	30.0
50–99	81.8	44.4	66.7	33.3
100 +	66.7	50.0	0.0	50.0

Notes:
[a] The percentage is calculated on the total number of firms for each category.
[b] The percentage is calculated on the number of firms having collaborations. Horizontal totals are higher than 100 because firms, on average, have more than one collaboration.

Table 10.10   *Innovative firms and collaborations (%)*

	More innovative	Less innovative	Non-innovative
Collaborating firms/total[a]	62.5	53.3	50.0
Firms collaborating with regional partners[b]	40.0	68.8	62.5
Firms collaborating with national partners[b]	40.0	62.5	50.0
Firms collaborating with international partners[b]	33.3	12.5	50.0

Notes:
[a] The percentage is calculated on the total number of firms for each category.
[b] The percentage is calculated on the number of firms of each group having collaborations. Columns sum higher than 100 because firms, on average, have more than one collaboration.

group); furthermore, if one looks at the geographical location of partners, a remarkable difference among firms which have a different level of innovation emerges. Less innovative firms (more than 60 per cent) have collaborative relationships with regional or national partners, whereas for more innovative firms collaborations with foreign partners are higher than 30 per cent (20 per cent with European and 13.3 per cent with extra-European firms); the collaborations with other Italian firms are only 40 per cent.

Significantly, non-innovative firms show an attitude towards collaboration relationships not too dissimilar from the one shown by the less-innovative firms group.

Data on collaboration with public entities have also been collected, but only seven firms in the whole sample have declared that they have experienced such collaboration.

Innovative Activity: Sources and Obstacles

To investigate the nature of innovative activity, data on the relevance attributed by firms to some sources of technical information for the introduction of innovation deserve to be considered (Figure 10.3). First of all, an overwhelming majority of more innovative firms consider their own internal human resources ('internal functions') precious sources of technical information for introducing innovation.

Conversely, for the less innovative firms, equipment suppliers, consulting and service companies as well as raw material and components suppliers are crucial as information sources for innovation. This set of data fully reflects the nature of innovations introduced within this last group of firms and corresponds to such firms' characteristics.

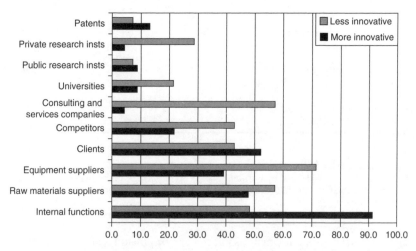

*Figure 10.3   Factors considered relevant as sources of technical
            information for introducing innovations (only innovative firms
            considered)*

The importance attributed to the market players is worth mentioning too. On the one hand, less innovative firms attribute more importance to competitive pressure; on the other, over 50 per cent of the more innovative firms receive from their customers information they consider relevant for innovation.

Variables usually taken into consideration in the study of innovation seem to play a limited role in the Sicilian case. The minimum relevance attributed by more innovative firms to universities and to research institutions (both public and private) are quite unexpected, as is the very limited number of firms which attribute some relevance to patents as a source of information.

Further heterogeneity elements among the two different groups emerge when we analyse the obstacles to innovation (Figure 10.4).

Financial problems and innovation costs seem to affect significantly the innovative behaviour of most less innovative firms; these factors are considered as the most relevant ones. On the other hand, for more innovative firms, the lack of qualified personnel and innovation costs heavily hamper innovation.

Apart from an immediate interpretation, the data below need to be read in the light of the fact that they reflect subjective evaluations by firms whose individual innovative choices correspond to different strategies. In this sense, the relevance of any single obstacle has to be considered in relation

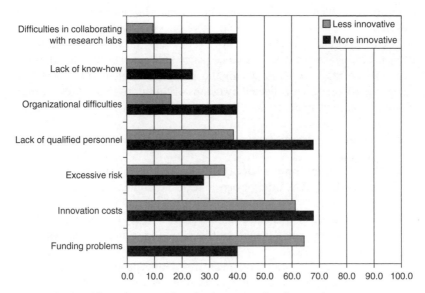

Figure 10.4   Obstacles considered relevant in the choice about innovation
(only innovative firms considered)

to the kind and technological content of the innovation introduced. Therefore, in this view, the value attributed by the more innovative firms to the negative role of innovation costs, far from being a weakness, corresponds to the attitudes of those firms to innovative choices.

The same interpretation should be given to the somehow greater importance attributed by more innovative firms, if compared to the other groups, to organizational difficulties and to difficulties in collaborating with public and private laboratories; these kinds of obstacle are less likely to be encountered by firms introducing marginal innovations.

SICILIAN FIRMS AND THE SYSTEM OF INNOVATION

The descriptive analysis of the data provides a basis for identifying an interpretative model of innovative behaviour of firms located in a lagging region. In particular the main question addressed concerns the role of variables internal or external to the firms but embodied in the regional 'system'.

Innovations, classified by degree of newness, are the dependent variables. Structure, relational factors (as in the literature on systems of innovation and *milieux innovateurs*) and factors relevant for innovation have been considered as independent variables.

Given the nature of the considered system – a lagging one – particular attention has been paid to the variables measuring internal and external obstacles for firms and some aspects of public intervention.

The independent variables considered account for structural characteristics (size, age, sector), performance (sales and exports) and for the relevance of some factors in influencing the innovative behaviour of firms. This last group of variables, collected by means of qualitative measures of interviewees' opinions, relate to:

- resources generating innovation, grouped under 'in-house' and 'extra-mural';
- the role for innovative activity of some sources of technical–scientific knowledge.[10] The interviewees had to attribute a score of 1 to 5 to each source;
- the relevance of obstacles to innovative activity (for both innovative and non-innovative firms). In this case, too, opinions are expressed on a scale of 1 to 5;
- the use of public funds and incentives. This is particularly relevant for a lagging region that has traditionally relied on public policy for growth. As regards this aspect, the institutional nature of incentives has been specified (regional, national and European);

- qualitative information about the firm. In this category details are included on entrepreneurs and firms' managements and participation in industrial associations or other consortia;
- data on the interactions between firms and with institutions. Given the relevance attributed to various types of relationships by approaches based on systems of innovation and *milieux innovateurs*, interactions have also been classified according to their spatial dimension (regional, national and international);
- information about the functioning of the labour market, in particular, specific questions referring to difficulties in finding qualified personnel. Such an aspect is crucial, given, first, the relevance of qualified personnel for innovation and, second, the high unemployment rate and low labour cost that are typical of a lagging region and that specifically characterize Sicily;
- position in the final product market and in the supply markets;
- dummies relating to the location in the two principal provinces (Palermo and Catania) or in other provinces.

The analysis was carried out in successive steps. At the beginning, linear regressions relative to the four main dependent variables (innovations new to the firm, new to the region, to the nation and to the world) were run for each of the two considered periods (1981–90; 1991–95) to verify the existence of any similarity of results across them. This in effect highlighted the existence of some regularities in the causal relationships that were then tested through linear and logit estimates on the whole sample.

The results were synthesized in the following tables (Tables 10.11–10.14). The plus and minus signs refer to the existence of positive or negative impact of the exogenous variables. A double sign shows a higher impact (in terms of the regression coefficient). Dependent variables (innovations with different degrees of novelty) refer to the data considered: innovation in period 1 (1981–90), innovation in period 2 (1991–95), and innovation in general.[11] Definitions of exogenous variables and results of the estimates are reported in the Appendix.

Table 10.11 summarizes the impact of the independent variables on the introduction of innovations new at the firm level. *INNF1* and *INNF2* refer respectively to the first period (1981–90) and to the second period (1991–95), while *INNF* (tested both through linear regression and logit estimates) refers to this group of innovations, without considering the time period.

Some expected results have surfaced from the analysis. First, the high dependence of innovation with a low degree of newness from acquisition of equipment (*PROVACE*) and regional public incentives and funds

Table 10.11   Factors influencing innovations new at the firm level

Independent variables	Dependent variables: innovations new to the firm			
	INNF1	*INNF2*	*INNF*	*INNF*
	Linear			Logit
PROVACE	++	++	+	+
INCOREG	++	++	++	+
RELSCSF	+	+	+	
FMSEUR	+		+	+
FMSWOR	+			+
FAMILY	+			
INNPP	−			
RELSSEQ		− −		
SMSWOR		+		
RELOFP	+			
RELOLQP		−		
RELOER		+		

Table 10.12   Factors influencing innovations new at the regional level

Independent variables	Dependent variables: innovations new to the region		
	INNR1	*INNR2*	*INNR*
	Linear		Logit
PROVII	+ +		
PROVPD		+	
PROVRD		+ +	
KNOWPER			+
QUALSERS	+	+	+
SMSREG	+ +	+	+
RELOIC	−	− −	−
DIFFQP	−	−	
SMSEUR	−		
RELOFP		− −	
COLLOFW	− −		

Table 10.13 *Factors influencing innovations new at the national level*

Independent variables	Dependent variables: innovations new to the nation			
	INNN1	*INNN2*	*INNN*	*INNN*
	Linear			Logit
PROVII		+ +	+	+
PROVPD	+			
PROVRD		−		+
PROVACK	+ +		+	
RELSSEQ	+			
RELSCUS	−			
RELSUNI	+	+		
RELSCOM		+	+	+
RELSCSF		−		
COLLOFE		+ +		
FMWOR		+ +		
INNS	+	+ +		
INNW				−
INCOREG	−			
RELOFP		−		

Table 10.14 *Factors influencing radically new innovations*

Independent variables	Dependent variables: innovations new to the world		
	INNW1	*INNW2*	*INNW*
	Linear		Logit
PROVII	+ +	+	
KNOWPER			+
PROVPD	−		
COLLOFW	+	+	
COLLOFE		+ +	+
COLLOFN	−	+ +	
COLLOFR	−		
QUALSERS	+	−	−
FMNAT	+		
FMEUR	−		
RELOFP			−

(*INCOREG*) is evident. In both the periods considered, and also in the estimates (linear and logistic) on the whole sample, the strong impact of these variables, whose importance also emerged in the descriptive analysis, is confirmed.

Moreover, the relevance of service and consultant companies as sources of technical information for innovations (*RELSCSF*) seems to be significant in positively affecting this type of innovation.

The picture that emerges from these results shows an innovative adaptive behaviour, brought on mainly by the acquisition of equipment supported by information obtained by external consultants and strongly encouraged (or perhaps determined) by public regional funding. This interpretative framework is completed by other interesting evidence on the positive role of the firm's presence on the international market (*FMSEUR* and *FMSWOR*).

In the second period, innovations seem to be influenced by the quota of international suppliers (*SMSWOR*); this could explain the negative sign associated with *RELSSEQ*, which refers to the relevance of equipment suppliers as a source of information. Physical distance and cultural barriers could have halted flows of information between equipment suppliers and their customers.

The unexpected results marked by the positive sign for *RELOER* (obstacles should discourage innovations) in the second period plus the positive sign of *RELOFP* in the first period could be explained by the behaviour of less innovative firms which introduce innovations just to remain in the market and depend very heavily on public support. These firms are therefore unaffected by obstacles in the form of finding financial resources and by the risk associated with innovations and as they innovate by introducing new pieces of equipment without any substantial learning from equipment suppliers.

In Table 10.12 data on innovations new to the region are summarized. In contrast to the previous category of innovations, it seems that in this case innovative activity is pursued within specific strategic behaviour.

Innovations are strongly affected by internal resources. This is evident from the positive signs corresponding to individual initiative (*PROVII*) in the first case, to the firms' production department (*PROVPD*) and R&D department (*PROVRD*) in the second, and to a more general variable measuring the role of the knowledge of internal personnel (*KNOWPER*) in the logit estimate.

Moreover, the existence of efficient user–producer interactions at the regional level can also be inferred from the relevance for innovation of the quota of suppliers located in the region (*SMSREG*). The role of 'context' variables is further emphasized by the corresponding results on the relevance of the quality of public services and utilities available in the region

(*QUALSERS*) and the negative impact of the difficulty in finding qualified personnel (*DIFFQP*).

The innovation costs, as evident in the aggregate data on more innovative firms discussed in the descriptive overview, exert an influence in discouraging innovation (*RELOIC*) and this, in my opinion, is a correct signal for dynamic, efficient firms.

With regard to innovations new at the country level (Table 10.13), the estimates results are not as self-evident as in the previous cases; in spite of this, they signal some interesting causal relationships. Internal resources and functions appear to play, here too, a positive role, as evidenced by the positive impact of individual initiative and, limited to the first dependent variable, of the production department. These internal resources, however, are coupled in stimulating innovation by the acquisition of knowledge from outside, signalled in two estimates by the positive sign associated with *PROVACK*, that is, the importance of acquisition of knowledge for the introduction of innovation. Among the vehicles of technical information relevant for innovation, university and competing firms appear to have, in this case, a positive impact (*RELSUNI* and *RELSCOM*). In this group of innovations, therefore, some of the mechanisms considered crucial by the literature on national systems of innovation seem to play a significant role.

The positive impact of variables related to the quota of firm sales coming from the international market (*FMSWOR*) and from the collaboration with European firms (*COLLOFE*), even if limited to the second period, constitutes an interesting outcome.

Finally, the analysis of the role of independent variables on radically new innovations (Table 10.14) shows some peculiar characteristics. First of all, the role of knowledge embedded in the firms' human resources emerges from all the estimates (individual initiative in the linear regressions and knowledge of personnel in the logit one). Collaborations with international partners (*COLLOFE* and *COLLOFW*) also exert an influence on the introduction of this type of innovations.

CONCLUSIONS

The results discussed above seem to support the main research hypothesis that, in a lagging region, context variables play a role in influencing innovative activity. In this case, however, such variables may constitute 'ties' or may trigger vicious mechanisms, instead of promoting dynamic positive synergies.

This does not deny that innovative behaviour is influenced by other factors characterizing individual firms, their productive activities and their strategies.

A second important outcome of the study consists in the identification of a more detailed method of analysing innovations in lagging regions. Differentiating innovations according to their degree of novelty has proved to be correct, even if it still deserves some reviewing for more accurate estimates.

Empirical results, in detail, furnish evidence on specific differences in innovative behaviour and relevant factors among firms with different degrees of innovation. These, in my view, can constitute a reference point for normative purposes.

It is thus possible to distinguish two main typologies of firms. The first group comprises more innovative firms, which depend heavily on internal resources, which generally receive the impulse to innovation from collaboration with other firms and are very sensitive to the presence of qualified personnel and to the quality of external services and utilities.

The second group, constituted by firms which introduce innovations new merely to themselves, is influenced by the availability of public funds (especially those awarded by the regional authorities) and by the acquisition of new pieces of equipment.

Therefore, a dual 'system' can be identified: its principal elements are those considered in the literature on systems of innovation and *milieux innovateurs* but its functioning is asymmetric, leading to either vicious or virtual dynamics.

Therefore policy-making should primarily identify the target of its intervention. If innovation as a general improvement in techniques is the policy target, then a general funding intervention which reduces the costs of acquiring new pieces of equipment is sufficient.

If, on the contrary, a process of diffused economic growth through innovative change is the first priority, then a more articulated plan of intervention should be followed. The actions that should be taken are confirmed by the results summarized above:

- encourage investments in human capital internal to firms;
- encourage labour mobility and processes of skills formation;
- render interactions and access to public institutions more efficient and transparent;
- support the productive sphere with efficient services and utilities;
- support firms' cooperative interactions;
- facilitate flows of information.

NOTES

1. Trust is, therefore, necessary for the success of dynamic interactive processes of innovation and diffusion.
2. In particular, Sicily is one of the four autonomous Italian regions; this gives the regional Parliament the legislative power in some matters which are fundamental for economic growth, among which industry and commerce (*Statuto Siciliano*, art. 14).
3. The incidence of local units in the public sector is in line with the national data (7.7 per cent in Sicily vs 7 per cent in the whole nation) while the public employees' quota is much higher in Sicily than in other Italian regions (in Sicily 33.9 per cent of employees work in the public sector while nationally it absorbs only 19.7 per cent of total employment).
4. On a national level the incidence of industry is 24 per cent in terms of local units and 33 per cent measured in terms of employees.
5. The percentage remains almost identical if single-employee firms are excluded; it decreases to 95 per cent.
6. While food-processing and mechanical industries are relevant in terms of size, the textile & clothing industry is interesting for the role that it can play in the growth of the small manufacturing local system (as evidenced in industrial districts cases).
7. The response rate is therefore approximately 100 per cent.
8. This can be calculated by the ratio between the sum of innovations for each group of firms and the correspondent number of firms.
9. This evidence emerges from the examination of individual data of firms.
10. They are similar to those considered in ISTAT surveys on innovation and are specified in the Appendix.
11. The time period is indicated by the numerical suffix to the variable's name.

REFERENCES

Becattini, G. (ed.) (1987), *Mercato e forze locali: il distretto industriale*, Bologna: Il Mulino.

Breschi, S. and Malerba, F. (1997), 'Sectoral innovation systems: Technological regimes, Schumpeterian dynamics and spatial boundaries', in C. Edquist (ed.), *Systems of Innovation*, London: Pinter, pp. 130–56.

Brusco, S. (1983), 'Flessibilità e solidità del sistema: l'esperienza emiliana', in G. Fuà and C. Zacchia (eds), *Industrializzazione senza fratture*, Bologna: Il Mulino.

Camagni, R. (ed.) (1991), *Innovation Networks: Spatial Perspectives*, London: Belhaven Press.

Camagni, R. and Capello, R. (eds) (2002), *Apprendimento collettivo e competitività territoriale*, Milan: F. Angeli.

Carlsson, B. (ed.) (1997), *Technological Systems and Industrial Dynamics*, Dordrecht: Kluwer.

Cooke, P., and Morgan, K. (1998), *The Associational Economy: Firms, Regions and Innovation*, Oxford: Oxford University Press.

Epifanio, R., Fazio, V. and Mazzola, F. (2002), 'Gli ostacoli all'apprendimento collettivo: il caso Sicilia', in R. Camagni and R. Capello (eds), *Apprendimento collettivo e competitività territoriale*, Milan: F. Angeli, pp. 211–41.

Freeman, C. (1987), *Technology Policy and Economic Performance: Lessons from Japan*, London: Pinter.

ISTAT (2002), *Indicatori di contesto chiave regionali QCS 2000–2006*, novembre, www.istat.it.

ISTAT (anni vari), *Censimento dell'industria e dei servizi*.

Lundvall, B.-A. (ed.) (1992), *National Systems of Innovation: Towards a Theory of Innovation and interactive learning*, London: Pinter.

Mazzola, F. and Asmundo, A. (1999), 'I sistemi locali manifatturieri in Sicilia: analisi dei potenziali distretti industriali', in *Quaderni di Ricerca del Banco di Sicilia*, no. 2.

Nelson, R. (ed.) (1993), *National Innovation Systems: A comparative analysis*, Oxford: Oxford University Press.

Pyke, F. and Sengenberger, W. (eds) (1992), *Industrial Districts and Local Economic Regeneration*, Geneva: International Institute for Labour Studies.

APPENDIX

*Table 10A.1   Factors influencing innovations new at the firm level**

Independent variables	Dependent variables			
	INNF1	*INNF2*	*INNF*	*INNF*
	Linear			Logit*
PROVACE	0.472	0.464	0.363	1.6541
	(5.624)	(6.341)	(2.769)	(3.46)
INCOREG	0.449	0.888	0.519	2.3203
	(5.250)	(11.383)	(3.964)	(2.71)
RELSCSF	0.218	0.295	0.275	
	(2.394)	(4.063)	(1.939)	
FMSEUR	0.266		0.173	5.4311
	(2.925)		(1.230)	(1.69)
FMSWOR	0.181			1.9680
	(2.402)			(1.13)
FAMILY	0.325			
	(3.649)			
INNPP	−0.291			
	(−3.197)			
RELSSEQ		−0.425		
		(−4.563)		
SMSWOR		0.177		
		(2.363)		
RELOFP	0.215			
	(2.801)			
RELOLQP		−0.262		
		(−3.535)		
RELOER		0.209		
		(2.523)		
Adj. R²	0.866	0.896	0.527	
SE	0.1632	0.4513	0.3240	
F	22.084	30.570	9.625	
	(0.00)	(0.00)	(0.00)	
Correct cases				80%

Note: *z-values in parentheses.

*Table 10A.2   Factors influencing innovations new at the regional level**

Independent variables	Dependent variables		
	INNR1	*INNR2*	*INNR*
	Linear		Logit*
PROVII	0.792		
	(24.582)		
PROVPD		0.244	
		(2.245)	
PROVRD		0.670	
		(5.958)	
KNOWPER			6.6236
			(1.38)
QUALSERS	0.231	1.376	2.5527
	(6.606)	(8.909)	(1.34)
SMSREG	0.649	0.219	9.1891
	(18.585)	(2.099)	(1.47)
RELOIC	−0.190	−0.739	−2.935
	(−5.306)	(−4.418)	(−1.27)
RELOFP		−0.620	
		(−3.438)	
DIFFQP	−0.238	−0.309	
	(−7.001)	(−2.922)	
SMSEUR	−0.229		
	(−5.244)		
COLLOFW	−0.544		
	(−15.625)		
Adj. R^2	0.913	0.892	
SE	0.1290	0.2742	
F	34.552	17.496	
	(0.00)	(0.00)	
Correct cases			94.4%

Note: *z-values in parentheses.

Table 10A.3   *Factors influencing innovations new at the national level**

Independent variables	Dependent variables			
	INNN1	*INNN2*	*INNN*	*INNN*
	Linear			Logit*
PROVII		0.486	0.369	2.1560
		(6.746)	(2.645)	(1.75)
PROVPD	0.302			
	(4.118)			
PROVRD		−0.880		1.7764
		(−5.563)		(1.42)
PROVACK	0.591		0.242	
	(6.668)		(1.737)	
RELSSEQ	0.130			
	(2.013)			
RELSCUS	−0.170			
	(−2.598)			
RELSUNI	0.109	0.216		
	(1.538)	(1.724)		
RELSCOM		0.263	0.400	0.5808
		(2.898)	(2.863)	(1.49)
RELSCSF		−0.550		
		(−4.609)		
COLLOFE		0.604		
		(6.331)		
FMWOR		0.453		
		(4.057)		
INNS	0.302	0.482		
	(4.196)	(5.128)		
INNW				−2.8751
				(−1.29)
INCOREG	−0.190			
	(−3.079)			
RELOFP		−0.241		
		(−3.343)		
Adj. R^2	0.939	0.891	0.300	
SE	0.047	0.006	0.2316	
F	50.955	23.164	6.132	
	(0.00)	(0.00)	(0.00)	
Correct cases				92.3%

Note: *z-values in parentheses.

*Table 10A.4   Factors influencing radically new innovations**

Independent variables	Dependent variables		
	INNW1	*INNW2*	*INNW*
	Linear		Logit*
PROVII	0.496	1.118	
	(5.262)	(11.044)	
KNOWPER			1.0017
			(2.00)
PROVPD	−0.596		
	(−5.603)		
COLLOFW	0.376	0.399	
	(4.004)	(2.216)	
COLLOFE		0.424	1.6849
		(4.716)	(1.17)
COLLOFN	−0.212	0.633	
	(−2.208)	(7.256)	
COLLOFR	−0.412		
	(−4.451)		
QUALSERS	0.306	−0.947	−0.9266
	(3.272)	(−6.412)	(−1.55)
FMSNAT	0.342		
	(3.632)		
FMSEUR	−0.322		
	(−3.710)		
SMSNAT		−0.638	
		(−4.783)	
SMSEUR		0.863	
		(4.287)	
SMSWOR		1.185	
		(7.209)	
RELOIC		−0.768	
		(−5.806)	
RELOFP		1.107	−0.6280
		(6.678)	(−1.21)
INNPP		1.083	
		(7.018)	
Adj. R^2	0.890	0.958	
SE	0.1072	0.005	
F	18.211	29.806	
	(0.00)	(0.00)	
Correct cases			90.0%

Note: *z-values in parentheses.

Tables 10.11–10.14: Definition of Variables

PROVII:	Introduction of innovation by means of individual initiative (usually the manager)
PROVPD:	Introduction of innovation as a result of production department/section activity
PROVRD:	Introduction of innovation as a result of R&D department/section activity
PROVACE:	Introduction of innovation through acquisition of equipment
KNOWPER:	Relevance of knowledge embedded in firm personnel for the introduction of innovation
RELSSEQ:	Relevance as source of technical information for innovation of equipment suppliers
RELSCSF:	Relevance as source of technical information for innovation of services and consultant firms
RELSCUS:	Relevance as source of technical information for innovation of customers
RELSCOM:	Relevance as source of technical information for innovation of competitors
RELSUNI:	Relevance as source of technical information for innovation of local university
RELOLQP:	Relevance of lack of qualified personnel as obstacle to innovation
RELOER:	Relevance of excessive risk as obstacle to innovation
RELOFP:	Relevance of funding problems as obstacle to innovation
RELOIC:	Relevance of innovation costs as obstacle to innovation
INCOREG:	Obtaining of regional public funds
FMSREG:	Share of firm output destined for regional market
FMSNAT:	Share of firm output destined for national (extra-regional) market
FMSEUR:	Share of firm output destined for European market
FMSWOR:	Share of firm output destined for extra-European market
SMSWOR:	Share of firm input acquired in the extra-European market
FAMILY:	Dummy indicating if the firm is family owned and managed
INNPP:	Product and process innovations

11. Universities and economically depressed regions: how strong is the influence of the University of Évora on the human capital of the region?

Maria da Conceição Rego

1. INTRODUCTION

In the last 30 years, the expansion of higher education has been one of the most important events in Portugal in social terms. This expansion has come about in three ways: the creation of new public universities; the creation of public polytechnic institutions; and the development of private universities. This evolution has changed, in a substantial way, the panorama of higher education in Portugal: this subsystem, initially elitist, has become an education of the masses; the number of pupils, teachers and educational establishments has increased exponentially; these establishments, originally located only in the large cities on the Portuguese coast (Lisbon, Coimbra and Porto), started to emerge in the cities of the interior, modifying them fundamentally and allowing access to this level of education on the part of innumerable students who otherwise would not have had the economic means to enjoy it.

The changes that have occurred in the domain of higher education have influenced the functions that these institutions have to perform. The universities currently fulfil three primary functions (Geoideia, 1993):

1. The development of highly qualified human resources: the university trains graduates, masters and doctors generally required in the labour market, the educational system and the scientific and technological system.
2. The accomplishment of R&D activities: the goal of the university is to generate new knowledge and sustain the chain of knowledge; the product of university research, scientific and technological knowledge,

is transferred to the public domain in a multiplicity of forms: published books, monographs, articles, reports and other documents.

3. The synergistic relationship with the surrounding society: through the public use of the scientific and technological potential of the university, from the accomplishment of research projects in cooperation or contracted by industry to the provision of services and consultancies.

The university has focused discussion of the relationship between economic activity and the university on this third function, originating in the need to maximize the use of financial and human resources, knowledge and scientific and technical information, through the implementation of efficient mechanisms of transference between the university and the productive sector. This transference implies, however, the existence, in the industry, of human resources capable of absorbing the products of the university, as well as the capacity for formulating questions and presenting problems at university level.

In Évora, as in other small cities of the interior where higher educational institutions have been located, since the establishment of the university in 1979, there have been fundamental changes in the profile and the daily rhythms of city life. The following is a survey of the characteristics that dominated the city until the 1970s.

> The city of Évora was historically affirmed as a pole of administrative functions (district headquarters) and as the main agglomeration of a vast agricultural area marked by great properties (large estates) and by a strong economy centred on three products: wheat, cork-oak and pigs. The history of the natural capital of the Alentejo, a region traditionally considered as the granary of Portugal, is dominated, up to 1974, by two social groups – landowners, and employees of public administration – both particularly averse to innovation. (Ferrão, 1997, p. 33).

From the 1980s, through social and political factors at national and local level, the expansion of the University of Évora has contributed decisively to the alteration of the dynamic of the city through the increasingly significant presence of students coming from outside. Currently, the University of Évora is one of the main public institutions in the city. Apart from the importance that it has in terms of the direct creation of jobs, with about one thousand employees, and as an integral entity within local economic activity, with an annual total budget in the order of €40 million, we must recognize the dynamics generated by its students. During the 1990s, the importance of university students in the city of Évora was strongly increasing: the 4229 students who at the beginning of the 1990s represented 7.9 per cent of the resident population in the city became 7859 students registered in the academic year 1999/2000, and already they represent 13.9 per cent of the residents of Évora. This expansion, of course, has made the relationship between the city and the university more intense.

The institutions of higher education in general, and the universities in particular, where they exist, are promotional agents for the development of the regions. The universities are fundamental entities within the development process, capable of generating positive externalities in improving the performance of human capital through exercise of the functions of education, R&D and community service.

> Human capital is a fundamental variable in the economic development process: the education of the citizens, more than any material wealth, is the force that mobilizes the cultural spread of a country, gives it influence between nations and attributes to it the aptitude to cooperate in the development of a world that is becoming, with each day that passes, closer and more interdependent. (Crespo, 1993, p. 12).

It is in this sense that we approach the relations between education and economic development: on the one hand, education is responsible for increases in private incomes by enhancing the capacity for obtaining jobs and wages; on the other hand, it generates collective externalities and it stimulates the competitiveness of companies and territories. The relationship between the economic and social actors and the universities, privileged entities in terms of the scope of production and diffusion of innovative knowledge and technology, is developed in the theoretical framework of a learning region: where the actors within the system are involved in processes of learning, they provide an opportunity for the development of knowledge, of know-how and of the abilities necessary for innovation and for the maintenance of conditions of sustainable development.

In this chapter, we propose to analyse the contribution of the University of Évora to the improvement of the human capital of the region, through the graduates who remain in the region and through the relationship between the university and other regional agents. To do this, we present some theoretical developments that show how universities can relate to the surrounding region and contribute to the improvement of its competitive capacity and its economic performance. At the same time, we characterize, briefly, the Alentejo region, where the University of Évora is located, and the institution itself, to provide a better understanding of the effect of its existence and functioning.

2. THE UNIVERSITY AND THE REGION: THEORETICAL FRAMEWORK

The economic development of countries and regions can be defined as the increase, supported and irreversible, of the real income of its inhabitants (Polèse, 1998). This concept assumes that there is justice, harmony and balance from two perspectives: space and time. A developed society is not one whose forms of life are supported by the exploitation of the resources of others, just as it cannot be one whose standards of living had been created or maintained at the cost of consumption of resources that are not renewable, or consumption of renewable resources that are consumed at a rate higher than their capacity for renewal (Simões Lopes, 1984).

Regional development is, basically, the construction of a propitious way to innovation, and the sharing of it with local agents. Thus regional policies will not only have to be centred on the company, but must also privilege the territorial system of production as well as the endogenous mechanisms for creating synergies and relationships between the actors, with the aim of stimulating capacity for innovation and adaptation through nominated innovative regional agglomerations (Cooke, 1998, p. 10). These are constituted by large and small companies in the productive sector, where such relationships exist or can be stimulated commercially, through research activity in institutions of higher education, private R&D laboratories, agencies of technology transfer, associations, governmental organizations and institutes for professional training.

Some studies by the OECD (1997, 1998) demonstrate that countries' development directly related to their level of education and R&D: more developed countries are, generally, those that have a higher level of education or those that spend relatively more on education and R&D. As a correlative, any insufficiency in these areas constitutes an obstacle to development.

Education is the legacy of one generation to the following one; this is its main social function (Thomas, 1995). It is a medium-term investment, made for society in general and for families in particular, to the extent that expectations of stronger contributions in the future mean forgoing the productive contribution of the young in the present (Lopes, 2001). Parents want their children to receive a high-quality education because they understand that in this way they are preparing them better for the labour market. They realize that unemployment rates are higher among unqualified workers and those of lower educational levels. However, we do not always observe a positive correlation between vocational/professional qualifications and wages, to the extent that, at times, workers of similar age, qualifications and labour activity can be remunerated differently.

The systematic application of scientific knowledge to the production of goods and services increases the value of education, if it takes into account the component of technical or professional training, to the extent that the knowledge is internalized by scientists, teachers, technicians, managers and others. Qualified human resources will have a more significant role in the development of society, in so far as they become more dependent on knowledge. Innovation, and new products and processes, will come to have a greater importance in companies. Research and knowledge will tend to increase, and companies will have to strengthen their labour force with researchers, engineers and other technically specialized staff (Shelton, 1997, p. 16).

The accumulation of capital, physical and human, is a basic condition for sustainable economic growth in the long run, and for the reduction of the divergences of income between countries. Improvement in the standard of living of populations is directly related to productivity. Economic success, the first condition for the improvement of the standard of living of the population, translates into the capacity of regions or organizations to mobilize different institutions (companies, organizations, infrastructures of information, systems of incentives, etc.) to support learning. The relation between the acquisition of knowledge and institutional education is decisive. The training of abilities results (Lundvall, 2000) from the institutional training acquired from diverse educational establishments (schools and universities), and also through the learning that occurs through the pursuit of professional activity.

The component of research in higher education institutions (HEIs) can be seen as universal, without regard to regional variations. Goddard (1998) asserts that it is in the level of education and the employment of graduates in the regional labour market, as well as the level of programmes of professional improvement, that the effects of these institutions will be more significant. This effect is clear in relation to the local economies where they are located, in that it is positive and increases with time (Hedrick et al., 1990, pp. 17–18).

There are several ways in which HEIs can influence the functioning of the local labour markets (Beeson and Montgomery, 1993). On the one hand, in the performance of the role of educators, HEIs increase job prospects and the chances of earning higher wages for their graduates; on the other hand, by increasing the average level of knowledge, HEIs can, as said previously, promote an increase in local productivity, and in the capacity to develop and to implement new technologies, depending on the average level of human capital in the economy. To restate the argument: the knowledge of the active population influences the technology used by companies, as well as by workers, to the extent that people with raised levels of education are better able to implement new technologies.

One of the factors in the economic success of a region is the extent it can attract or retain graduates, in that these citizens generally become more productive. A great part of the economic effect of the HEI depends on the decisions of its graduates not to migrate (Brown and Heaney, 1997). It must be admitted that higher education increases the probability of migration, in so far as graduates are better equipped to compete in the national and international labour markets and thus leave the region where they have studied. Migration decisions are based on job chances: if a given region does not have a tradition of growth of jobs in specific sectors, but has graduates in these areas, then these will be potential emigrants. At the same time, the increase in the knowledge of the HEI cannot influence the development of economies if there is a lack of adequate and available jobs for graduates.

The retention of graduates is one of the main means that the region can adopt to hold on to those endowed with sensitivity to innovation, enterprise spirit and management capacity. Retention rates show, however, a relationship of many factors: the capacity of the HEI to offer studies and training that take into account the needs of the regional economy: stability, diversity and importance of the economic regional base, the context of the national economy, the origin of the students, the type of educational establishment and the economic and social context of the students.

However, the contribution to the relationship between the universities and the companies must be greater than the availability of training, and should include, for example, the availability of grants for R&D or the acquisition of consultancy services from the universities. In a scenario where the universities do not make more use of the monopoly of the production of scientific knowledge, to remain in the vanguard of knowledge, university researchers will have to exchange knowledge with others, including producers of knowledge such as companies or other organizations (Schuetze, 2000, p. 189). Both institutions gain from the establishment of diverse relations between universities and companies (Antonelli, 2001, p. 26–7). In the universities, teachers and researchers are presented with specific technological problems, which has a positive effect on the research undertaken. The companies, in their turn, have access, at reduced cost, to a body of ability in relation to advanced techniques and to a specialized infrastructure that is often characterized by great coherence and strong fixed costs.

The relations between pure and applied research, and the consequent diffusion of knowledge jointly through partnerships between the units producing new scientific knowledge and local companies and institutions, can

encourage training in relation to research contracts, consultancies, science
parks, joint creation of companies of R&D, commercialization of research
through businesses, and so on.

The effect of the research done in the HEI, or other units, is particularly important for SMEs – the predominant companies in the Alentejo,
as well as in the majority of the regions in the interior of Portugal – in
so far as these are the companies that most need to look to the exterior
for technological developments capable of promoting improvements in
the efficiency of their productive processes. Large companies, in their
turn, if they do not have R&D units, look for these processes near to
their headquarters, or in companies of the same group, or in companies
where such units exist, using acquisition mechanisms, cooperation or
other means.

In the most peripheral regions (Rosa Pires et al., 1998, p. 3), the concept
of the triple helix, a metaphor illustrative of the relations between higher
education, the productive system and the government, has come to be considered as an essential factor in stimulating and/or strengthening development strategies. The main argument developed presents the idea that the
installation of innovative dynamics in a regional economy depends on the
capacity of the region to synthesize three pairs of attributes:

- coherence and diversity of the regional productive system;
- competition and cooperation;
- access to tacit and codified economic knowledge.

With the attributes indicated, the universities can contribute to improving and to consolidating the regional capacity for innovation, through
mechanisms in the area of education and research. The coherence of the
regional system will become more robust through a rigorous selection of
courses and curricula adapted to regional technological needs, and by supporting the development of a culture using local techniques (accumulation
of codified knowledge). At the same time, the processes of creation, acquisition, adaptation and diffusion of new knowledge developed in the universities can consolidate the relationship capacity of the region where
they are located, developing projects that involve cooperation between
companies. This can contribute to diminishing the distance between
science, technology and society, between pure and applied research and
between the discovery of new technologies and the development of products and viable processes of production (facilitating the accumulation of
tacit knowledge).

3. SOME FEATURES OF THE ALENTEJO AND THE UNIVERSITY OF ÉVORA

3.1 The Alentejo[1]

The Alentejo, with its 535 000 inhabitants (5 per cent of the total population of Portugal), occupying one-third of the country, is the least densely populated Portuguese region. The increasingly aged population lives in urban agglomerations of small to medium size, while the agricultural areas are losing population. Évora, with its 56 525 inhabitants, is the biggest city of the region.

The active population is also tiny, not exceeding about 220 000 individuals. Until the 1990s, the Alentejo was a predominantly agricultural region, with this activity employing the majority of the active population. Since then, the tertiary sector has become the main employer. In characterizing the employed population, two main aspects stand out: on the one hand, the large amount of unqualified labour; on the other, the importance of directors, controllers and specialists. This second characteristic is related to the importance that public administration has in the regional job market, the educational qualifications of employees in Alentejan companies being weak, with few of the workers having middle- and upper-level qualifications. The low average level of qualifications of the employed population results from the low levels of education of the resident population in the region: in 2001, 35.8 per cent had, as a qualification, only the first level of basic education. Only 7.6 per cent of the residents have higher-level training.

In 1999, the rate of unemployment in the Alentejo was 6.7 per cent (in Portugal it was 4.4 per cent), which reflects the evolution of the agricultural sector as a result of the implementation of reform of agricultural policies by the EU. Apart from this particularity, unemployment in the Alentejo presents similar characteristics to those of the rest of the country: it affects all women over 25 years and looking for a new job. These characteristics allow us to classify the unemployment as structural.

Because the active population of the Alentejo, employed or unemployed, is under-qualified, this has consequences at three levels:

- it affects the establishment of new economic companies, particularly those most demanding in terms of training;
- it limits the capacity to promote self-employment;
- it influences the competitive capacity of local companies.

The industry of the Alentejo constitutes only a small part (3.4 per cent) of the Portuguese total. These companies are small to medium size, in terms of staff employed (6.2 people) and in terms of sales (about €450 000). The companies of the Alentejo, of small size and with fragile capital structures, basically target the local and regional market. The share of the Alentejo economy in international markets has been deficient, even though some regional products and resources are gaining an increasing position in foreign countries. On the other hand, some significant investment has been made in modern industries with appreciable technological intensity, associated with external capital.

The low level of economic activity results in a lower quality of life for the residents of the region. In terms of the income of the region and its residents, the available data for GDP per capita show that the Alentejo is one of the 25 poorest regions of the EU, and is the one furthest from the average for the country. Also, disposable family income presents values lower than the rest of the country while prices for the consumer are, on average, higher. Regional purchasing power is only 68 per cent of the national rate, this being the worst result presented by all the regions of the country. Another index, the Composed Indices of Human Development, is only 76.

The quality of life of the population of the Alentejo can also be evaluated through the infrastructure of the region. If, on the one hand, the region is reasonably well provided for in the area of basic infrastructures and has a very significant level of environmental and cultural preservation, the same is not true as far as social provision is concerned, especially in the areas of health and support to the elderly, which assumes particular importance in an aged region such as the Alentejo. Data show that this coincides with the main urban agglomerations, creating problems of access to this provision, in that it is the aged who mostly inhabit the agricultural areas.

In the domain of communication infrastructures, the region is reasonably well endowed, with a road network that fulfils, the goal of guaranteeing good access to the bordering regions (Lisbon, Spain and the Algarve), but there is a lack of intra-regional accessibility, with links between the agricultural areas and the headquarters of the region being poor. The railway network is obsolete, and none of it fulfils its function of transporting passengers and goods. The port infrastructures serve only for the transportation of specific goods, and the airports are still to be developed. This scenario makes the region dependent on road links for the transport of goods and people, both in the interior of the territory and in links with the exterior, which is not economically the most efficient solution from the point of view of residents and companies.

The Alentejo, from the point of view of provision and support infrastructures for the population and for economic activity, offers a picture with reasonable prospects for the future, but it continues to present great weaknesses in respect of its basic resource, the population, in so far as this continues the trend to ageing and low qualifications. In this context, it cannot be expected that the region's economic dynamics will change in a significant way through the activities promoted by regional economic agents, which makes the region dependent on external initiatives for its development.

3.2 The University of Évora

Since its reopening at the end of the 1970s, the University of Évora (UE) has gained status in the context of Portuguese higher education, where it currently occupies a medium position, with successively more students and teachers. However, the UE, with about 8000 students and more than 600 teachers and researchers, is the main higher education institution and the only public university in the region: in the year 2000, it had 39.9 per cent of the students in public higher education in the Alentejo, and 55 per cent of the teachers.[2]

The UE is installed in nine buildings in the historical centre of Évora[3] and its environs, where the teaching and all the other services function. This location provides it with an excellent historical and patrimonial setting, contributing to the concept of a 'university city'. The effect is strengthened by the fact that the students who are not resident in Évora choose to live in the centre of the city in term-time, contributing to the occupation of the buildings as well as to the incomes of the families who receive them.

Most of the students on undergraduate courses (95 per cent) are women, not resident in the region of Évora, who have been placed on courses different from the ones they desired, and for whom this university was not the first choice. The location factor is pointed to as most influential in the choice of the UE. In fact, just 30 per cent of the UE students come from the Évora region. The courses that traditionally have more students are education (25 per cent), economics and management (14.3 per cent) and agricultural engineering (15.7 per cent). The number of students on courses of advanced training, still small, has seen a positive evolution in recent years. These data suggest that, with the current scene of a falling number of people seeking undergraduate places in HEIs, and the excess of offers existing in public institutions, the UE must carefully evaluate its education policies, particularly in terms of choices for undergraduates, and in attracting a new public, for example, post-secondary education or other fields of education and training that do not have as their purpose the award of an academic degree.

This institution has in its service about 1000 employees, the majority of them teachers. Its functioning is ensured by an annual budget of around €40 million, mainly from the government, and comprising to a large extent (about 80 per cent of the academic budget) the payment of wages, which limits the capacity for investment and improvement in its conditions of study and work. The annual budget, together with the personal expenditure of students over the year, has a multiplying effect on gross domestic product and disposable local income with a value of 1.2 per cent. At the same time, we conclude that the activity involving the UE is equivalent to 1.5 per cent of the GDP of the Alentejo.

As the main institution of R&D located in the Alentejo, the UE has increased responsibilities in the areas of the research and community service. With reference to research, the areas prioritized for development are natural sciences, social and human sciences, and agrarian and veterinary sciences, which reflects the fact that these are the areas with more teachers with PhDs. The research is financed, basically, by European programmes such as PRAXIS and PAMAF, and is developed, predominantly, in studies led by the institution itself, with a few cases of partnerships with foreign entities.

In the scope of the activities of community service, the UE offers services at the level of training and consultancy, or by promoting the entry of graduates in the regional labour market. It participates in many regional entities, at the level of the respective administrations, seeks regional partners for the institution through participation in education or research activities, and maintains a special relationship with the schools involved in other levels of education. Organization or promotion of cultural and similar activities has been one of the most systematic ways used to involve the city. In terms of international cooperation, the UE has not been very active: neither the students nor the teachers have made significant use of the many European mobility programmes.

In terms of development strategy over the next few years, this institution will have to seek to consolidate its position in the framework of Portuguese HEIs, adapting its activities in accordance with the process begun by the Bologna Declaration, and diversifying them with the aim of attracting a new public, strengthening its activities in the area of research and publishing its results, developing cooperation and internationalization, with the underlying idea that while the university is a scientific institution, it is also a school, and a cultural agent for the development of the territory where it is located.

4.   EFFECTS OF THE UNIVERSITY OF ÉVORA ON THE REGION

4.1   Methodology

The analysis of the effect of the UE on the improvement of the human capital of the region and the transfer of innovative knowledge and technology to other economic agents was made using two instruments of information gathering: questionnaires and content analysis of protocols.

The questionnaires were applied to many public targets: local and regional companies, other institutions, graduates and teachers at the UE. These questionnaires allowed us to evaluate the relationship with a diversified set of regional and local agents, including employers and employees, teachers and graduates, and effective or potential partners in the activities of education, research and community service.

The protocols signed by the UE with external organizations were studied with the aim of identifying the links between this institution and the region, through the main characteristics of the content of signed documents. These documents are the written expression of the involvement of the UE, through its teachers, researchers and infrastructure, with the surrounding economic and social organizations.

To analyse the collected information, we proceeded to a descriptive analysis of the data acquired by these instruments, with a view to making evident its basic characteristics through evaluating the frequencies of the answers, as well as measuring the average value and the standard deviation, when this was relevant. At the same time, an analysis was made of the relationship between the variables to complement the treatment of the collected data. The techniques of descriptive statistics were complemented by techniques of content analysis, particularly in the treatment of some of the questions in the questionnaires, and in the treatment of the protocols. In the content analysis, the technique of categorial analysis[4] was used.

4.2 Contribution to the Human Capital of the Region

The contribution of the UE to the improvement in regional human capital is particularly important in a region such as the Alentejo, where the qualifications of the population are very low.

The first contribution that the UE makes to the qualifications of the human capital of Évora results from the direct creation of jobs. Of its 1000 employees, the majority are teachers. Of the remaining employees, 15 per cent are graduates and 26 per cent have technical training. In this institution, therefore, the degree of qualification for jobs is very high. At the same time, as a result of its economic activity, the UE produces a multiplying effect on jobs, creating more than 2000 indirect jobs, mainly (60 per cent) in sector III (see Appendix Table 11A.1).

Apart from the effect on jobs described above, we will also seek to evaluate whether the graduates of this institution, after finishing their training, remain in the region, in the local and regional labour market. From the results of the questionnaire carried out in various institutions, we conclude

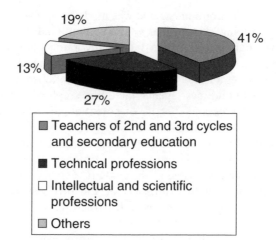

19%

41%

13%

27%

■ Teachers of 2nd and 3rd cycles
   and secondary education

■ Technical professions

□ Intellectual and scientific
   professions

■ Others

Figure 11.1   Professions of the graduates of the UE

that, among the employees with a university education, 27.8 per cent were graduates of UE. This value, apparently low, is explained by the age of the institution, which is only 20 years old, and by the fact that a large number of its graduates are not from the region.

In the questionnaire applied to the graduates of UE,[5] one of the pieces of information that we looked for was aimed at evaluating at what point the students, some time after graduating, sought and obtained a job in Évora or the Alentejo. In this area we can conclude that 39.1 per cent of the graduates looked for a job in Évora and that 37.4 per cent tried to find employment in the Alentejo. Of these, 20.2 per cent decided to take a job in Évora and 30.4 per cent in the Alentejo.

Of the graduates who work in Évora, teachers of higher education, teachers of the second and third cycles and in secondary education, as well as those in administrative and supervisory jobs, have a very similar weighting (about 14 per cent) in this subgroup of respondents. Among those working in the Alentejo, almost half (48.9 per cent) are teachers of the second and third cycles and secondary education (Figure 11.1).

The main employer of UE graduates is the Education Ministry; the number involved in technical jobs is also very significant. As well as education, agriculture and fishing, financial activities and commerce, hotels and restaurants are the other sectors of activity using many UE graduates (Figure 11.2).

The relationship between the UE and the biggest companies of the Alentejo[6] is basically the entry of trainees or students into work, as well as

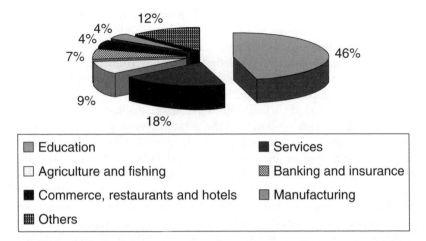

Figure 11.2   Branch of activity where UE graduates work

provision of graduate-level staff for the company. However, variations can be seen in the appreciation of these issues: on the one hand, the companies consider that, in the case of the entry of trainees, the partnership conforms in a reasonable way to their expectations, while in the case of graduate entry, the degree of satisfaction does not reflect expectations. Those questioned expressed themselves very satisfied with the partnerships related to the entry of graduates, with the support of specific programmes for that effect.

The entry of graduates into regional economic activity is one way to ensure contact between higher education and the region. The companies that answered the questionnaire had, on average, 146 employees, of whom eight were graduates of an HEI (about 5.5 per cent of the total), which reveals the weak participation of graduates in total workers in these companies. A large number of the companies (71.9 per cent) had graduates in their service, mainly those (62.8 per cent) who had been trained in the UE, in the poly-technics of Beja and of Portalegre, and in the Technical University of Lisbon. The scientific areas providing most of these graduates are econom-ics, management, and industrial, civil and agricultural engineering.

The institutions and companies that answered the questionnaire con-sidered their employees as having adequate training for the functions they performed. The teachers of the UE, in their turn, considered that the train-ing offered to undergraduates or postgraduates allows a satisfactory adjust-ment to the needs of the regional and national labour markets. This affirms that the performance of the respective UE departments contributes to the improvement of the qualifications of the human resources within the local labour market.

The regional institutions, although claiming to know, in a general way and to a reasonable degree, some of the activities developed in the UE, particularly education, research, community service and training, show that they have a higher level of knowledge concerning education, but they do not have a clear idea of the graduate specializations required to meet the needs of the region or the institutions themselves.

All those questioned are unanimous in considering that the UE must give priority to developing education in the areas of computer science, research and community service. As well as this, there must be more emphasis on studies in the area of health and well-being, the place of private ownership in an ageing region such as the Alentejo, and in the current national context of lack of health professionals. Companies, in their turn, mention the need for the UE to invest in the scientific area of engineering, from which they recruit many of their technicians. Economics and management, life sciences, geography and the environment, as well as the traditional sectors of agriculture and fishing, are other areas that particularly the teachers of the institution and the other entities affirm to be basic to the development of the region and of the institution itself.

A broader analysis, elaborated through questionnaires used with the graduates from the Alentejo in the academic year 1994/95 (from all institutions of public and private higher education) concluded that those questioned (based on birth and residence during the secondary cycle), after completing their degrees, returned to the place where they lived until their secondary education (Cerdeira, 1999, pp. 251–3). This interregional movement was positive for the Alentejo, which not only retained the students who came from this zone, but also gained some who came from outside and ended up looking for work in the region, with the district of Évora contributing most to this situation.

This study further concludes that there is still some uncertainty concerning work among those questioned. The tertiary sector was the one that absorbed most graduates (81.2 per cent), distributed among schools (49 per cent), health establishments (12 per cent) and public administration (12 per cent), which means that the absorption of qualified and trained human resources in year 1994/95 was done in order to create conditions of access for the population to 'essential public goods' (education, health and public administration), because that shows the state to be active in job creation and, simultaneously, the creation of better conditions of life for the population.

4.3   Contribution to Innovation and Technology Transfer

The best way to analyse the transfer of innovative knowledge and technology to the surrounding region is through the protocols signed by the UE.

In summary, we can say that the diverse protocols signed between the UE and external entities, the majority in the second half of the 1990s, have translated into a relationship with both public and private entities, basically nationwide. Initially, Rendering of Services Protocols were established, together with contract activities in the areas of research and community service. Most of the activities were related to agricultural sciences, the traditional activity in the region, natural sciences and environmental and social sciences.

The region of Lisbon and the Tejo valley is preponderant in relation to signed documents, while the relations with the Alentejo are only concentrated at the level of the city of Évora. These documents are, basically, bilateral: they involve only one department or departmental area and only one external entity. At the same time, the degree of internationalization is very weak, as are the relationships with entities or localities situated at the border between Alentejo and Extremadura (Spain). The UE carries out its research in a somewhat isolated way: it is the leader in 57 per cent of the projects in which it participates; cooperation with other universities or R&D centres, national or foreign, has little significance.

The documents signed with local and regional entities are mainly in the form of Rendering of Services Protocols (61.3 per cent), basically involving the departmental areas of natural sciences and environmental and social sciences. These contracts also involved the areas of agricultural sciences, economics and management sciences. The regional entities that signed these documents are diverse: city councils and associations of cities, public institutions of regional scope, regional delegations of some ministries, professional associations of regional scope, particularly in the area of agriculture, local development associations, companies with headquarters in the region, other educational establishments and cultural entities, among others.

The documents signed with local and regional entities relate to activities in the area of research, education, training and community service. The participation of the UE in these partnerships has taken different forms, among which we highlight specific training activities, consultancy and other provision of services close to the contracting entities, as well as the integration of the social agencies of other institutions.

Research carried out in the UE in the year 2000 had financing equivalent to 20 per cent of the total budget of the institution, and took place in departments and research centres. Despite this, research and community services stand out as characteristic of the basic fact that the research developed is applied to national and international questions, reflecting the concerns and the interests of the investigators, such as the possibility of securing financing. Thus, this activity does not reflect the regional context where the institution is located. The Alentejo would have much to gain if the teachers and researchers of the UE applied the scientific method of research to dealing with regional problems. This is teamwork, together with members of the same department or of other national or regional institutions, its results being divulged predominantly at conferences in Portugal or other similar sessions. Community services, in their turn, have responded to the needs presented by regional partners, and have become a team based on members of the same department.

Despite this, the regional institutions value highly the contribution of the UE to the development of the city and the region (between 6 and 8 on a scale of 0 to 10). If an analysis is made of the performance of the various functions developed (education, research, community services and training), or of impacts on specific areas (economic, demographic, cultural, and technical and scientific), generally the classification is the highest in Évora, in comparison with the Alentejo, which suggests that the perception among most of those questioned is that the impact of the institution is limited to the territory of the city.

However, the respondents evaluate with a higher than average score (between 7 and 9 on a scale of 0 to 10) the engagement that the UE should have in its diverse areas of activity, which is taken to mean that they consider that the institution can still improve its contribution to the region.

A more detailed evaluation of the sectors where the influence of the UE is more significant demonstrates that its main contributions are:

- to the improvement of the qualifications of the active population and of the labour market, which strengthens the link between the region and the other institutions in terms of the performance of the education function:
- to the information society and to the definition of a strategy for the region, as well as in the promotion of or contribution to regional artistic and cultural life, due to the existence of frequent activities of this nature: exhibitions, concerts, theatre and cinema, among others, which the members of the UE and the public in general can share.

The UE is considered by those questioned as a moderately active partner in the relationship, showing, however, some difficulties in relation to the lack of information about various agents, to a lack of motivation, and to a lack of tradition in the establishment of partnerships characteristic of the region. As to promoting the approach between higher education and the region, those questioned are unanimous in the measures proposed: more and better information, and the promotion of the activities developed, in terms of both education or research.

The regional institutions still consider that the UE contributes, in a moderate way, to the locating of new companies or other entities in Évora. This evaluation leads us to conclude that the presence of the UE is not seen as having the effect of attracting new economic units to the Alentejo.

5.   FINAL REMARKS

The UE is the only public institution for university education in the Alentejo. Its students account for 4 per cent of Portuguese students in higher education, 40 per cent of students in HEIs in the Alentejo, and 14 per cent of the residents in Évora. Thus, despite the low profile that it has in national terms, its regional weight in the area of education is quite important. On the other hand, being the highest educational institution in the region, with more human resources and having the best levels of qualification, it has an increased responsibility in the areas of research and community service. Here, some partnerships are registered in the areas of social sciences, agricultural sciences, natural sciences and the environment.

The main relationship between the graduates of the UE and the surrounding region consists of participation in periods of training for the staff of both institutions and companies, in the city and in the region, in the areas of economics and management, pure sciences and agricultural sciences. In the activities of research and community services, the partnerships with regional and local entities give priority to local authorities, decentralized public institutions, professional associations, local development associations and regional associations.

Although we have exposed many gaps in the relationship between the UE and the region, we also conclude that this institution promotes various initiatives which regularly deepen its relationship with the region. The departments and research centres have undertaken many initiatives, such as clarification and promulgation sessions, participation in fairs, as well as partnerships with professional associations, companies and establishments of other levels of education.

In terms of the link to the region, we can give several examples: the initiative of 'Science Day', when the institution opens its doors to the students of the other levels of education; the community services provided by the Water Laboratory or the Veterinary Hospital; the research developed in areas of regional interest such as irrigated land, forests, cheese or wine.

The performance of the UE in the area of the transfer of innovative knowledge to regional companies and other institutions is reactive, stemming from isolated contributions and not from a strategically institutional perspective. However, we cannot ignore the fact that the first contract for community services, signed by the UE in the 1970s, was in the area of wine, transferring and applying innovations developed in the laboratories of the institution to regional agricultural exploitation, giving rise to the market success that the wines of the Alentejo now know.

NOTES

1. Some data on regional characterization can be seen in Table 11A.1 in the Appendix.
2. In the Alentejo, there are two public polytechnic institutions and three institutions of private higher education.
3. The city of Évora was classified as a World Heritage Site by UNESCO in 1986.
4. The technique of categorial analysis 'consists of calculating and comparing the frequencies of certain characteristics, previously grouped in significant categories' (Quivy and Campenhoudt, 1992, p. 226).
5. This was a postal questionnaire to graduates of UE for whom the academic services of the institution knew the address. This questionnaire was answered by 26 per cent of those questioned (more than 750 answers), representing the qualifications offered by the UE. The majority of those questioned graduated in the second half of the 1990s.
6. We asked the companies with headquarters in the Alentejo and more than 50 workers.

REFERENCES

Antonelli, C. (2001), 'Distritos industriais e conhecimento tecnológico localizado', in C. Antonelli and J. Ferrão (eds), *Comuniação, conhecimento colectivo e inovação, As vantagens da aglomeração geográfica*, Lisbon: Imprensa das Ciências Sociais, Estudos e Investigações, no. 17, pp. 19–28.
Beeson, R.J. and Montgomery, E. (1993), 'The effect of college and universities on local labour markets', *Review of Economics and Statistics*, **75** (4), 753–61.
Brown, R.H. and Heaney, M.T. (1997), 'A note on measuring the economic impact of institutions of higher education', *Research in Higher Education*, **38** (2), 229–40.
Cerdeira, M.L. (1999), 'Da contribuição das instituições de ensino superior para o desenvolvimento de uma região – o Alentejo, o caso dos diplomadas do ensino superior – ano lectivo 1994/95', Masters thesis, unpublished, Universidade de Évora.
Cooke, P. (1998), 'Introduction – origins of the concept, Regional Innovation Systems', in Braczyk, H.-J., Cooke, P. and Heidenreich, M. (eds), *Regional Innovation Systems*, London: UCL Press, pp. 2–25.
Crespo, V. (1993), *Uma Universidade para os anos 2000, O Ensino Superior numa perspectiva de futuro*, Lisbon: Editorial Inquérito.
Ferrão, J. (1997), 'Meios inovadores em cidades de média dimensão: uma utopia razoável? O caso de Évora', in João Ferrão (ed.), *Política de inovação e desenvolvimento regional e local*, Lisbon: Instituto de Ciências Sociais da Universidade de Lisboa, Estudos e Investigações, pp. 31–51.
Geoideia (1993), *Um Enquadramento para o Plano de desenvolvimento Estratégico da Universidade de Évora*, volume 1, Lisbon: Geoideia, Estudos de Organização do Território, Ldª.

Goddard, J. (1998), 'Contribution au développement national et regional', UNESCO, Conférence mondiale sur l'enseignement supérieur, Paris.

Hedrick, D.W., Henson, S.E. and Mack, R.S. (1990), 'The effects of the universities on local retail, service, and F.I.R.E. employment: some cross-sectional evidence', *Growth and Change*, Summer, 9–20.

Lopes, Raul (2001), *Competitividade, Inovação e Territórios*, Lisbon: Celta Editora.

Lundvall, B.-A. (2000), 'L'économie apprenante et certaines de ses conséquences pour la base de savoir du système de santé et du système éducatif', *Société du savoir et gestion des connaissances*, Centre pour la Recherche et l'Innovation dans l'Enseignement, Paris: OECD, pp. 143–62.

OECD (1997), *Éducation et équité dans les pays de l'OCDE*, Paris: OECD.

OECD (1998), *L'investissement dans le capital human, une comparaison internationale*, Centre pour la Recherche et l'Innovation dans l'Enseignement, Paris: OECD.

Polèse, M. (1998), *Economia Urbana e Regional*, Coimbra: Colecção APDR.

Quivy, M. and Campenhoudt, L.V. (1992), *Manual de investigação em ciências sociais*, Lisbon: Gradiva.

Rosa Pires, A., Rodrigues, C.J. and Castro, E.A. (1998), 'A Cooperação Universidade–Sociedade em Portugal: Inovação Institucional ou Social?', comunicação apresentada ao V Encontro da APDR, Coimbra.

Schuetze, H.G. (2000), 'L'innovation industrielle, la création et la dissémination des connaissances: implications pour les relations université/industrie', *Société du savoir et gestion des connaissances*, Centre pour la Recherche et l'Innovation dans l'Enseignement, Paris: OECD, pp. 183–98.

Shelton, J.R. (1997), 'Economic growth and the importance of people in regional competitiveness', in *Regional Competitiveness and Skills*, Paris: OECD, pp. 15–19.

Simões Lopes, A. (1984), *Desenvolvimento Regional – problemática, teoria e modelos*, 2nd edn, Lisbon: Fundação Calouste Gulbenkian.

Thomas, D.J. (1995), 'Education and the role of the university in economically developing regions', *Higher Education Policy*, **8** (2), 51–62.

APPENDIX

Table 11A.1   Some data on regional characterization

Variable	Year	Unit	Portugal	Alentejo
Resident population	2001	1000 hab.	10 355 824	535 507
Population density	1998	Hab./km^2(%)	112.7	19.8
Activity rate	1999	(%)	50.5	44.7
Population of activity sector	1999	(%)		
Sector I			12.7	12.9
Sector II			35.1	26.2
Sector III			52.2	60.9
Unemployment rate	1999	(%)	4.4	6.7
GDP/per capita	1997	10^3 esc.	1.797	1.574
Disposable family income	1995	10^9 esc.	11.290	506
Regional purchasing power	1997		100	68
Composed Human Development Index	1997		81.6	76
Literacy Index	1997		91.1	80.5
Life Expectancy Index	1997		84.9	86.2
Comfort Index	1997		94.7	91.5
GDP/per capita Index	1997		55.6	45.8
Educational level	2001	(%)		
Illiterate			9.0	17.1
Secondary education			16.0	13.9
Higher education			10.6	7.6
Currently in education			20.6	18.3

Source: INE, IEFP, Department of Statistics of Work, Jobs and Professional Training, PDR 2000–2006.

Index